Snooker

Records · Facts and Champions

Snooker

Records · Facts and Champions

Ian Morrison

GUINNESS BOOKS

Project Editor: Honor Head
Editor: Anne Marshall
Design and Layout: Alan Hamp

Published in Great Britain by Guinness Publishing Ltd,
33 London Road, Enfield, Middlesex

Typeset in Melior and Helvetica
by Ace Filmsetting Ltd, Frome, Somerset
Printed and bound in Great Britain by
Butler & Tanner Ltd, Frome, Somerset

British Library Cataloguing in Publication Data
Morrison, Ian
   Snooker: records, facts & champions.
   1. Snooker, to 1989.
   I. Title
   794.7'35'09

   ISBN 0-85112-364-3

Facing title page: John Pulman held the world title
between 1964–8 when it was organised on a challenge
basis. He successfully overcame six challenges.

Contents

Special Features

Biographies

Acknowledgements
The author would like to thank
the following for their cooperation
in compiling this book: David
Ford and the staff at the Billiards
& Snooker Control Council, Mike
Watterson, Norman Mcleod and
Scotts Bar in Santa Ponsa.

Picture Credits
All-Sport
Colorsport
Roger Lee, RoLee Promotions
    Ltd.
Terry Smith
Eric Whitehead

Abbreviations
Aus. . . Australia
Bel. . . Belgium
Can. . . Canada
Cey. . . Ceylon
Eng. . . England
FRG. . . West Germany
HK. . . Hong Kong
Ind. . . India
IoM. . . Isle of Man
Ire. . . Northern Ireland
Mal. . . Malta
Nor. . . Norway
NZ. . . New Zealand
Pak. . . Pakistan
RoI. . . Republic of Ireland
SAf. . . South Africa
Sco. . . Scotland
Sin. . . Singapore
Sri. . . Sri Lanka
Tha. . . Thailand
Wal. . . Wales

CHAPTER ONE

History and Development of Snooker

Unlike many other sports, snooker can pinpoint its exact beginnings to a day in 1875 when Neville Bowes Chamberlain and fellow army officers at Jubbulpore, India, added a bit of variety to Black Pool by adding additional colours.

Black Pool was played with a white cue ball, 15 reds and a black. It was primarily a potting game and boredom soon set in amongst Chamberlain and his fellow officers. To add variety they added three extra colours: yellow, green and pink. The brown and blue followed later and the complement of 22 balls as exists in the present-day game was reached. Having to pot different coloured balls offered more skill than Black Pool. The new game remained nameless – but not for long.

The credit for naming the game goes to Neville Chamberlain. One day he referred to a playing partner as a 'snooker' after he missed an easy shot. The term snooker at that time referred to a first-year recruit at the Woolwich Academy. It was agreed that as all players were 'snookers' themselves at this new game then that is what it should be called. And so snooker was born.

The new game was inevitably brought to England. But it had to live in the shadow of billiards which, at that time, remained the more popular and more skilful of the two games. Snooker was regarded as a potting game, whereas billiards was considered to be more scientific.

The English Amateur Snooker Championship was inaugurated in 1916 but it was not until the arrival of Joe Davis in the 1920s that snooker's popularity increased.

Davis was the first player to see how important it was to control the cue-ball in order to develop big breaks. Prior to his arrival, breaks of 20 and 30 were acceptable, but he soon added a new dimension to the game.

His expertise attracted crowds whenever he played and in 1924 Tom Dennis, a professional from Nottingham, suggested to the Billiards Association and Control Club (BA & CC) that a world championship should be held. They rejected the idea on the grounds that snooker was

not popular enough. Davis and a friend, billiard-hall owner Bill Camkin from Birmingham, then applied pressure on the controlling body. They eventually succumbed and on 26 November 1926 the first match for the Professional Championship of Snooker's Pool got under way at Thurston's Hall, London.

Davis, predictably, won the first final six months later when he beat Dennis in the final at Camkin's Hall, Birmingham.

That win was to herald the start, not only of snooker's premier event, but of a domination over the rest of the world that Joe Davis was to hold until he retired from world championship play in 1946. In all that time he never lost to any player under level conditions. He did, however, lose in handicapped events which were popular

The grandfather of billiards, John Roberts Senior, at Burroughes & Watts in 1880.

Joe Davis, the first of the great snooker champions.

● ● ● ● ● ● ● ● ● ● ● ● ● ● ● ● ●

JOE DAVIS

Born: 15 April 1901, Whitwell, Derbyshire
Died: 10 July 1978

Joe Davis was the first of the great snooker champions. He was also the man who popularized the game in the 1920s when it lived in the shadow of billiards.

Apart from being the finest exponent of snooker, Davis was also an innovator and it was thanks largely to his efforts that the world professional championship was born in 1926-7. Davis predictably won that inaugural championship and every subsequent one up to 1940. After the war he won the title again in 1946 but then retired from world championship play.

He continued playing and won the other prestigious events of the day, such as the *Daily Mail* Gold Cup, *Empire News* Tournament, and *News of the World* Tournament.

A prolific break-builder he compiled 687 century breaks between 1928, when he made the first against Fred Pugh at Manchester, and 1965. But one of the highlights of his great career was in 1955 when he compiled the first official maximum.

Joe was awarded the OBE in 1963 shortly before his retirement. He collapsed while watching brother Fred in the 1978 world championship at The Crucible and two months later died.

● ● ● ● ● ● ● ● ● ● ● ● ● ● ● ● ●

in the pre-war and early post-war days. Furthermore, they were necessary. The gap between the best and next-best players was a wide one in those days. Today, the gap between any of the top 64 professionals is nowhere near as wide.

After Joe retired from world championship play it was left to the rest to fight it out for supremacy. Walter Donaldson was Joe's first successor, and he was followed by Joe's younger brother Fred. But the early fifties saw a decline in interest in both billiards and snooker. Joe's dominance of the game, originally the reason for the sport's growth, probably had the adverse effect of causing its downfall. While Joe was a great player, he was also invincible and that is not good for any game.

A split amongst the governing body and professional players in 1952 was the start of the decline and the last championship to bear the title 'World Professional Championship' was held that year when colonials, Horace Lindrum and Clark McConachy, contested a two-man championship.

A world matchplay championship existed until 1957, but after that snooker was restricted to the working men's clubs, pubs, and billiards halls. Long gone were the days of packed houses at Thurston's, Burroughes Hall and Leicester Square Hall when the fans would pack in for days on end to watch Joe Davis and the other professionals.

Thanks largely to the efforts of current professional Rex Williams, the world championship was revived in 1964. Williams was also responsible for the revival of the world professional billiards championship. At the Rex Williams Snooker Centre, Blackheath, between 16 and 23 March 1964 four men – Rex Williams, Fred Davis, Jackie Rea and John Pulman – took part in the Conayes £200 Professional Tournament. It was significant because it was the first commercially-sponsored snooker event since 1960.

When the snooker world championship was reinstated it was as a series of challenge matches. The first match was between John Pulman, the winner of the world match-play title in 1957, and Fred Davis. Pulman won and subsequently went on to make six further successful defences between 1964 and 1968. The world championship was back, and so was the interest.

In the 1968–9 season the championship reverted to its knockout formula and for the first time received sponsorship, from John Player and Son. Suddenly the prospects looked healthier than ever for the sport Neville Chamberlain invented nearly 100 years earlier.

Only eight professionals took part in that 1969 championship and two of them were men with outstanding amateur records: John Spencer and Ray Reardon. They both turned professional because they had the foresight to see a possible 'second coming' of snooker, and they were right. The final session of the 1969 world championship between Spencer and Gary Owen at London's Victoria Hall saw hundreds of fans turned away. Ample proof that snooker had returned as a spectator sport.

The year 1969 was certainly a significant one in snooker history. Not only had the world cham-

Rex Williams has given so much to snooker during his 40 years or so.

Below: After Joe Davis (centre) retired from world championship play in 1946 it was down to brother Fred (left) and Walter Donaldson to fight out the 1947 final. Donaldson won.

The Wythenshawe Forum, home of the 1976 world championship final, the first under Embassy's sponsorship.

pionship returned to a knockout format but, following the arrival of colour television, it became popular television viewing.

BBC producers were looking at new events that would fit nicely into the technological breakthrough of colour television. Snooker was an obvious sport and Phillip Lewis set about putting together a programme. Commentator Ted Lowe was given the job of getting the contestants together, and *Pot Black* was created. But, more significantly, snooker was reborn.

Gradually the image of snooker being a sign of a misspent youth and played only in dingy, smoke-filled billiard halls disappeared. The clean-cut image of the snooker player made the public more aware of the sport and its newly-discovered personalities. As for the players, they were astounded by the sudden upsurge of interest in their game. However, they had problems coping with the demands that television and the new breed of snooker fan were putting on them.

Television coverage was very limited in those pre-*Pot Black* days. The sport was given the odd slot 'here and there' but, because of the lack of time and the sophisticated editing machines of today, matches had to last as long as the programme required. Allegations of match-fixing to enable the sport to be projected in the right manner were admitted by the leading players of the day. The television companies wanted entertainment. They got it, and happily for snooker the game was projected in an entertaining manner to its audience.

The players who became household names had to make the transition from playing in the smoke-filled billiard halls to playing under the heat and pressure of the television lights, which posed all sorts of major problems for TV producers and players alike. Conventional billiard-table lighting was unsuitable for the cameras and the television companies experimented with various systems, often resulting in blown bulbs dur-

TOTAL 1988 VIEWING FIGURES FOR SPORT (All channels)					
Sport	Total viewers (000s)	% of men viewers	% of women viewers	% of viewers made up AB adults	% of viewers made up 16–24s
American Football . . .	81,578	50.96	36.76	13.20	15.26
Athletics	208,003	43.56	46.73	13.54	7.73
Badminton	3,446	48.43	39.29	15.99	14.68
Baseball	4,736	52.72	34.63	11.06	20.50
Basketball	14,426	47.21	40.52	14.81	13.63
Boating	17,768	46.29	43.76	17.14	10.39
Bowls	93,343	47.81	48.03	11.64	3.69
Boxing	86,940	48.78	42.93	8.70	9.92
Cricket	230,375	55.25	38.71	13.81	6.74
Curling	3,895	46.26	44.42	13.97	13.45
Cycling	32,000	48.32	38.81	17.41	14.18
Darts	88,609	46.75	46.01	7.55	8.62
Equestrian	37,172	39.66	53.40	12.28	7.59
Football	320,875	51.47	38.17	11.82	10.21
Golf	119,023	50.67	44.45	17.67	6.28
Gymnastics	13,554	33.57	45.64	10.33	11.94
Hockey	3,684	42.59	42.92	9.17	8.71
Horse Racing	181,489	48.80	45.97	10.89	5.92
Ice Skating	71,567	36.29	57.15	12.84	8.00
Modern Pentathlon . .	855	36.26	46.08	10.18	16.61
Motor Racing	56,269	49.05	38.56	14.27	11.48
Olympics	652,375	42.23	48.11	12.40	10.21
Roller Skating	2,021	35.77	47.15	6.68	12.82
Rugby (Union & League)	57,847	55.69	35.27	21.69	8.14
Skiing	25,775	44.69	39.74	21.64	10.29
Snooker	697,834	45.00	40.00	11.94	5.69
Street Hockey	3,334	45.80	38.12	10.50	13.65
Sumo Wrestling	25,262	42.79	43.50	10.83	14.65
Swimming	1,745	40.63	39.60	13.81	16.68
Table Tennis	2,336	47.47	31.93	17.04	15.07
Tennis	159,417	38.60	55.48	17.81	8.69
Various	1,123,456	48.05	42.48	12.08	8.48
Volleyball	5,983	40.10	34.65	8.54	12.07
Windsurfing	595	34.96	55.80	13.61	10.25
Wrestling	107,448	45.75	41.34	5.91	10.13

Source: AGB Sports Watch/RARB

Alex Higgins took the snooker world by storm when he won the 1972 world championship and he has constantly hit the headlines since then.

ing matches which resulted in scorched cloths. Eventually they got it right and to a standard that was acceptable to both player and producer.

Snooker's image changed dramatically in those early years of televised events and in the 1970s the trend was to take snooker away from the billiard halls of old and move it into modern, purpose-built snooker centres which not only catered for the enthusiast's playing needs but also became places of leisure and relaxation.

Television popularized the likes of Reardon and Spencer, and David Taylor, Eddie Charlton, Patsy Fagan and others. The clean-cut, well-dressed image of the snooker player fitted ideally into the BBC's schedule and the response from the public was such that *Pot Black* remained on the screens until 1986 when Jimmy White potted the last black. The real success of the series, however, stemmed from the fact that the average man no longer associated snooker with spit-and-sawdust pubs and backstreet dives. At last the game had lost its disreputable, down-at-heel image. Consequently, men and boys wanted to try their hand at snooker and emulate the feats of their new heroes, Spencer and Reardon being the market leaders in the hero stakes! (See the feature on *Pot Black* on p. 64.)

By the mid-seventies, the number of professionals had increased fourfold and was up to about 30. Most of them made a reasonable living, either from exhibition matches or via the holiday-camp circuit where they became popular attractions with holidaymakers.

The year 1977 was also important for the growth of snooker. The world championship, having been sponsored by W. D. & H. O. Wills for the first time in 1976 (nearly disastrously, one might add), was again sponsored by the tobacco company under its Embassy brand name. Thanks to the persuasive powers of promoter Mike Watterson, Wills stuck with the sport, and Watterson took the world championship to The Crucible Theatre in Sheffield, its current home. The venue is now as synonymous with snooker as Wimbledon is with tennis.

Television coverage of the event was

increased substantially in 1978 and since then the 17 days at The Crucible is one of the major televised events of the sporting calendar.

The Crucible's arrival into the world of snooker came at roughly the same time as one of the game's greatest players, Steve Davis. He turned professional in 1978, won his first major title in 1980 and was world champion in 1981. Since then his record has been second to none as he has become one of the highest-paid sportsmen in Britain. But the fortune amassed by Davis, and the money available to the other 140-plus professionals, is thanks to the never-ending flow of big money sponsors prepared to lend their names to televised snooker events.

Snooker is a great advertising platform for big companies and it remains the most popular televised sport in terms of viewing audiences. It is second only to cricket in terms of viewing hours.

The sport has never looked back from the day in 1969 when *Pot Black* was launched. It has gone from strength to strength. Its popularity has spread to all corners of the globe. The Far East is a great growth area, so is Europe. The 1988-9 season saw two ranking tournaments taken abroad for the first time, to Canada and France. Teething problems may have been experienced but the 1989-90 season sees the professional game extending to even wider horizons with ranking events in Hong Kong, Thailand and Dubai, to confirm snooker as a truly international sport.

CHAPTER TWO

Embassy World Professional Championship

The world professional championship is professional snooker's oldest surviving tournament, dating to the 1926-7 season. Its long history, however, has not been a smooth-running one and it is only since the mid-seventies that it has grown in stature to become one of sport's great annual events.

Ten players entered the first championship which started on 26 November 1926 and Joe Davis, predictably, won the first final by beating Tom Dennis 20-11 at Camkin's Hall, Birmingham. For his efforts Davis collected the princely sum of £6 10s (£6.50).

Davis dominated the event and won the trophy 15 times before his retirement from the championship in 1946.

Despite Davis's brilliance, interest in the championship declined in the 1930s, and on two occasions, in 1931 and 1934, the world championship consisted of a single match between Davis and a challenger: Tom Dennis in 1931 and Tom Newman three years later.

Between 1927 and 1940 a total of 100 men took part in the championship, an average of approximately seven per year. In 1989 the number of entrants, all hoping to win the most prestigious trophy in snooker, totalled a record 142.

Following Joe Davis's retirement from the championship after beating Horace Lindrum in the 1946 final, the way was open for his younger brother Fred to succeed him. However, Scotland's first world champion, Walter Donaldson, put paid to those family ambitions by beating Fred in the 1947 final.

It was after Fred's last success in 1951 that a split between the professional players and the Billiards Association and Control Club (BA & CC) developed. The result was a boycott of the 1952 world championship with only two men left to contest the title. Horace Lindrum (Aus) and Clark McConachy (NZ) fought out a long battle which the Australian eventually won 94-49.

Matches were certainly longer than those of today and week-long matches were commonplace in the early championship days.

Lindrum was the last champion for 12 years because the world championship was abandoned after the boycott. However, the professionals organized their own world championship under the name of the Professional Match-Play Championship (see p. 88), but it folded after the 1957 championship when John Pulman beat Jackie Rea in the last final.

Snooker went into decline in the late fifties and early sixties. But eventually the rift between the professionals and the BA & CC was healed and, thanks largely to the efforts of current professional Rex Williams, the world champion-

The world championship trophy; the most sought after trophy in professional snooker.

ships were revived in 1964, albeit on a challenge basis.

It was decided that John Pulman, the last World Match-Play champion in 1957, should meet a challenge from Fred Davis. Pulman won 19–16 and then successfully fended off six other challenges before the championship was restored to a knockout basis in 1969 when new professional John Spencer beat world amateur champion Gary Owen in the final at London's Victoria Hall.

Gradually, as the number of professionals increased, and thanks to the advent of *Pot Black*, snooker gained in popularity. Tobacco companies saw snooker, like other sporting events, as an advertising platform, particularly with the added television interest. Player's No. 6 sponsored the 1969 and 1970 championships and

Gallahers, using its 'Park Drive' brand name, sponsored the event in 1973 and 1974. After a year without sponsorship, W. D. & H. O. Wills, manufacturers of the famous Embassy brand, stepped in to help in 1976. Because of poor organization, the event was little short of a disaster and the company was ready to pull the plug on snooker.

However, promoter Mike Watterson persuaded the company to give it another try. This time it was a success, after Watterson took the sport to its current home at The Crucible. Television interest increased rapidly and Embassy was only too pleased to retain its sponsorship. The rest of the world championship and its trials, tribulations, great characters and great moments are now an integral part of snooker history. The sport can rest safe in the knowledge that the world championship will be known as the Embassy World Professional Snooker Championship well into the 1990s.

One of snooker's most imposing arenas, The Crucible Theatre, Sheffield, home of the world championship.

Joe Davis (left) and Willie Smith contested the 1933 and 1935 finals. They are seen here reminiscing in 1953.

1927

Round one Tom Carpenter beat Nat Butler 8–3; Melbourne Inman beat Tom Newman 8–5

Round two Tom Carpenter beat Melbourne Inman 8–3; Albert Cope beat Alec Mann 8–6; Joe Davis beat Joe Brady 10–5; Tom Dennis beat Fred Lawrence 8–7

Semi-finals Joe Davis beat Albert Cope 16–7; Tom Dennis beat Tom Carpenter 12–10

Final Joe Davis beat Tom Dennis 20–11

1928

Round one Alec Mann beat Albert Cope 14–9; Tom Newman beat Frank Smith 12–6

Round two Fred Lawrence bet Alec Mann 12–11; Tom Newman beat Tom Dennis 12–5

Round three Fred Lawrence beat Tom Newman 12–7

Final Joe Davis beat Fred Lawrence 16–13

1929

Round one Fred Lawrence beat Alec Mann 13–12

Semi-finals Joe Davis beat Fred Lawrence 13–10; Tom Dennis beat K. Prince 14–6

Final Joe Davis beat Tom Dennis 19–14

1930

Round one Nat Butler beat Tom Newman 13–11; Fred Lawrence beat Alec Mann 13–11

Semi-finals Joe Davis beat Fred Lawrence 13–2; Tom Dennis beat Nat Butler 13–11

Final Joe Davis beat Tom Dennis 25–12

1931

Final Joe Davis beat Tom Dennis 25–21

1932

Round one Clark McConachy beat Tom Dennis 13–11

Final Joe Davis beat Clark McConachy 30–19

1933

Round one Walter Donaldson beat Willie Leigh 13–11

Semi-finals Joe Davis beat Walter Donaldson 13–1; Willie Smith beat Tom Dennis 16–9

Final Joe Davis beat Willie Smith 25–18

1934

Final Joe Davis beat Tom Newman 25–23

Benson and Hedges – Snooker's Longest Continuous Sponsorship

Tobacco company Gallahers first became involved with snooker in 1971 when, using their Park Drive brand name, they sponsored the Park Drive 2000. This four-man round-robin tournament with matches played around the country proved to be successful. In 1973 Gallahers switched their sponsorship to the world championship, again using the Park Drive name. But after a disastrous championship in 1974 they withdrew their sponsorship and in 1975 switched their attention to a a new tournament using their Benson and Hedges brand name. The new event was to be called the Benson and Hedges Masters. The tournament is still in existence today and the Masters has become the longest-running sponsored event in snooker.

The first tournament was played at the West Centre Hotel in Fulham but was not a great success. The table was not satisfactory, and the location was too far out of central London to attract the large crowds that were anticipated. Nevertheless, Ray Reardon and John Spencer provided the crowd with a thrilling final which Spencer won 9–8.

When the event moved to the New London Theatre in 1976 full houses were a regular sight. That has been a feature of the Benson and Hedges Masters ever since.

The Wembley Conference Centre became the tournament's new, and present, home in 1979 and even bigger crowds flocked to the North London venue to see the best players in the world. Crowds of more than 2000 are not uncommon at Wembley and they help to make it the sport's second most prestigious event after the Embassy World Championship.

It has always been an invitation-only event. Originally with ten invited professionals It was increased to 12 in 1981 and to its present complement of 16 in 1983. Entry is now only open to players ranked in

The 1986 Benson and Hedges final at Wembley between Cliff Thorburn and Jimmy White. The Canadian won 9–5.

The imposing Wembley Arena, snooker's biggest venue.

Cliff Thorburn after capturing his third Benson and Hedges title in 1986.

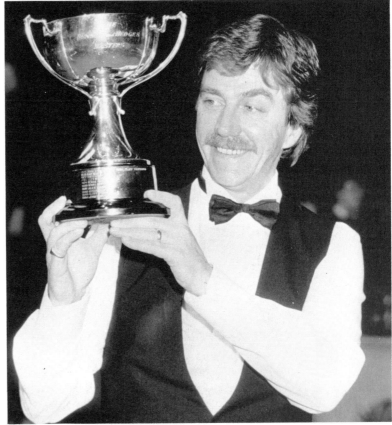

the top 16. However, the sponsors reserve the right to issue two wild-card invitations.

Over the years the Masters has seen some of the sport's greatest moments. And there was none finer than Kirk Steven's 147 maximum against Jimmy White in 1984.

It is not only at Wembley that the Benson and Hedges name can be seen every year but also at the unusual setting of the Goff's Sales Ring at Kill, County Kildare in Ireland. It has been the home of the Benson and Hedges Irish Masters since its inauguration in 1978.

The Masters at Wembley is, happily, assured until 1996 because Benson and Hedges signed a new six-year contract with the BBC in 1989. And that will mean 21 years of the Masters: the longest continuous sponsorship in snooker.

Fred Davis has graced the world championship with his presence for over 50 years. He made his debut in 1937.

1935

Round one Willie Smith beat Con Stanbury 13–12

Semi-finals Joe Davis beat Tom Newman 15–10; Willie Smith beat Alec Mann 13–4

Final Joe Davis beat Willie Smith 25–20

1936

Round one Joe Davis beat Tom Newman 29–2; Horace Lindrum beat Harold Terry 20–11; Clare O'Donnell beat Sydney Lee 16–15; Willie Smith beat Sidney Smith 16–15; Con Stanbury beat Alec Mann 22–9

Round two Alec Brown beat Con Stanbury 16–15; Joe Davis beat Willie Smith 22–9; Horace Lindrum beat Clare O'Donnell 19–6 (O'Donnell retired); Stan Newman bye

Semi-finals Joe Davis beat Alec Brown 21–10; Horace Lindrum beat Stan Newman 29–2

Final Joe Davis beat Horace Lindrum 34–27

1937

Round one Bill Withers beat Fred Davis 17–14

Round two Joe Davis beat Bill Withers 30–1; Horace Lindrum beat Sydney Lee 20–11; Sidney Smith beat Alec Brown 18–13; Willie Smith beat Tom Newman 16–15

Semi-finals Joe Davis beat Sidney Smith 18–13; Horace Lindrum beat Willie Smith 20–11

Final Joe Davis beat Horace Lindrum 32–29

FRED DAVIS

Born: 14 August 1913, Whittingham Moor, Chesterfield

Fred Davis has been a professional for 60 years and has been nothing but a credit to the game. Today, although his appearances are limited, he remains one of the game's most popular characters.

Fred had to live in the shadow of his elder brother Joe for many years and in 1940 the pair of them met in one of the great world championship finals – Joe won 37–36.

After Joe retired from world championship play Fred eventually maintained the family tradition by winning the title three times in 1948, 1949 and 1951. Fred also won the other leading tournaments of the day: the Professional Match-Play title five years in succession, 1952–6, and the *News of the World* tournament in 1958 and 1959.

Equally proficient at billiards, Fred won the UK professional title in 1951, but his finest hour came in 1980 when, at the age of 66, he captured the world professional billiards title.

In the modern era of snooker his best result was in reaching the semi-final of the Embassy World Professional Championship in 1978. He lost to Perrie Mans, and it was while watching the match that Fred's brother Joe collapsed and was to die two months later.

1938

Qualifying round one Herbert Holt beat C. W. Reid 21–10

Qualifying round two Fred Davis beat Herbert Holt 23–8

Round one Fred Davis beat Alec Brown 16–6 (Brown retired ill); Joe Davis beat Sydney Lee 24–7; Sidney Smith beat Con Stanbury 27–4; Willie Smith beat Tom Newman 16–15

Semi-finals Joe Davis beat Willie Smith 24–7; Sidney Smith beat Fred Davis 18–13

Final Joe Davis beat Sidney Smith 37–24

1939

Qualifying round one Walter Donaldson beat Herbert Holt 18–13; Dicky Laws beat Stan Newman 19–12

Qualifying round two Walter Donaldson beat Dicky Laws 18–13

Round one Fred Davis beat Con Stanbury 19–12; Walter Donaldson beat Claude Falkiner 21–10; Tom Newman beat Alec Mann 19–12; Sidney Smith beat Sydney Lee 21–10

Round two Alec Brown beat Horace Lindrum 17–14; Fred Davis beat Tom Newman 20–11; Joe Davis beat Willie Smith 19–12; Sidney Smith beat Walter Donaldson 16–15

Semi-finals Joe Davis beat Fred Davis 17–14; Sidney Smith beat Alec Brown 20–11

Final Joe Davis beat Sidney Smith 43–30

1940

Qualifying round one Herbert Holt beat Con Stanbury 18–13

Round one Fred Davis beat Sydney Lee 20–11; Joe Davis beat Alec Brown 20–11; Walter Donaldson beat Herbert Holt 24–7; Sidney Smith beat Tom Newman 22–9

Semi-finals Fred Davis beat Sidney Smith 17–14; Joe Davis beat Walter Donaldson 22–9

Final Joe Davis beat Fred Davis 37–36

1946

Qualifying round one Kingsley Kennerley beat Fred Lawrence 22–9; Stan Newman beat Willie Leigh 16–15; Con Stanbury beat John Barrie 18–13

Qualifying round two Kingsley Kennerley beat Tom Reece 8–2 (Reece retired); Stan Newman beat Con Stanbury 17–14

Qualifying round three Stan Newman beat Kingsley Kennerley 21–10

Round one Fred Davis beat Alec Brown 24–7; Joe Davis beat Walter Donaldson 21–10; Horace Lindrum beat Herbert Holt 17–14; Stan Newman beat Sydney Lee 19–12

Semi-finals Joe Davis beat Stan Newman 21–10; Horace Lindrum beat Fred Davis 16–12

Final Joe Davis beat Horace Lindrum 78–67

1947

Qualifying round one Albert Brown beat John Pulman 21–14; Kingsley Kennerley beat Con Stanbury 23–12; Sydney Lee beat Jim Lees 19–16; Willie Leigh beat H. F. Francis 19–16; Eric Newman beat Herbert Holt w.o.

Qualifying round two John Barrie beat Fred Lawrence 25–10; Albert Brown beat Eric Newman 28–7; Kingsley Kennerley beat Alec Mann 23–12; Willie Leigh beat Sydney Lee 25–10

Qualifying round three Albert Brown beat John Barrie 24–11; Kingsley Kennerley beat Willie Leigh 21–14

Qualifying round four Albert Brown beat Kingsley Kennerley 21–14

Round one Fred Davis beat Clark McConachy 53–20; Walter Donaldson beat Stan Newman 46–25; Horace Lindrum beat Albert Brown 39–34; Sidney Smith beat Alec Brown 43–28

Semi-finals Fred Davis beat Sidney Smith 39–32; Walter Donaldson beat Horace Lindrum 39–32

Final Walter Donaldson beat Fred Davis 82–63

1948

Qualifying round one John Barrie beat H. F. Francis 19–16; Willie Leigh beat Herbert Holt 18–17; John Pulman beat Sydney Lee w.o.; Con Stanbury beat Eric Newman 28–7

Qualifying round two Willie Leigh beat John Barrie 21–14; John Pulman beat Con Stanbury 19–16

Qualifying round three John Pulman beat Willie Leigh 18–17

Round one Albert Brown beat Sidney Smith 36–35; Fred Davis beat Alec Brown 43–28; Walter Donaldson beat Kingsley Kennerley 46–25; Clark McConachy beat John Pulman 42–29

Semi-finals Fred Davis beat Clark McConachy 43–28; Walter Donaldson beat Albert Brown 40–31

Final Fred Davis beat Walter Donaldson 84–61

1949

Qualifying round one Con Stanbury beat H. F. Francis 18–17

Qualifying round two Con Stanbury beat Jackie Rea 18–17

Qualifying round three Con Stanbury beat Herbert Holt 18–17

Round one Fred Davis beat Kingsley Kennerley 50–21; Walter Donaldson beat Con Stanbury 58–13; John Pulman beat Albert Brown 42–29; Sidney Smith beat Alec Brown 41–30

Semi-finals Fred Davis beat Sidney Smith 42–29; Walter Donaldson beat John Pulman 49–22

Final Fred Davis beat Walter Donaldson 80–65

1950

Qualifying round one Herbert Holt beat Dicky Laws 26–9; Kingsley Kennerley beat John Barrie 21–14; Sydney Lee beat Con Stanbury 20–15; Willie Smith beat Bill Withers 28–7

Qualifying round two Kingsley Kennerley beat Willie Smith 22–13; Sydney Lee beat Herbert Holt 16–8 (retired ill)

Qualifying round three Kingsley Kennerley beat Sydney Lee 21–14

Round one Albert Brown beat John Pulman 37–34; George Chenier beat Peter Mans 37–34; Fred Davis beat Alec Brown 44–27; Walter Donaldson beat Kingsley Kennerley 42–29

Semi-finals Fred Davis beat George Chenier 43–28; Walter Donaldson beat Albert Brown 37–34

Final Walter Donaldson beat Fred Davis 51–46

1951

Qualifying round one John Barrie beat Sydney Lee 23–12

Qualifying round two John Barrie beat Dicky Laws 28–7

Round one Fred Davis beat John Barrie 42–29; Walter Donaldson beat Kingsley Kennerley 41–30; Horace Lindrum beat Albert Brown 43–28; John Pulman beat Sidney Smith 38–33

Semi-finals Fred Davis beat John Pulman 22–14 (retired ill); Walter Donaldson beat Horace Lindrum 41–30

Final Fred Davis beat Walter Donaldson 58–39

1952

Final Horace Lindrum beat Clark McConachy 94–49

1964
(challenge matches)

John Pulman beat Fred Davis 19–16
John Pulman beat Rex Williams 40–33

1965
(challenge matches)

John Pulman beat Fred Davis 37–36
John Pulman beat Rex Williams 25–22 (series of matches in South Africa)
John Pulman beat Freddie van Rensburg 39–12

1966
(challenge match)

John Pulman beat Fred Davis 5–2 (series of matches)

1967

No challenge offered

1968
(challenge match)

John Pulman beat Eddie Charlton 39–34

1969

Round one Fred Davis beat Ray Reardon 25–24; Gary Owen beat Jackie Rea 25–17; John Spencer beat John Pulman 25–18; Rex Williams beat Bernard Bennett 25–4

Semi-finals Gary Owen beat Fred Davis 37–24; John Spencer beat Rex Williams 37–12

Final John Spencer beat Gary Owen 37–24

1970

Round one David Taylor beat Bernard Bennett 11–8

Round two Gary Owen beat Rex Williams 31–11; John Pulman beat David Taylor 31–20; Ray Reardon beat Fred Davis 31–26; John Spencer beat Jackie Rea 31–15

Semi-finals John Pulman beat Gary Owen 37–12; Ray Reardon beat John Spencer 37–33

Final Ray Reardon beat John Pulman 37–33

1971
(played November 1970)

Round robin Eddie Charlton beat Perrie Mans 26–11; Eddie Charlton beat Gary Owen 23–14; Eddie Charlton beat Norman Squire 27–10; Paddy Morgan beat Warren Simpson

Two of snooker's 'senior' players Eddie Charlton (left) and John Spencer.

21–16; Gary Owen beat Paddy Morgan 26–11; Gary Owen beat Norman Squire 19–18; John Pulman beat Paddy Morgan 25–12; John Pulman beat Norman Squire 26–11; Ray Reardon beat Eddie Charlton 21–16; Ray Reardon beat Perrie Mans 22–15; Ray Reardon beat John Spencer 21–16; Ray Reardon v. Paddy Morgan not played; Warren Simpson beat Perrie Mans 19–18; Warren Simpson beat Gary Owen 19–18; Warren Simpson beat John Pulman 21–16; John Spencer beat Perrie Mans 20–17; John Spencer beat John Pulman 23–14; John Spencer beat Norman Squire 27–10

Final positions 1 Eddie Charlton; 2 John Spencer; 3 Ray Reardon; 4 Warren Simpson; 5 John Pulman; 6 Gary Owen; 7 Paddy Morgan; 8 Perrie Mans; 9 Norman Squire

Semi-finals Warren Simpson beat Eddie Charlton 27–22; John Spencer beat Ray Reardon 34–15

Final John Spencer beat Warren Simpson 37–29

1972

Qualifying round one John Dunning beat Pat Houlihan 11–10; Alex Higgins beat Ron Gross 15–6; Graham Miles beat Bernard Bennett 15–6; Maurice Parkin beat Geoff Thompson 11–10

Qualifying round two John Dunning beat Graham Miles 11–5; Alex Higgins beat Maurice Parkin 11–3

Round one Alex Higgins beat Jackie Rea 19–11; John Pulman beat John Dunning 19–7

Round two Eddie Charlton beat David Taylor 31–25; Alex Higgins beat John Pulman 31–23; John Spencer beat Fred Davis 31–21; Rex Williams beat Ray Reardon 25–23

Semi-finals Alex Higgins beat Rex Williams 31–30; John Spencer beat Eddie Charlton 37–32

Final Alex Higgins beat John Spencer 37–32

1973

Round one David Greaves beat Bernard Bennett 9–8; Pat Houlihan beat Jackie Rea 9–2; Perrie Mans beat Ron Gross 9–2; Graham Miles beat Geoff Thompson 9–5; Warren Simpson beat Maurice Parkin 9–3; David Taylor beat John Dunning 9–4; Cliff Thorburn beat Dennis Taylor 9–8; Jim Meadowcroft beat Kingsley Kennerley w.o.

Round two Eddie Charlton beat Perrie Mans 16–8; Fred Davis beat David Greaves 16–1; Alex Higgins beat Pat Houlihan 16–3; Graham Miles beat John Pulman 16–10; Gary Owen beat Warren Simpson 16–14; Ray Reardon beat Jim Meadowcroft 16–10; John Spencer beat David Taylor 16–5; Rex Williams beat Cliff Thorburn 16–15

Round three Eddie Charlton beat Graham Miles 16–6; Alex Higgins beat Fred Davis 16–14; Ray Reardon beat Gary Owen 16–6; John Spencer beat Rex Williams 16–7

Semi-finals Eddie Charlton beat Alex Higgins 23–9; Ray Reardon beat John Spencer 23–22

Final Ray Reardon beat Eddie Charlton 38–32

1974

Qualifying round John Dunning beat David Greaves 8–2; Jim Meadowcroft beat Pat Houlihan 8–5; Marcus Owen beat

Dennis Taylor 8–1; John Pulman beat Jack Karnehm 8–0; Warren Simpson beat Jackie Rea 8–3; David Taylor beat Ron Gross 8–7; Cliff Thorburn beat Alan McDonald 8–3

Round one Bernard Bennett beat Warren Simpson 8–2; John Dunning beat David Taylor 8–6; Perrie Mans beat Ian Anderson 8–1; Jim Meadowcroft beat Kingsley Kennerley 8–5; Paddy Morgan beat Cliff Thorburn 8–4; Marcus Owen beat Maurice Parkin 8–5; John Pulman beat Sydney Lee 8–0; Bill Werbeniuk beat Geoff Thompson 8–3

Round two Fred Davis beat Bill Werbeniuk 15–5; John Dunning beat Eddie Charlton 15–13; Alex Higgins beat Bernard Bennett 15–4; Perrie Mans beat John Spencer 15–13; Graham Miles beat Paddy Morgan 15–7; Marcus Owen beat Gary Owen 15–8; Ray Reardon beat Jim Meadowcroft 15–3; Rex Williams beat John Pulman 15–12

Round three Fred Davis beat Alex Higgins 15–14; Graham Miles beat John Dunning 15–13; Ray Reardon beat Marcus Owen 15–11; Rex Williams beat Perrie Mans 15–4

Semi-finals Graham Miles beat Rex Williams 15–7; Ray Reardon beat Fred Davis 15–3

Final Ray Reardon beat Graham Miles 22–12

1975

Qualifying round Lou Condo beat Maurice Parkin 15–8; David Greaves beat Jim Charlton 15–14; Phil Tarrant beat Bernard Bennett 15–8

Round one Ian Anderson beat Lou Condo 15–8; Gary Owen beat David Greaves 15–3; John Pulman beat Phil Tarrant 15–5; Warren Simpson beat Ron Mares 15–5; David Taylor beat Rex King 15–8; Dennis Taylor beat Perrie Mans 15–12; Cliff Thorburn beat Paddy Morgan 15–6; Bill Werbeniuk beat Jim Meadowcroft 15–9

Round two Eddie Charlton beat Bill Werbeniuk 15–11; Alex Higgins beat David Taylor 15–2; Gary Owen beat John Dunning 15–8; Ray Reardon beat Warren Simpson 15–11; John Spencer beat John Pulman 15–10; Dennis Taylor beat Fred Davis 15–14; Cliff Thorburn beat Graham Miles 15–2; Rex Williams beat Ian Anderson 15–4

Round three Eddie Charlton beat Cliff Thorburn 19–12; Alex Higgins beat Rex Williams 19–12; Ray Reardon beat John Spencer 19–17; Dennis Taylor beat Gary Owen 19–9

Semi-finals Eddie Charlton beat Dennis Taylor 19–12; Ray Reardon beat Alex Higgins 19–14

Final Ray Reardon beat Eddie Charlton 31–30

1976

Qualifying round one Lou Condo beat Marcus Owen 8–6; David Greaves beat Jim Charlton 8–5; Ron Gross beat Maurice Parkin 8–5; Jim Meadowcroft beat Dennis Wheelwright 8–1; Jackie Rea beat Ian Anderson 8–5

Qualifying round two Jim Meadowcroft beat Ron Gross 8–4; Jackie Rea beat Bernard Bennett 8–5; David Taylor beat David Greaves 8–1; Willie Thorne beat Lou Condo 8–3

Qualifying round three Jim Meadowcroft beat Willie Thorne 8–5; David Taylor beat Jackie Rea 8–7

Round one Eddie Charlton beat John Pulman 15–9; Fred Davis beat Bill Werbeniuk 15–12; Alex Higgins beat Cliff Thorburn 15–14; Perrie Mans beat Graham Miles 15–10; Jim Meadowcroft beat Rex Williams 15–7; Ray Reardon beat John Dunning 15–7; John Spencer beat David Taylor 15–5; Dennis Taylor beat Gary Owen 15–9

Round two Eddie Charlton beat Fred Davis 15–13; Alex Higgins beat John Spencer 15–14; Perrie Mans beat Jim Meadowcroft 15–8; Ray Reardon beat Dennis Taylor 15–2

Semi-finals Alex Higgins beat Eddie Charlton 20–18; Ray Reardon beat Perrie Mans 20–10

Final Ray Reardon beat Alex Higgins 27–16

1977

Qualifying round one John Virgo beat Roy Andrewartha 11–1

Qualifying round two Patsy Fagan beat Jim Meadowcroft 11–9; Doug Mountjoy beat Jackie Rea 11–9; John Pulman beat Maurice Parkin w.o.; David Taylor beat David Greaves

11–0; Dennis Taylor beat Jack Karnehm 11–0; Cliff Thorburn beat Chris Ross 11–0; Willie Thorne beat Bernard Bennett 11–4; John Virgo beat John Dunning 11–6

Round one Eddie Charlton beat David Taylor 13–5; Graham Miles beat Willie Thorne 13–4; Doug Mountjoy beat Alex Higgins 13–12; John Pulman beat Fred Davis 13–12; Ray Reardon beat Patsy Fagan 13–7; John Spencer beat John Virgo 13–9; Dennis Taylor beat Perrie Mans 13–11; Cliff Thorburn beat Rex Williams 13–6

Round two John Pulman beat Graham Miles 13–10; John Spencer beat Ray Reardon 13–6; Dennis Taylor beat Doug Mountjoy 13–11; Cliff Thorburn beat Eddie Charlton 13–12

Semi-finals John Spencer beat John Pulman 18–16; Cliff Thorburn beat Dennis Taylor 18–16

Final John Spencer beat Cliff Thorburn 25–21

1978

Qualifying round one Roy Andrewartha beat Jack Karnehm 9–0; John Barrie beat David Greaves 9–3; Pat Houlihan beat Chris Ross 9–1; Maurice Parkin beat Bernard Bennett 9–4

Qualifying round two Fred Davis beat John Virgo 9–8; Patsy Fagan beat John Dunning 9–5; Pat Houlihan beat Jim Meadowcroft 9–6; Perrie Mans beat John Barrie 9–6; Doug

Until the arrival of Steve Davis, Welshman Ray Reardon was the most successful modern-day player.

Mountjoy beat Roy Andrewartha 9–3; David Taylor beat Paddy Morgan 9–7; Willie Thorne beat Rex Williams 9–3; Bill Werbeniuk beat Maurice Parkin 9–2

Round one Eddie Charlton beat Willie Thorne 13–12; Fred Davis beat Dennis Taylor 13–9; Patsy Fagan beat Alex Higgins 13–12; Perrie Mans beat John Spencer 13–8; Graham Miles beat David Taylor 13–10; Ray Reardon beat Doug Mountjoy 13–9; Cliff Thorburn beat Pat Houlihan 13–8; Bill Werbeniuk beat John Pulman 13–4

Round two Eddie Charlton beat Cliff Thorburn 13–12; Fred Davis beat Patsy Fagan 13–10; Perrie Mans beat Graham Miles 13–7; Ray Reardon beat Bill Werbeniuk 13–6

Semi-finals Perrie Mans beat Fred Davis 18–16; Ray Reardon beat Eddie Charlton 18–14

Final Ray Reardon beat Perrie Mans 25–18

1979

Qualifying round one Roy Andrewartha beat Ray Edmonds 9–8; Steve Davis beat Ian Anderson 9–1; John Dunning beat Jackie Rea 9–5; Terry Griffiths beat Bernard Bennett 9–2; Pat Houlihan beat John Barrie 9–5; Jim Meadowcroft beat Jimmy van Rensburg 9–7; Doug Mountjoy beat Derek Mienie 9–1; Kirk Stevens beat Roy Amdor 9–1; Willie Thorne

● ● ● ● ● ● ● ● ● ● ● ● ● ● ● ●

RAY REARDON

Born: 8 October 1932, Tredegar, Wales

Ray Reardon was the 'Mr Snooker' of the 1970s, and between 1973 and 1976 won the world title in four successive years; even Steve Davis has not managed that . . . yet.

Reardon learned his skills in the Welsh valleys where he was a miner. He won the Welsh amateur title six times. The family moved to Stoke-on-Trent in the 1950s and, following an accident, Reardon quit the colliery job to become a policeman. He won the 1964 English amateur title and the following year won the prestigious WMC & IU title.

He became a professional in 1968 and won the first of his world titles in 1970 when he beat John Pulman 37–33. After his four successive titles in the mid-seventies he won his sixth title in 1978 when Perrie Mans was his victim.

Number one in the world rankings every year from 1976 to 1980 and again in 1982, when he reached his seventh world final before losing to Alex Higgins, he has since slipped down the rankings. He has not registered a major win since 1983 when he won the Yamaha International Masters and Welsh professional titles.

Reardon was awarded the MBE for his services to snooker in 1985.

● ● ● ● ● ● ● ● ● ● ● ● ● ● ● ●

beat Jim Charlton 9–3; John Virgo beat Maurice Parkin 9–0; Rex Williams beat David Greaves 9–2

Qualifying round two Steve Davis beat Patsy Fagan 9–2; Terry Griffiths beat Jim Meadowcroft 9–6; Graham Miles beat Rex Williams 9–5; Doug Mountjoy beat Pat Houlihan 9–6; Kirk Stevens beat John Pulman 9–0; David Taylor beat John Dunning 9–8; John Virgo beat Willie Thorne 9–8; Bill Werbeniuk beat Roy Andrewartha 9–2

Round one Eddie Charlton beat Doug Mountjoy 13–6; Fred Davis beat Kirk Stevens 13–8; Terry Griffiths beat Perrie Mans 13–8; Alex Higgins beat David Taylor 13–5; Ray Reardon beat Graham Miles 13–8; Dennis Taylor beat Steve Davis 13–11; John Virgo beat Cliff Thorburn 13–10; Bill Werbeniuk beat John Spencer 13–11

Round two Eddie Charlton beat Fred Davis 13–4; Terry Griffiths beat Alex Higgins 13–12; Dennis Taylor beat Ray Reardon 13–8; John Virgo beat Bill Werbeniuk 13–9

Semi-finals Terry Griffiths beat Eddie Charlton 19–17; Dennis Taylor beat John Virgo 19–12

Final Terry Griffiths beat Dennis Taylor 24–16

1980

Qualifying group one Jackie Rea beat Bernard Bennett 9–1; Willie Thorne beat Kevin Robitaille 9–4; Willie Thorne beat Jackie Rea 9–1

Qualifying group two Steve Davis beat Chris Ross 9–3; Paddy Morgan beat Paul Thornley 9–4; Steve Davis beat Paddy Morgan 9–0

Qualifying group three Mike Hallett beat Kingsley Kennerley 9–2; Kirk Stevens beat David Greaves 9–3; Kirk Stevens beat Mike Hallett 9–3

Qualifying group four Joe Johnson beat Roy Andrewartha 9–5; Pat Houlihan beat Joe Johnson 9–6; Tony Meo beat Jimmy van Rensburg 9–1; Tony Meo beat Pat Houlihan 9–1

Qualifying group five Roy Amdor beat Bernie Mikkelsen 9–7; Rex Williams beat Roy Amdor 9–4; Jim Wych beat John Bear 9–5; Jim Wych beat Rex Williams 9–7

Qualifying group six Frank Jonik beat Mark Wildman 9–7; Cliff Wilson beat Frank Jonik 9–6

Qualifying group seven Ray Edmonds beat Maurice Parkin 9–2; Sid Hood beat John Dunning 9–7; Ray Edmonds beat Sid Hood 9–6

Qualifying group eight Eddie Sinclair beat Mario Morra 9–5; Eddie Sinclair beat Derek Mienie 9–7; Jim Meadowcroft beat Eddie Sinclair 9–1

Round one Steve Davis beat Patsy Fagan 10–6; Alex Higgins beat Tony Meo 10–9; Doug Mountjoy beat Cliff Wilson 10–6; Kirk Stevens beat Graham Miles 10–3; David Taylor beat Ray Edmonds 10–3; John Virgo beat Jim Meadowcroft 10–2; Bill Werbeniuk beat Willie Thorne 10–9; Jim Wych beat John Pulman 10–5

Round two Eddie Charlton beat John Virgo 13–12; Steve Davis beat Terry Griffiths 13–10; Alex Higgins beat Perrie Mans 13–6; Ray Reardon beat Bill Werbeniuk 13–6; Kirk Stevens beat John Spencer 13–8; David Taylor beat Fred Davis 13–5; Cliff Thorburn beat Doug Mountjoy 13–10; Jim Wych beat Dennis Taylor 13–10

Terry Griffiths, the 1979 world champion. He certainly had the world in his hands that year.

Round three Alex Higgins beat Steve Davis 13–9; Kirk Stevens beat Eddie Charlton 13–7; David Taylor beat Ray Reardon 13–11; Cliff Thorburn beat Jim Wych 13–6

Semi-finals Alex Higgins beat Kirk Stevens 16–13; Cliff Thorburn beat David Taylor 16–7

Final Cliff Thorburn beat Alex Higgins 18–16

1981

Qualifying group one David Greaves beat Maurice Parkin 9–5; Willie Thorne beat Mario Morra 9–5; Willie Thorne beat David Greaves 9–3

Qualifying group two Jimmy White beat Bernie Mikkelsen 9–4; Jimmy White beat Jim Meadowcroft 9–8

Qualifying group three Ray Edmonds beat Mark Wildman 9–3; Rex Williams beat Sid Hood 9–4; Ray Edmonds beat Rex Williams 9–7

Qualifying group four Mike Hallett beat Frank Jonik 9–1; Tony Meo beat Joe Johnson 9–8; Tony Meo beat Mike Hallett 9–4

Qualifying group five John Dunning beat Bernard Bennett 9–6; John Dunning beat Patsy Fagan 9–7

Qualifying group six Dave Martin beat Ian Anderson 9–3; Dave Martin beat John Pulman 9–2

Qualifying group seven Eddie Sinclair beat Paddy Morgan 9–8; Cliff Wilson beat Roy Andrewartha 9–4; Cliff Wilson beat Eddie Sinclair 9–4

Qualifying group eight Tony Knowles beat Chris Ross 7–0 (Ross retired); Tony Knowles beat Jim Wych 9–3

Round one Steve Davis beat Jimmy White 10–8; Tony Meo beat John Virgo 10–6; Graham Miles beat Tony Knowles 10–8; Doug Mountjoy beat Willie Thorne 10–6; Kirk Stevens beat John Dunning 10–4; John Spencer beat Ray Edmonds 10–9; David Taylor beat Cliff Wilson 10–6; Bill Werbeniuk beat Dave Martin 10–4

Round two Steve Davis beat Alex Higgins 13–8; Terry Griffiths beat Tony Meo 13–6; Ray Reardon beat John Spencer 13–11; David Taylor beat Fred Davis 13–3; Dennis Taylor beat Kirk Stevens 13–11; Cliff Thorburn beat Graham Miles 13–2; Bill Werbeniuk beat Perrie Mans 13–5; Doug Mountjoy beat Eddie Charlton 13–7

● ● ● ● ● ● ● ● ● ● ● ● ● ● ● ●

TERRY GRIFFITHS

Born: 16 October 1947, Llanelli, Wales

Terry Griffiths has appeared in two world championship finals, in 1979 and 1988. Remarkable as it may seem they were his only two ranking final appearances until he lined up against John Parrott in the 1989 ICI European Open final. However, Griffiths has been ranked in the top-16 every year since 1979 which highlights the consistency of the Welshman.

The Welsh amateur champion in 1975, he won the English title in 1977 and 1978 and shortly after that second success he turned professional. In his first professional event, the Coral UK Championship he led the experienced Rex Williams 8–2 before losing 9–8 in one of the biggest reversals in snooker history. But, a couple of months later, he gained ample compensation when he beat three former finalists, Perrie Mans, Alex Higgins and Eddie Charlton on his way to the Embassy World Professional final. In the final he beat Dennis Taylor 24–16 to end a remarkable debut season as a professional.

In the early eighties Griffiths was Steve Davis's biggest rival and won both the English and Irish versions of the Benson and Hedges Masters, and such other tournaments as the non-ranking Lada Classic and Coral UK Championship in 1982, and the Welsh professional championship in 1985, 1986 and 1988.

He reached his second world final in 1988 but lost to Matchroom stablemate Steve Davis, and in the 1989 European Open was beaten by first-time winner John Parrott.

● ● ● ● ● ● ● ● ● ● ● ● ● ● ● ●

Quarter-finals Steve Davis beat Terry Griffiths 13–9; Ray Reardon beat Bill Werbeniuk 13–10; Cliff Thorburn beat David Taylor 13–6; Doug Mountjoy beat Dennis Taylor 13–6

Semi-finals Steve Davis beat Cliff Thorburn 16–10; Doug Mountjoy beat Ray Reardon 16–10

Final Steve Davis beat Doug Mountjoy 18–12

1982

Qualifying group one John Bear beat Frank Jonik 9–4; John Bear beat Jim Wych 9–4

Qualifying group two Dennis Hughes beat Clive Everton 9–4; Tony Meo beat Dennis Hughes 9–4

Qualifying group three Dean Reynolds beat Dessie Sheehan 9–5; Dean Reynolds beat Ray Edmonds 9–6

Qualifying group four Eugene Hughes beat Derek Mienie w.o.; Tony Knowles beat Eugene Hughes 9–7

Qualifying group five Mark Wildman beat Geoff Foulds 9–8; Jimmy White beat Mark Wildman 9–4

Qualifying group six Colin Roscoe beat Bernie Mikkelsen 9–6; Willie Thorne beat Colin Roscoe 9–1

Qualifying group seven Paul Medati beat John Phillips 9–3; Cliff Wilson beat Paul Medati 9–5

Qualifying group eight Pat Houlihan beat Ian Anderson 9–5; Dave Martin beat Pat Houlihan 9–3

Qualifying group nine Murdo Macleod beat Eddie McLaughlin 9–8; John Dunning beat Murdo Macleod 9–4

Qualifying group ten Mike Watterson beat Bert Demarco 9–6; Jim Meadowcroft beat Mike Watterson 9–7

Qualifying group eleven Doug French beat Bernard Bennett 9–3; Patsy Fagan beat Doug French 9–6

Qualifying group twelve Ian Black beat Maurice Parkin 9–6; Rex Williams beat Ian Black 9–2

Qualifying group thirteen Joe Johnson beat Vic Harris 9–4; Mike Hallett beat Joe Johnson 9–8

Qualifying group fourteen Jim Donnelly beat Matt Gibson 9–8; Eddie Sinclair beat Billy Kelly 9–8; Jim Donnelly beat Eddie Sinclair 9–8

Qualifying group fifteen Silvino Francisco beat Chris Ross 9–0; Paddy Morgan beat David Greaves 9–2; Silvino Francisco beat Paddy Morgan 9–1

Qualifying group sixteen Jack Fitzmaurice beat John Pulman w.o.; Mario Morra beat Tommy Murphy 9–5; Jack Fitzmaurice beat Mario Morra 9–7

Round one Eddie Charlton beat Cliff Wilson 10–5; Patsy Fagan beat David Taylor 10–9; Silvino Francisco beat Dennis Taylor 10–7; Alex Higgins beat Jim Meadowcroft 10–5; Tony Knowles beat Steve Davis 10–1; Perrie Mans beat Tony Meo 10–8; Graham Miles beat Dave Martin 10–5; Doug Mountjoy beat Rex Williams 10–3; Ray Reardon beat Jim Donnelly 10–5; Dean Reynolds beat Fred Davis 10–7; John Spencer beat John Dunning 10–4; Kirk Stevens beat Jack Fitzmaurice 10–4; Willie Thorne beat Terry Griffiths 10–6; John Virgo beat Mike Hallett 10–4; Bill Werbeniuk beat John Bear 10–7; Jimmy White beat Cliff Thorburn 10–4

Round two Eddie Charlton beat Bill Werbeniuk 13–5; Silvino Francisco beat Dean Reynolds 13–8; Alex Higgins beat Doug Mountjoy 13–12; Tony Knowles beat Graham Miles 13–7; Ray Reardon beat John Virgo 13–8; Kirk Stevens beat Patsy Fagan 13–7; Willie Thorne beat John Spencer 13–5; Jimmy White beat Perrie Mans 13–6

Quarter-finals Eddie Charlton beat Tony Knowles 13–11; Alex Higgins beat Willie Thorne 13–10; Ray Reardon beat Silvino Francisco 13–8; Jimmy White beat Kirk Stevens 13–9

Semi-finals Ray Reardon beat Eddie Charlton 16–11; Alex Higgins beat Jimmy White 16–15

Final Alex Higgins beat Ray Reardon 18–15

1983

Qualifying group one Billy Kelly beat Bert Demarco 10–4; Silvino Francisco beat Billy Kelly 10–5

Qualifying group two Paddy Morgan beat Pascal Burke 10–9; Graham Miles beat Paddy Morgan 10–6

Qualifying group three Tommy Murphy beat Pat Houlihan 10–9; John Virgo beat Tommy Murphy 10–8

Qualifying group four Rex Williams beat Mike Darrington 10–0; Rex Williams beat Fred Davis 10–1

Qualifying group five Mark Wildman beat Bob Harris 10–7; Mark Wildman beat Jim Wych w.o.

Qualifying group six Ray Edmonds beat Frank Jonik 10–4; Dean Reynolds beat Ray Edmonds 10–6

Qualifying group seven Mick Fisher beat Patsy Fagan 10–8; Eddie McLaughlin beat David Greaves 10–7; Mick Fisher beat Eddie McLaughlin 10–9

Qualifying group eight Geoff Foulds beat Matt Gibson 10–6; Tony Meo beat Vic Harris 10–0; Tony Meo beat Geoff Foulds 10–4

Qualifying group nine Ian Black beat Mario Morra 10–9; Paul Medati beat John Bear 10–7; Ian Black beat Paul Medati 10–4

Qualifying group ten Joe Johnson beat Paul Watchorn 10–0; Cliff Wilson beat Clive Everton 10–1; Cliff Wilson beat Joe Johnson 10–8

Qualifying group eleven Murdo Macleod beat Marcus Owen 10–5; Dave Martin beat Maurice Parkin 10–1; Dave Martin beat Murdo Macleod 10–7

Qualifying group twelve Graham Cripsey beat Dennis Hughes 10–2; Jim Meadowcroft beat Bernard Bennett 10–3; Jim Meadowcroft beat Graham Cripsey 10–6

Qualifying group thirteen John Campbell beat Mike Watterson 10–6; Jim Donnelly beat Dessie Sheehan 10–6; John Campbell beat Jim Donnelly 10–2

Qualifying group fourteen Les Dodd beat John Dunning w.o.; Ian Williamson beat Doug French 10–8; Les Dodd beat Ian Williamson 10–9

Qualifying group fifteen Mike Hallett beat Roy Andrewartha 10–7; Warren King beat Ian Anderson 10–6; Mike Hallett beat Warren King 10–6

Qualifying group sixteen Eugene Hughes beat Jack Fitzmaurice 10–7; Eddie Sinclair beat Colin Roscoe 10–2; Eugene Hughes beat Eddie Sinclair 10–8

Round one Eddie Charlton beat Les Dodd 10–7; Steve Davis beat Rex Williams 10–4; Terry Griffiths beat Mark Wildman 10–8; Alex Higgins beat Dean Reynolds 10–4; Tony Knowles beat Graham Miles 10–3; Perrie Mans beat Ian Black 10–3; Tony Meo beat Jimmy White 10–8; Doug Mountjoy beat Cliff Wilson 10–2; Ray Reardon beat Eugene Hughes 10–7; John Spencer beat Mike Hallett 10–7; Kirk Stevens beat Mick Fisher 10–2; David Taylor beat Jim Meadowcroft 10–2; Dennis Taylor beat Silvino Francisco 10–9; Cliff Thorburn beat John Campbell 10–5; Willie Thorne beat John Virgo 10–3; Bill Werbeniuk beat Dave Martin 10–4

Round two Eddie Charlton beat John Spencer 13–11; Steve Davis beat Dennis Taylor 13–11; Alex Higgins beat Willie Thorne 13–8; Tony Knowles beat Ray Reardon 13–12; Tony Meo beat Doug Mountjoy 13–11; Kirk Stevens beat Perrie Mans 13–3; Cliff Thorburn beat Terry Griffiths 13–12; Bill Werbeniuk beat David Taylor 13–10

Quarter-finals Steve Davis beat Eddie Charlton 13–5; Alex Higgins beat Bill Werbeniuk 13–11; Tony Knowles beat Tony

Meo 13–9; Cliff Thorburn beat Kirk Stevens 13–12

Semi-finals Steve Davis beat Alex Higgins 16–5; Cliff Thorburn beat Tony Knowles 16–15

Final Steve Davis beat Cliff Thorburn 18–6

1984

Qualifying group one John Parrott beat Dennis Hughes 10–3; John Parrott beat Clive Everton 10–2; John Parrott beat Perrie Mans 10–0

Qualifying group two Bernie Mikkelsen beat Paul Medati 10–8; Bernie Mikkelsen beat Frank Jonik 10–9; Willie Thorne beat Bernie Mikkelsen 10–3

Qualifying group three Mario Morra beat Geoff Foulds 10–2; Tommy Murphy beat Jack Fitzmaurice 10–8; Mario Morra beat Tommy Murphy 10–5; Mario Morra beat Dean Reynolds 10–7

Qualifying group four Paul Mifsud beat Eugene Hughes 10–5; Wayne Sanderson beat Paddy Morgan 10–8; Paul Mifsud beat Wayne Sanderson 10–5; Paul Mifsud beat Cliff Wilson 10–8

Qualifying group five Ray Edmonds beat David Greaves 10–0; Jimmy van Rensburg beat Vic Harris 10–7; Jimmy van Rensburg beat Ray Edmonds 10–9; Silvino Francisco beat Jimmy van Rensburg 10–3

Qualifying group six Mike Hines beat Ian Black 10–5; Ian Williamson beat Pat Houlihan 10–5; Ian Williamson beat Mike Hines 10–6; Graham Miles beat Ian Williamson 10–6

Qualifying group seven Mick Fisher beat Paul Thornley 10–8; Matt Gibson beat Gino Rigitano 10–7; Matt Gibson beat Mick Fisher 10–7; Joe Johnson beat Matt Gibson 10–3

Qualifying group eight Roy Andrewartha beat John Bear w.o.; Eddie McLaughlin beat John Hargreaves 10–5; Roy Andrewartha beat Eddie McLaughlin 10–8; Roy Andrewartha beat Mark Wildman 10–9

Qualifying group nine George Scott beat Leon Heywood 10–7; Jim Wych beat George Ganim 10–1; Jim Wych beat George Scott 10–6; Jim Wych beat Patsy Fagan 10–3

Qualifying group ten Paddy Browne beat Steve Duggan 10–9; Colin Roscoe beat Bert Demarco 10–7; Paddy Browne beat Colin Roscoe 10–4; Eddie Sinclair beat Paddy Browne 10–1

Qualifying group eleven Graham Cripsey beat Maurice Parkin 10–4; Marcel Gauvreau beat John Campbell 10–7; Marcel Gauvreau beat Graham Cripsey 10–1; Marcel Gauvreau beat Murdo Macleod 10–6

Qualifying group twelve Ian Anderson beat Gerry Watson 10–4; Jim Donnelly beat Paul Watchorn 10–7; Jim Donnelly beat Ian Anderson 10–6; Fred Davis beat Jim Donnelly 10–5

Qualifying group thirteen Warren King beat Tony Jones 10–9; Mike Watterson beat Bernard Bennett 10–5; Warren King beat Mike Watterson 10–8; Warren King beat Dave Martin 10–8

Qualifying group fourteen Joe Caggianello beat Mike Darrington 10–7; Bill Oliver beat John Dunning 10–3; Bill Oliver beat Joe Caggianello 10–7; Rex Williams beat Bill Oliver 10–8

● ● ● ● ● ● ● ● ● ● ● ● ● ● ●

TONY KNOWLES

Born: 13 June 1955, Bolton, Greater Manchester

Tony Knowles was the 'Golden Boy' of snooker in the early-eighties. Today he remains just as popular, certainly amongst the female fans, even though he has not won a tournament since the 1984 Winfield Australian Masters.

The under-19 snooker champion in both 1972 and 1974 he was accepted as a professional at his second attempt in 1980. After a consolidatory first season in 1980–1 there followed a great second season.

He reached the quarter-final of the Coral UK Championship and then beat defending champion Steve Davis 10–1 in the Embassy World Championship before losing 13–11 to Eddie Charlton in the quarter-final.

A first success was not far away and it came in the following season's Jameson International when he beat David Taylor 9–6 in the final. He beat Joe Johnson to win the 1983 Professional Players' Tournament and that season climbed to number four in the rankings. He moved up two places in 1983–4 and has since maintained a position in the top-16 despite not winning a ranking event since 1983.

● ● ● ● ● ● ● ● ● ● ● ● ● ● ●

Qualifying group fifteen Les Dodd beat James Giannaros 10–1; Neal Foulds beat Doug French 10–5; Neal Foulds beat Les Dodd 10–4; Neal Foulds beat Jim Meadowcroft 10–2

Qualifying group sixteen Pascal Burke beat Billy Kelly 10–7; Bob Harris beat Dessie Sheehan 10–3; Pascal Burke beat Bob Harris 10–4; Mike Hallett beat Pascal Burke 10–5

Round one Eddie Charlton beat Roy Andrewartha 10–4; Steve Davis beat Warren King 10–3; Neal Foulds beat Alex Higgins 10–9; Silvino Francisco beat Tony Meo 10–5; Terry Griffiths beat Paul Mifsud 10–2; Doug Mountjoy beat Mike Hallett 10–4; John Parrott beat Tony Knowles 10–7; Ray Reardon beat Jim Wych 10–7; John Spencer beat Graham Miles 10–3; Kirk Stevens beat Eddie Sinclair 10–1; Dennis Taylor beat Joe Johnson 10–1; Cliff Thorburn beat Mario Morra 10–3; Willie Thorne beat John Virgo 10–9; Bill Werbeniuk beat Fred Davis 10–4; Jimmy White beat Rex Williams 10–6; David Taylor beat Marcel Gauvreau 10–5

Round two Steve Davis beat John Spencer 13–5; Terry Griffiths beat Bill Werbeniuk 13–5; Doug Mountjoy beat Neal Foulds 13–6; Ray Reardon beat Silvino Francisco 13–8; Kirk Stevens beat David Taylor 13–10; Dennis Taylor beat John Parrott 13–11; Cliff Thorburn beat Willie Thorne 13–11; Jimmy White beat Eddie Charlton 13–7

Quarter-finals Steve Davis beat Terry Griffiths 13–10; Kirk Stevens beat Ray Reardon 13–2; Dennis Taylor beat Doug Mountjoy 13–8; Jimmy White beat Cliff Thorburn 13–8

Semi-finals Steve Davis beat Dennis Taylor 16–9; Jimmy White beat Kirk Stevens 16–14

Final Steve Davis beat Jimmy White 18–16

1985

Qualifying group one Gino Rigitano beat Dessie Sheehan 10–9; Gino Rigitano beat Bob Harris 10–4; Gino Rigitano beat Billy Kelly 10–6; Gino Rigitano beat Mick Fisher 10–2; Neal Foulds beat Gino Rigitano 10–8

Qualifying group two Dene O'Kane beat Jack McLaughlin w.o.; Dene O'Kane beat Vic Harris 10–5; Dene O'Kane beat Frank Jonik 10–5; Dene O'Kane beat Les Dodd 10–7; Dene O'Kane beat Dave Martin 10–8

Qualifying group three Steve Longworth beat James Giannaros 10–1; Steve Longworth beat Graham Cripsey 10–8; Jimmy van Rensburg beat Steve Longworth 10–7; Marcel Gauvreau beat Jimmy van Rensburg 10–9; Dean Reynolds beat Marcel Gauvreau 10–1

Qualifying group four Bob Chaperon beat Roger Bales 10–4; Bob Chaperon beat Leon Heywood 10–1; Bob Chaperon beat Paddy Morgan 10–3; Fred Davis beat Bob Chaperon 10–9; Rex Williams beat Fred Davis 10–6

Qualifying group five Dennis Hughes beat Doug French 10–5; Steve Newbury beat Dennis Hughes 10–9; Steve Newbury beat Pascal Burke 10–3; Steve Newbury beat George Scott 10–2; Eugene Hughes beat Steve Newbury 10–6

Qualifying group six Mike Hines beat Tony Chappel 10–8; Mike Hines beat Paul Watchorn 10–4; Matt Gibson beat Mike Hines 10–7; Patsy Fagan beat Mike Gibson 10–8; Patsy Fagan beat Cliff Wilson 10–9

Qualifying group seven Danny Fowler beat John Hargreaves 10–0; Danny Fowler beat Gerry Watson w.o.; Danny Fowler beat Joe Caggianello w.o.; Danny Fowler beat Jim Donnelly 10–0; John Parrott beat Danny Fowler 10–2

Qualifying group eight Robbie Foldvari beat Paul Thornley w.o.; Robbie Foldvari beat Bill Oliver 10–3; Ray Edmonds beat Robbie Foldvari 10–3; Ray Edmonds beat Mark Wildman 10–7

Qualifying group nine Dave Chalmers beat David Greaves 10–3; Dave Chalmers beat Eddie McLaughlin 10–9; Dave Chalmers beat Ian Black 10–4; Mike Hallett beat Dave Chalmers 10–1

Qualifying group ten Geoff Foulds beat Maurice Parkin 10–6; Geoff Foulds beat Clive Everton 10–2; Geoff Foulds beat Colin Roscoe 10–7; Joe Johnson beat Geoff Foulds 10–6

Qualifying group eleven Paul Medati beat Bernard Bennett 10–4; Paul Medati beat Ian Williamson 10–8; Paul Medati beat Warren King 10–9; Silvino Francisco beat Paul Medati 10–7

Qualifying group twelve Ian Anderson beat Tony Kearney 10–8; Paddy Browne beat Ian Anderson 10–5; Mario Morra beat Paddy Browne 10–6; John Campbell beat Mario Morra 10–9

Qualifying group thirteen Wayne Jones beat John Rea 10–3; Wayne Jones beat John Dunning 10–6; Wayne Jones beat

Mike Watterson 10–5; Wayne Jones beat Graham Miles 10–8

Qualifying group fourteen Malcolm Bradley beat Derek Mienie 10–4; Malcolm Bradley beat Bernie Mikkelsen 10–9; Jim Wych beat Malcolm Bradley 10–7; John Virgo beat Jim Wych 10–4

Qualifying group fifteen Peter Francisco beat Bert Demarco 10–4; Peter Francisco beat Tommy Murphy 10–4; Peter Francisco beat Jim Meadowcroft 10–5; Murdo Macleod beat Peter Francisco 10–7

Qualifying group sixteen Tony Jones beat Mike Darrington 10–2; Tony Jones beat Steve Duggan 10–8; Tony Jones beat Jack Fitzmaurice 10–4; Tony Jones beat Eddie Sinclair 10–2

Round one Eddie Charlton beat John Campbell 10–3; Steve Davis beat Neal Foulds 10–8; Patsy Fagan beat Willie Thorne 10–6; Terry Griffiths beat Rex Williams 10–3; Alex Higgins beat Dean Reynolds 10–4; Tony Knowles beat Tony Jones 10–8; Tony Meo beat John Virgo 10–6; Doug Mountjoy beat Murdo Macleod 10–5; John Parrott beat John Spencer 10–3; Ray Reardon beat Eugene Hughes 10–9; Kirk Stevens beat Ray Edmonds 10–8; David Taylor beat Dene O'Kane 10–4; Dennis Taylor beat Silvino Francisco 10–2; Cliff Thorburn beat Mike Hallett 10–8; Bill Werbeniuk beat Joe Johnson 10–8; Jimmy White beat Wayne Jones 10–4

Round two Steve Davis beat David Taylor 13–4; Terry Griffiths beat Alex Higgins 13–7; Tony Knowles beat Doug Mountjoy 13–6; John Parrott beat Kirk Stevens 13–6; Ray Reardon beat Patsy Fagan 13–9; Dennis Taylor beat Eddie Charlton 13–6; Cliff Thorburn beat Bill Werbeniuk 13–3; Jimmy White beat Tony Meo 13–11

Quarter-finals Steve Davis beat Terry Griffiths 13–6; Tony Knowles beat Jimmy White 13–10; Ray Reardon beat John Parrott 13–12; Dennis Taylor beat Cliff Thorburn 13–5

Semi-finals Steve Davis beat Ray Reardon 16–5; Dennis Taylor beat Tony Knowles 16–5

Final Dennis Taylor beat Steve Davis 18–17

1986

Qualifying round one Dave Gilbert beat Roger Bales 10–7; Omprakash Agrawal beat Dennis Hughes 10–6; Anthony Kearney beat Glen Wilkinson 10–5; Bill Oliver beat Joe O'Boye 10–8; Dessie Sheehan beat Pat Houlihan 10–7; Matt Gibson beat Greg Jenkins 10–4; Satchai Simngam beat Bernard Bennett 10–0; Jim Bear beat Pascal Burke 10–8; Tony Drago beat Graham Cripsey 10–4; Martin Smith beat David Greaves 10–4; Barry West beat James Giannaros w.o.; Paul Thornley beat Derek Mienie 10–3; Robbie Grace beat Maurice Parkin 10–8; Stephen Hendry beat Bert Demarco 10–7; Paul Watchorn beat Jim Rempe w.o.; Bernie Mikkelsen beat John Hargreaves 10–7; Mike Darrington beat Wayne Sanderson w.o.

Qualifying round two Jim Wych beat Tony Chappel 10–6; Steve Duggan beat Mick Fisher 10–3; Tony Jones beat Vic Harris 10–7; Dave Gilbert beat Malcolm Bradley 10–7; Steve Newbury beat Omprakash Agrawal 10–5; Ian Black beat Bob Harris 10–8; George Scott beat Anthony Kearney 10–8; Danny Fowler beat Bill Oliver 10–8; Colin Roscoe beat Geoff

Foulds 10–3; Warren King beat Dessie Sheehan 10–4; Matt Gibson beat Mario Morra 10–9; Paul Medati beat Satchai Simngam 10–9; Bob Chaperon beat Frank Jonik 10–8; Marcel Gauvreau beat Jim Bear 10–5; Fred Davis beat Dave Chalmers 10–6; Peter Francisco beat Tony Drago 10–4; Barry West beat John Dunning 10–3; Wayne Jones beat Robbie Grace 10–3; Steve Longworth beat Paul Watchorn 10–7; Mike Watterson beat Bernie Mikkelsen 10–2; Les Dodd beat Jack Fitzmaurice 10–6; Mike Darrington beat Jim Meadowcroft 10–6; John Rea beat Eddie McLaughlin 10–6; Jim Donnelly beat Martin Smith 10–6; Stephen Hendry beat Paddy Browne 10–9; Eddie Sinclair beat Paddy Morgan 10–8; Tommy Murphy beat Jack McLaughlin 10–7; Paul Thornley beat Patsy Fagan 10–7; Graham Miles beat Clive Everton 10–3; Robbie Foldvari beat Gino Rigitano 10–6; Ray Edmonds beat Billy Kelly 10–0; Jimmy van Rensburg beat Ian Williamson 10–9

Qualifying round three Stephen Hendry beat Wayne Jones 10–8; Barry West beat Jim Donnelly 10–5; Tommy Murphy beat Paul Thornley 10–3; Jim Wych beat Steve Duggan 10–5; Dave Gilbert beat Tony Jones 10–7; Steve Newbury beat Ian Black 10–2; Danny Fowler beat George Scott 10–7; Warren King beat Colin Roscoe 10–5; Paul Medati beat Matt Gibson 10–6; Marcel Gauvreau beat Bob Chaperon 10–8; Peter Francisco beat Fred Davis 10–1; Jimmy van Rensburg beat Eddie Sinclair 10–2; Steve Longworth beat John Rea 10–4; Robbie Foldvari beat Graham Miles 10–7; Les Dodd beat Mike Watterson 10–1; Ray Edmonds beat Mike Darrington 10–5

Qualifying round four Mike Hallett beat Jim Wych 10–7; Dave Martin beat Dave Gilbert 10–5; John Spencer beat Steve Newbury 10–7; Danny Fowler beat Murdo Macleod 10–6; Dean Reynolds beat Warren King 10–7; Cliff Wilson beat Paul Medati 10–6; Rex Williams beat Marcel Gauvreau 10–3; Neal Foulds beat Peter Francisco 10–9; Bill Werbeniuk beat Barry West 10–8; Eugene Hughes beat Tommy Murphy 10–7; Stephen Hendry beat Dene O'Kane 10–9; John Campbell beat Jimmy van Rensburg 10–6; John Virgo beat Steve Longworth 10–8; John Parrott beat Robbie Foldvari 10–6; Perrie Mans beat Les Dodd 10–7; Ray Edmonds beat Mark Wildman 10–9

Round one Mike Hallett beat Dennis Taylor 10–6; Joe Johnson beat Dave Martin 10–3; Alex Higgins beat John Spencer 10–7; Terry Griffiths beat Danny Fowler 10–2; Kirk Stevens beat Dean Reynolds 10–6; Eddie Charlton beat Cliff Wilson 10–6; Silvino Francisco beat Rex Williams 10–4; Tony Knowles beat Neal Foulds 10–9; Cliff Thorburn beat Bill Werbeniuk 10–5; Eugene Hughes beat David Taylor 10–7; Willie Thorne beat Stephen Hendry 10–8; John Campbell beat Ray Reardon 10–8; Jimmy White beat John Virgo 10–7; John Parrott beat Tony Meo 10–4; Doug Mountjoy beat Perrie Mans 10–3; Steve Davis beat Ray Edmonds 10–4

Round two Joe Johnson beat Mike Hallett 13–6; Terry Griffiths beat Alex Higgins 13–12; Cliff Thorburn beat Eugene Hughes 13–6; Willie Thorne beat John Campbell 13–9; Jimmy White beat John Parrott 13–8; Steve Davis beat Doug Mountjoy 13–5; Kirk Stevens beat Eddie Charlton 13–12; Tony Knowles beat Silvino Francisco 13–10

Quarter-finals Joe Johnson beat Terry Griffiths 13–12; Tony Knowles beat Kirk Stevens 13–9; Cliff Thorburn beat Willie Thorne 13–6; Steve Davis beat Jimmy White 13–5

Bradford's Joe Johnson shares his 1986 world championship glory with wife Terryl.

Semi-finals Joe Johnson beat Tony Knowles 16–8; Steve Davis beat Cliff Thorburn 16–12

Final Joe Johnson beat Steve Davis 18–12

1987

Qualifying round one Geoff Foulds beat Paul Watchorn 10–6; Dennis Hughes beat Maurice Parkin 10–5; Colin Roscoe beat Terry Whitthread 10–2; Mario Morra beat Paul Gibson 10–6; Steve James beat Mike Watterson 10–2; Greg Jenkins beat Robbie Grace 10–9; David Greaves beat Paul Thornley 10–6; Mike Darrington beat Bert Demarco 10–6; Jim Rempe beat Martin Smith 10–9; Ken Owers beat Mick Fisher 10–5; Mark Bennett beat John Hargreaves 10–6; Billy Kelly beat Bernard Bennett 10–0; Jim Meadowcroft beat Derek Mienie 10–3; Bill Oliver beat Pascal Burke 10–5; Nigel Gilbert beat Dessie Sheehan 10–6; Jack Fitzmaurice beat Clive Everton 10–2; John Dunning beat Joe Caggianello 10–7; Jon Wright beat Pat Houlihan 10–4; Jim Bear beat Jackie Rea 10–5; Gino Rigitano beat Paddy Morgan 4–0 (Morgan retired); Dave Chalmers beat Eddie McLaughlin w.o.; David Roe beat Omprakash Agrawal w.o.; Tony Kearney beat Frank Jonik w.o.; Brian Boswell beat Satchai Simngam w.o.

Qualifying round two Steve Newbury beat Les Dodd 10–7; Bill Oliver beat Patsy Fagan 10–2; Marcel Gauvreau beat Jim Bear 10–3; Ray Edmonds beat Steve James 10–1; John Spencer beat Roger Bales 10–3; Steve Duggan beat Colin Roscoe 10–7; George Scott beat John Dunning 10–7; Gino

JOE JOHNSON

Born: 29 July 1952, Bradford

Joe Johnson took on the world and beat them in 1986. He then went away, had a disastrous season, but then returned to The Crucible and nearly repeated his performance.

The national under-19 snooker champion in 1971, he was runner-up to Cliff Wilson in the 1978 world amateur championship. A year later he joined the professional ranks. A grossly-underrated player Joe never had any major successes in the professional game. The nearest he came to a win was in the 1983 Professional Players' Tournament at Bristol when he lost 9–8 to Tony Knowles.

But, at The Crucible in 1986 Joe enjoyed the greatest 17 days of his life as he went all the way to the final where he beat Steve Davis 18–12. The following year after a terrible season he came through the pack as an outsider to reach his second successive final in the first-ever repeat final at The Crucible. This time Davis reversed the tables and won 18–14.

Joe has since won the Langs Scottish Masters and maintained his position amongst the top-16.

Rigitano beat Vic Harris 10–6; Bob Chaperon beat Jack Fitzmaurice 10–2; Malcolm Bradley beat Brian Rowswell 10–6; Tommy Murphy beat Greg Jenkins 10–4; Dene O'Kane beat Dave Gilbert 10–2; Matt Gibson beat Billy Kelly 10–9; Warren King beat David Roe 10–4; Wayne Jones beat Jim Donnelly 10–3; Ken Owers beat Fred Davis 10–5; Mark Wildman beat Robbie Foldvari 10–5; Jon Wright beat Paddy Browne 10–6; Joe O'Boye beat Nigel Gilbert 10–5; Graham Miles beat David Greaves 10–7; Stephen Hendry beat Mike Darrington 10–7; Jimmy van Rensburg beat Jack McLaughlin 10–6; Graham Cripsey beat Jim Meadowcroft 10–9; Ian Black beat Ian Williamson 10–8; Mark Bennett beat Bernie Mikkelsen 10–4; Jim Rempe beat John Rea 10–9; Tony Chappel beat Mario Morra 10–8; Paul Medati beat Tony Kearney 10–8; Danny Fowler beat Geoff Foulds 10–6; Eddie Sinclair beat Tony Drago 10–9; Tony Jones beat Dave Chalmers 10–1; Bob Harris beat Dennis Hughes 10–2

Qualifying round three Danny Fowler beat Bob Harris 10–6; Tony Chappel beat Steve Duggan 10–3; Tony Jones beat Jimmy van Rensburg 10–0; Paul Medati beat Marcel Gauvreau 10–3; Graham Cripsey beat Matt Gibson 10–4; Ray Edmonds beat Eddie Sinclair 10–6; Jon Wright beat Mark Wildman 10–0; Mark Bennett beat Wayne Jones 10–3; Warren King beat Ken Owers 10–4; Dene O'Kane beat Ian Black 10–2; Steve Newbury beat Gino Rigitano 10–4; Stephen Hendry beat Jim Rempe 10–4; Bill Oliver beat George Scott 10–5; John Spencer beat Bob Chaperon 10–4; Tommy Murphy beat Graham Miles 10–7; Malcolm Bradley beat Joe O'Boye 10–7

Qualifying round four John Parrott beat Danny Fowler 10–3; John Campbell beat Tony Chappel 10–6; John Virgo beat Tony Jones 10–9; Eugene Hughes beat Paul Medati 10–2; David Taylor beat Graham Cripsey 10–7; Murdo Macleod beat Ray Edmonds 10–7; Jon Wright beat Cliff Wilson 10–4; Mark Bennett beat Bill Werbeniuk 10–8; Warren King beat Eddie Charlton 10–4; Dene O'Kane beat Peter Francisco 10–5; Mike Hallett beat Steve Newbury 10–4; Stephen Hendry beat Dave Martin 10–7; Dean Reynolds beat Bill Oliver 10–7; Barry West beat John Spencer 10–5; Steve Longworth beat Tommy Murphy 10–2; Jim Wych beat Malcolm Bradley 10–7

Round one Steve Davis beat Warren King 10–7; Joe Johnson beat Eugene Hughes 10–9; Ray Reardon beat Barry West 10–5; Murdo Macleod beat Rex Williams 10–5; Terry Griffiths beat Jim Wych 10–4; Stephen Hendry beat Willie Thorne 10–7; Steve Longworth beat Kirk Stevens 10–4; Alex Higgins beat Jon Wright 10–6; Mike Hallett beat Tony Knowles 10–6; Jimmy White beat Dean Reynolds 10–8; John Parrott beat Tony Meo 10–8; Silvino Francisco beat John Campbell 10–3; Neal Foulds beat John Virgo 10–4; Doug Mountjoy beat David Taylor 10–5; Dennis Taylor beat Mark Bennett 10–4; Dene O'Kane beat Cliff Thorburn 10–5

Round two Joe Johnson beat Murdo Macleod 13–7; Steve Davis beat Ray Reardon 13–4; Terry Griffiths beat Alex Higgins 13–10; Stephen Hendry beat Steve Longworth 13–7; Jimmy White beat John Parrott 13–11; Mike Hallett beat Silvino Francisco 13–9; Neal Foulds beat Dennis Taylor 13–10; Dene O'Kane beat Doug Mountjoy 13–5

Quarter-finals Joe Johnson beat Stephen Hendry 13–12; Jimmy White beat Dene O'Kane 13–6; Steve Davis beat Terry Griffiths 13–5; Neal Foulds beat Mike Hallett 13–9

Semi-finals Joe Johnson beat Neal Foulds 16–9; Steve Davis beat Jimmy White 16–11

Final Steve Davis beat Joe Johnson 18–14

1988

Preliminary round Anthony Harris beat Steve Mizerak 10–2

Qualifying round one Graham Miles beat Dennis Hughes 10–3; Nigel Gilbert beat John Rea 10–5; Colin Roscoe beat Eddie McLaughlin 10–1; Paul Gibson beat Des Sheehan 10–9; Billy Kelly beat Tony Kearney 10–4; Bill Oliver beat Dave Chalmers 10–9; Brian Rowswell beat Paul Thornley 10–7; Jason Smith beat Jim Donnelly 10–4; Gino Rigitano beat John Dunning 10–7; Martin Clark beat Mike Darrington 10–5; Paul Watchorn beat Matt Gibson 10–7; Glen Wilkinson beat Clive Everton 10–2; Mario Morra beat Steve Meakin 10–5; Dave Gilbert beat Derek Heaton 10–2; Patsy Fagan beat David Greaves 10–3; Eddie Sinclair beat Pascal Burke 10–2; David Roe beat Bert Demarco 10–2; Paul Medati beat Gary Wilkinson 10–9; Jim Chambers beat Mike Watterson 10–3; Jack Fitzmaurice beat Maurice Parkin 10–6; Anthony Harris beat Mick Fisher 10–4; Ian Williamson beat Joe Caggianello w.o., Alain Robidoux beat Frank Jonik w.o.; Steve James beat Terry Whitthread w.o.; Martin Smith beat Vic Harris 10–6; Eric Lawlor beat Jimmy van Rensburg w.o.; Bernie Mikkelsen beat Jack Rea 10–3; Robbie Foldvari beat Jim Rempe 10–4; Jim Meadowcroft beat Bernard Bennett 10–5; Ian Black beat John Hargreaves w.o.; Jim Bear beat Derek Mienie 10–4

Qualifying round two Steve Duggan beat Anthony Harris 10–4; Paul Gibson beat Marcel Gauvreau 10–9; Steve James beat Joe O'Boye 10–7; Warren King beat Paul Watchorn 10–4; Martin Clark beat George Scott 10–4; Mark Bennett beat Gino Rigitano 10–4; Paddy Browne beat Billy Kelly 10–9; Bob Chaperon beat Robert Marshall 10–3; Graham Miles beat Roger Bales 10–7; Tony Chappel beat Nigel Gilbert 10–8; Malcolm Bradley beat Ian Williamson 10–9; Bill Werbeniuk beat Brian Rowswell 10–6; Wayne Jones beat Glen Wilkinson 10–4; Martin Smith beat Jack McLaughlin 10–3; Jim Wych beat Jason Smith 10–3; Bill Oliver beat Ray Reardon 10–6; Steve Newbury beat Eric Lawlor 10–3; Robbie Foldvari beat Tony Jones 10–9; Les Dodd beat Paul Medati 10–6; Jim Bear beat Geoff Foulds 10–2; Ken Owers beat David Roe 10–7; Eddie Sinclair beat Dene O'Kane 10–9; Bob Harris beat Patsy Fagan 10–1; Jon Wright beat Jim Chambers 10–2; Fred Davis beat Jack Fitzmaurice 10–8; Mark Wildman beat Bernie Mikkelsen 10–5; Tommy Murphy beat Colin Roscoe 10–8; Alain Robidoux beat Robbie Grace w.o.; Mario Morra beat Ray Edmonds 10–8; Graham Cripsey beat Jim Meadowcroft 10–3; Pat Houlihan beat Dave Gilbert w.o.; Danny Fowler beat Ian Black 10–1

Qualifying round three Tony Chappel beat Graham Miles 10–7; Bill Oliver beat Alain Robidoux 10–2; Bob Chaperon beat Tommy Murphy 10–5; Bill Werbeniuk beat Malcolm Bradley 10–8; Mark Bennett beat Jim Wych 10–5; Steve James beat Paddy Browne 10–1; Bob Harris beat Eddie Sinclair 10–0; Jon Wright beat Ken Owers 10–8; Fred Davis beat Jim Bear 10–4; Graham Cripsey beat Pat Houlihan 10–4; Steve Newbury beat Martin Smith 10–9; Robbie Foldvari beat Mark Wildman 10–1; Danny Fowler beat Les Dodd 10–8; Wayne Jones beat Mario Morra 10–8; Steve Duggan beat Paul Gibson 10–9; Warren King beat Martin Clark 10–9

● ● ● ● ● ● ● ● ● ● ● ● ● ● ● ●

STEVE JAMES

Born: 2 May 1961, Cannock, Staffordshire

West-Midlander Steve James came into the professional game as one of the first intakes via the pro-ticket series in 1986. It has taken him a couple of years to adjust to the new environment but he showed in 1988-9 that he is capable of pushing the best of players.

He first gave warning of his talent in the 1988 world championship when he was one of the stars at The Crucible. Not only did he beat Rex Williams and former champion Joe Johnson before losing to Cliff Thorburn in the quarter-final, but he compiled the highest break of the tournament, 140, which earned him a £9500 prize.

Carrying on where he left off, Steve reached the semi-final of the first ranking tournament of the next season, the Fidelity International at Trentham Gardens, but lost heavily 9-1, to Steve Davis. A steady collection of ranking points, however, lifted him up the rankings from 32 into the top-16.

● ● ● ● ● ● ● ● ● ● ● ● ● ● ● ●

Qualifying round four Tony Drago beat Tony Chappel 10-7; Bill Werbeniuk beat Tony Meo 10-4; Warren King beat John Spencer 10-7; Bob Chaperon beat David Taylor 10-6; Steve James beat Eugene Hughes 10-6; Danny Fowler beat Murdo Macleod 10-3; Cliff Wilson beat Bill Oliver 10-6; Kirk Stevens beat Mark Bennett 10-7; Steve Longworth beat Graham Cripsey 10-2; John Campbell beat Fred Davis 10-3; Stephen Hendry beat Jon Wright 10-4; Eddie Charlton beat Bob Harris 10-4; Wayne Jones beat Dave Martin 10-5; Peter Francisco beat Robbie Foldvari 10-5; Barry West beat Steve Newbury 10-8; John Virgo beat Steve Duggan 10-5

Round one Terry Griffiths beat Steve Longworth 10-1; Mike Hallett beat Bob Chaperon 10-2; Tony Drago beat Alex Higgins 10-2; Jimmy White beat John Campbell 10-3; John Parrott beat Warren King 10-4; Stephen Hendry beat Dean Reynolds 10-6; Willie Thorne beat Peter Francisco 10-6; Steve James beat Rex Williams 10-6; Doug Mountjoy beat Barry West 10-6; Cliff Thorburn beat Kirk Stevens 10-6; Eddie Charlton beat Silvino Francisco 10-7; Neal Foulds beat Wayne Jones 10-7; Tony Knowles beat Danny Fowler 10-7; Joe Johnson beat Cliff Wilson 10-7; Steve Davis beat John Virgo 10-8; Dennis Taylor beat Bill Werbeniuk 10-8

Round two Steve Davis beat Mike Hallett 13-1; Neal Foulds beat Doug Mountjoy 13-1; Tony Drago beat Dennis Taylor 13-5; Tony Knowles beat Eddie Charlton 13-7; Steve James beat Joe Johnson 13-9; Terry Griffiths beat Willie Thorne 13-9; Cliff Thorburn beat John Parrott 13-10; Jimmy White beat Stephen Hendry 13-12

Quarter-finals Steve Davis beat Tony Drago 13-4; Jimmy White beat Tony Knowles 13-6; Terry Grifffiths beat Neal Foulds 13-9; Cliff Thorburn beat Steve James 13-11

Semi-finals Steve Davis beat Cliff Thorburn 16-8; Terry Griffiths beat Jimmy White 16-11

Final Steve Davis beat Terry Griffiths 18-11

1989

Qualifying round one Nick Terry beat Maurice Parkin 10-0; Craig Edwards beat James Giannaros 10-4; Mark Rowing beat Steve Mizerak 10-1; Bernard Bennett beat Clive Everton 10-4; Paul Thornley beat Bert Demarco 10-3; Tony Wilson beat Mannie Francisco 10-5; Derek Mienie beat Wally Postanik 10-6; Mark Johnston-Allen beat Eddie McLaughlin 10-3; Ian Graham beat David Greaves 10-0; Joe Grech beat Derek Heaton 10-6; Robert Marshall beat Mike Hines 10-1; Darren Morgan beat Sam Frangie 10-5; Steve Campbell beat Gerry Watson w.o.; Mick Price beat Paddy Morgan w.o.

Qualifying round two Nick Terry beat Paul Medati 10-8; Craig Edwards beat Jim Bear 10-7; Mark Rowing beat John Dunning 10-9; Fred Davis beat Bernard Bennett 10-4; Paul Thornley beat Malcolm Bradley 10-7; Patsy Fagan beat Geoff Foulds 10-6; Bill Oliver beat Jim Rempe 10-5; Paul Watchorn beat Robbie Grace 10-6; Mario Morra beat Bernie Mikkelsen 10-4; Matt Gibson beat Mike Darrington 10-0; Terry Whitthread beat Jim Donnelly 10-7; Tony Wilson beat George Scott 10-4; Jim Meadowcroft beat Derek Mienie 10-7; Steve Meakin beat Tony Kearney 10-3; Jack Fitzmaurice beat Colin Roscoe 10-9; Vic Harris beat Mike Watterson 10-5; Anthony Harris beat Jimmy van Rensburg 10-7; Mark Johnston-Allen beat Gino Rigitano 10-3; Ian Graham beat Bob Harris w.o.; Martin Smith beat Steve Campbell 10-9; Jason Smith beat Robbie Foldvari 10-4; Jim Chambers beat Ian Anderson 10-7; Joe Grech beat Ian Williamson 10-7; Glen Wilkinson beat Billy Kelly 10-2; John Rea beat Dennis Hughes 10-3; Ian Black beat Dessie Sheehan 10-8; Mick Price beat Eddie Sinclair 10-9; Brian Rowswell beat Pascal Burke 10-0; Paul Gibson beat Robert Marshall 10-3; Darren Morgan beat Eric Lawlor 10-2; François Ellis beat Mark Wildman 10-7; Alain Robidoux beat Graham Miles 10-8

Qualifying round three Nigel Gilbert beat Nick Terry 10-5; Craig Edwards beat Tony Chappel 10-7; Mark Rowing beat Warren King 10-7; Steve Duggan beat Fred Davis 10-3; Paul Thornley beat Bill Werbeniuk w.o.; Dave Gilbert beat Patsy Fagan 10-4; Tommy Murphy beat Bill Oliver 10-8; David Roe beat Paul Watchorn 10-5; Martin Clark beat Mario Morra 10-6; Dave Martin beat Matt Gibson 10-7; Danny Fowler beat Terry Whitthread 10-6; Joe O'Boye beat Tony Wilson 10-8; Murdo Macleod beat Jim Meadowcroft 10-9; Paddy Browne beat Steve Meakin 10-9; Ray Reardon beat Jack Fitzmaurice 10-5; Gary Wilkinson beat Vic Harris 10-6; Wayne Jones beat Anthony Harris 10-4; Jim Wych beat Mark Johnston-Allen 10-3; Ian Graham beat Graham Cripsey 10-2; Martin Smith beat Jon Wright 10-7; Tony Jones beat Jason Smith 10-7; Kirk Stevens beat Jim Chambers 10-8; Les Dodd beat Joe Grech 10-9; Glen Wilkinson beat Roger Bales 10-1; John Rea beat Pat Houlihan 10-5; Ray Edmonds beat Ian Black 10-3; Mick Price beat Mark Bennett 10-9; Brian Rowswell beat Marcel Gauvreau 10-7; Ken Owers beat Paul Gibson 10-8; Darren Morgan beat John Campbell 10-4; Jack McLaughlin beat François Ellis 10-9; Alain Robidoux beat Mick Fisher 10-2

Steve Davis and the world championship trophy are inseparable, as is Steve from manager Barry Hearn (left).

Qualifying round four Nigel Gilbert beat Craig Edwards 10–8; Steve Duggan beat Mark Rowing 10–6; Dave Gilbert beat Paul Thornley 10–4; David Roe beat Tommy Murphy 10–7; Martin Clark beat Dave Martin 10–2; Joe O'Boye beat Danny Fowler 10–6; Paddy Browne beat Murdo Macleod 10–6; Gary Wilkinson beat Ray Reardon 10–5; Wayne Jones beat Jim Wych 10–9; Ian Graham beat Martin Smith 10–6; Tony Jones beat Kirk Stevens 10–2; Les Dodd beat Glen Wilkinson 10–4; John Rea beat Ray Edmonds 10–7; Brian Rowswell beat Mick Price 10–6; Darren Morgan beat Ken Owers 10–8; Alain Robidoux beat Jack McLaughlin 10–2

Qualifying round five Steve Newbury beat Nigel Gilbert 10–7; Steve Duggan beat John Spencer 10–1; Doug Mountjoy beat Dave Gilbert 10–7; David Roe beat Rex Williams 10–3; Bob Chaperon beat Martin Clark 10–4; Joe O'Boye beat Barry West 10–7; Paddy Browne beat Steve Longworth 10–0; Joe O'Boye beat Tony Drago 10–9; Wayne Jones beat David Taylor 10–7; Dean Reynolds beat Ian Graham 10–5; Tony Meo beat Tony Jones 10–7; Eddie Charlton beat Les Dodd 10–6; Steve James beat John Rea 10–7; Eugene Hughes beat Brian Rowswell 10–9; Darren Morgan beat Alex Higgins 10–8; Dene O'Kane beat Alain Robidoux 10–5

Round one Steve Davis beat Steve Newbury 10–5; Jimmy White beat Dene O'Kane 10–5; Steve Duggan beat Cliff Wilson 10–1; John Virgo beat Darren Morgan 10–4; Mike Hallett beat Doug Mountjoy 10–7; David Roe beat Tony Knowles 10–6; John Parrott beat Steve James 10–9; Dennis Taylor beat Eugene Hughes 10–3; Eddie Charlton beat Cliff Thorburn 10–9; Terry Griffiths beat Bob Chaperon 10–6; Tony Meo beat Joe Johnson 10–5; Silvino Francisco beat Joe O'Boye 10–6; Willie Thorne beat Paddy Browne 10–5; Wayne Jones beat Neal Foulds 10–9; Stephen Hendry beat Gary Wilkinson 10–9; Dean Reynolds beat Peter Francisco 10–7

Round two Steve Davis beat Steve Duggan 13–3; Jimmy White beat John Virgo 13–12; Mike Hallett beat David Roe 13–12; John Parrott beat Dennis Taylor 13–10; Terry Griffiths beat Silvino Francisco 13–9; Tony Meo beat Eddie Charlton 13–8; Dean Reynolds beat Wayne Jones 13–3; Stephen Hendry beat Willie Thorne 13–4

Quarter-finals Steve Davis beat Mike Hallett 13–3; Stephen Hendry beat Terry Griffiths 13–5; John Parrott beat Jimmy White 13–7; Tony Meo beat Dean Reynolds 13–9

Semi-finals Steve Davis beat Stephen Hendry 16–9; John Parrott beat Tony Meo 16–7

Final Steve Davis beat John Parrott 18–3

The Crucible Finals 1977–89

1977

After a disastrous championship under their first sponsorship in 1976, W. D. & H. O. Wills nearly quit snooker. It was only Mike Watterson's persuasiveness that maintained Wills's interest. And under the Embassy banner the championship moved to the plush surroundings of The Crucible Theatre, Sheffield, in 1977.

That move was to be one of the best for both snooker and Embassy. The two are now closely associated with each other, and the 17 days at The Crucible each spring is one of the highlights of the sporting calendar.

The two men who had the privilege of fighting out The Crucible's first final were John Spencer of England and Canada's Cliff Thorburn.

For Thorburn his entry into the arena for the final came just 12 hours after a gruelling 34-frame match against his old friend and foe, Dennis Taylor.

Looking jaded, the Canadian soon fell away and let Spencer build up a 4–2 lead at the end of the first morning session in the best-of-49 frame match. Thorburn got his game together on the first afternoon and ended the session at 6-all. Thorburn led for the first time when he won the opening two frames in the evening but Spencer had a 105 break in the final session to end the first day level at 9–9. Spencer's 105 was to be the only century of the final.

The morning session on day two belonged to the Canadian and he edged in front 13–11 at the

John Spencer (left) and Cliff Thorburn before the start of the 1977 world final, the first at The Crucible.

● ● ● ● ● ● ● ● ● ● ● ● ● ● ● ●

CLIFF THORBURN

Born: 16 January 1948, Victoria, Canada

When the first ranking list was drawn up in 1976 Cliff Thorburn occupied 13th place. The following season he was sixth and since then his lowest position has been seventh which indicates how consistent a performer the Canadian has been.

A professional since 1973 he reached The Crucible's first world championship final in 1977 but lost to John Spencer. Three years later he was back and this time it was success as he beat Alex Higgins 18–16 in a great final.

The following season he climbed to number one in the world rankings. He won the first of a record three Benson and Hedges titles in 1983 and the following month he captivated The Crucible fans when he compiled the world championship's first maximum break during his 2nd round match with Terry Griffiths.

In recent years Cliff has captured the Benson and Hedges title twice (1985 and 1986), Langs Scottish Masters twice (also 1985 and 1986) and the Canadian professional title on three occasions. His last ranking tournament success was in the 1985 Goya Matchroom Trophy at Stoke-on-Trent.

Cliff has been awarded the Canadian Order of Merit (CM) for his services to snooker. In January 1988 he became the eighth member of the Matchroom team.

● ● ● ● ● ● ● ● ● ● ● ● ● ● ● ●

end of the first six frames of the day. Thorburn extended that lead to 15–11 in the afternoon but then Spencer strung together four consecutive frames to level it at 15-all.

In the evening Thorburn won the first, Spencer levelled and then he took the lead for the first time since the fourth session when he cleared up with a 78 when trailing 58–0. Spencer then opened up a two-frame gap but Thorburn won the last two frames of the day to make it all square once more at 18-all. And so to the last day.

The first two frames of the morning session were scrappy. Spencer managed to win both and take a two-frame lead. He then made it 21–18 and was in sight of the finishing post. Thorburn pulled it back to 21–20 before Spencer won the last frame of the session, thanks to a 67 break, to make it 22–20.

Thorburn clawed his way back to within one frame by winning the opening frame of the afternoon session but then Spencer won the next three, concluding with a 51 break, to become The Crucible's first world champion.

1978

South African Perrie Mans, one of the game's finest long potters, and Ray Reardon, one of snooker's all-time greats, did battle in the 1978 final.

The players exchanged the first four frames but then steady break-building by the Welshman took him to 5–2 at the end of the opening session. Mans won the first three frames of the evening session to level it again before Reardon went 6–5 up before re-establishing a two-frame lead with an 87 break in frame 12. But at the end of the session it was 8-all.

The opening session of the second day saw the South African twice take the lead, in frames 17 and 19, but Reardon levelled it at 10–10. Consecutive breaks of 41 and 49 helped Reardon to take the 21st and 22nd frames before Mans finished the session as he had started, with a win, to make it 12–11 to Reardon.

Breaks of 64, 42 and 66 took Reardon to 15–11 and for the first time since the opening session the scoreboard reflected the true difference between the two players. Mans kept reducing the gap but was never to close it completely. The second day ended with Reardon 18–14 ahead. The gap, however, was closed to just one frame after Mans won the first three frames of the third day, the first despite a break of 54 from the Welshman.

But the first nail was hammered in the coffin when Reardon compiled a century break in frame 36 to make it 19–17. That was the confidence booster he needed and he took the next two frames as well to make it 21–17 and within four frames of victory. The session ended at 22–18.

An 81 break by Reardon in the opening frame of the final session demoralized Mans and breaks of 36 and 35 by Reardon in frames 42 and 43 took him to the winning 25-frame target and to his sixth world title, a modern-day record. With it, Reardon collected the winner's cheque for £7500.

1979

The 1979 championship belonged to Welshman Terry Griffiths. A new professional, he was making his world championship debut and had to come through the qualifying rounds before beating such notables as 1978 finalist Perrie Mans, 1972 champion Alex Higgins, and twice-beaten semi-finalist Eddie Charlton. His semi-final win over Charlton ended at 1.40 in the morning, and the final session lasted 5 hours 25 minutes.

Griffiths's final opponent was Dennis Taylor, also making his first appearance in the final. But unlike Griffiths he had been trying since 1973 to win the title.

The final was played over the best-of-47 frames scheduled for six sessions. At the end of four sessions there was little knowing who the 1979 world champion would be. But then the Welshman pulled away for a memorable victory.

Griffiths opened up with the first two frames. Taylor reduced it to 2–1, but Griffiths went to 3–1 before compiling a 120 break and going to 4–1. A 41 break made it 5–1 and the Irishman was in all sorts of trouble. But a 71 clearance, when he was 65–0 down, changed the course of the game as Taylor won the final frame of the morning session.

Taylor came out in the evening full of confidence after his last frame win. He could have started the second session 6–1 down, which would have been disastrous. As it was, he was only 5–2 in arrears, but that gap soon reduced to 5–4, and then 6–5. Griffiths went to 7–6 but Taylor was level for the first time since the start of the match at 7-all before Griffiths ended the first day with a slight advantage at 8–7.

On the second day, Taylor took the lead for the first time at 9–8 thanks to a 70 break. And in frame 20 a break of 92 (with a break of 143 on) helped him establish a two-frame lead at 11–9. But two frames later the two men were level again at 11-all. It had certainly developed into a battle between them, both eager to win the title.

With Griffiths starting to look tired after his epic semi-final, Taylor again built up a two-frame lead at 14–12 but day two ended at 15–15. Despite Taylor putting together a 41 break in the opening frame of the final day, Griffiths got up on the final black to take the lead for the first time since the 15th frame. He built on that in frame 32 and went to 17–15 after breaks of 64 and 44. Taylor won the next frame to make it 17–16 but that was to be the last frame for the Irishman. Griffiths went into the final session leading 22–16 and needed just two more for the title.

Breaks of 37, 31 and 49 in frame 39 made it 23–16 and then a 56 was the final act of the 1979 championship as Terry Griffiths was crowned world professional snooker champion.

1980

The beaten finalist in The Crucible's first final, Cliff Thorburn, was making history as the first man to appear in two finals at the sport's best-known venue. His opponent was Alex Higgins, the winner of the title in 1972 when it was played at the Selly Park British Legion – a far cry from The Crucible.

The final had been reduced to a four-session best-of-35 frame match, and indeed all subsequent finals have been over the same distance. Like so many Crucible finals, this match provided all that is best in snooker. The play from both men was of a high standard, and a close tense battle left the fans wondering until the very last minute who the 1980 champion was going to be.

First blood went to Thorburn but then Higgins won five on the trot to go to 5–1. Higgins had been building breaks steadily in each frame, which culminated in a 93 in frame six. A 68 by Thorburn made it 5–2. After the frame Higgins complained that Thorburn had been standing in his line-of-sight when at the table. The complaint was unfounded.

Higgins made it 6–2 thanks to an 81 break which could, and should, have been a 140 clearance, but Higgins missed an easy red. The Canadian completed the opening session with a 62 break to close the session 6–3 behind.

A mistake by Thorburn on the final red enabled Higgins to take the opening frame of the evening session and the Ulsterman led by four frames at 7–3. Thorburn pulled two back but Higgins reasserted his lead at 9–5. Three years earlier Thorburn had held a four-frame lead over John Spencer but ended up as the beaten finalist. Was history going to repeat itself? Thorburn kept plugging away at Higgins's lead and at the half-way stage the two men were level at 9-all.

The Canadian won the opening frame of the third session to take the lead for the first time since the opening frame. He extended his run of successes to six consecutive frames as he built up a two-frame lead for the first time. Higgins pulled back those two frames to make it 11-all and had to come from behind to make it 12–12 and 13–13.

As the game went into the final session Higgins gained the first initiative but then Thorburn came back to make it 14-all. The fans were excited. It was certainly The Crucible's tensest battle so far. A 53 break by Thorburn made it 15–14, but then Higgins did the necessary after Thorburn missed an easy black, and they were level again. Once more Thorburn took the lead at 16–15 and once more he missed an easy ball, the brown, which would have left Higgins requiring a snooker. Instead, the Irishman cleared up and it was 16–16 with three frames to play.

After two disappointments, Thorburn immediately responded with a break of 119 to go one up with two to play. Higgins was faced with an uphill task again, but this time there was no comeback. Thorburn reaped the benefit of a carefully-laid snooker when leading 45–9 to gain a 51 break and conclude a breathtaking final.

The Crucible Theatre

The outside of snooker's best known venue . . .

Most sports have a venue that is regarded as its 'home'. In cricket it is Lord's; Wembley is soccer's home, Silverstone is the British home of motor racing, and Hickstead is the home of the equestrian world. Snooker is no different and its home is The Crucible Theatre in Sheffield.

The venue for the Embassy World Championships every April/May, the 17-day long tournament is regarded as one of the great events of the British sporting calendar and receives more than 100 hours of BBC television coverage.

Snooker is the only sporting event at The Crucible. The rest of the year it stages local and national drama productions and various concerts. It also has its own repertory company which is one of the largest in England. But each spring The Crucible converts into one of the finest snooker arenas.

Intimidating to the debutant, it is not as big as some venues; the main theatre seats just over 1000. But playing at The Crucible is a nerveracking business and it has

been the downfall of even the best of players. Remember the defending champion Steve Davis losing 10–1 to Tony Knowles in 1982?

For many years The Crucible had a bogey which saw no man successfully defend his title. That was eventually laid by Steve Davis when he retained his crown in 1984.

The first champion at the famous venue was John Spencer in 1977. But had it not been for a current professional's wife the tournament may never have gone to The Crucible in the first place.

Mike Watterson, who hailed from nearby Chesterfield, was a leading amateur player at the time. He was also a promoter, and after his wife Carol attended a play at the Theatre she suggested it as a possible snooker venue. Mike was suitably impressed and made the necessary arrangements for the 1977 Embassy World Professional Championship to be staged at the new venue. And so The Crucible became the home of snooker—all thanks to Carol Watterson.

(For Crucible records see pp. 48–56.)

. . . and inside, waiting for the action to begin.

1981

The defending champion Cliff Thorburn went out to the youngster Steve Davis in the semi-final. Davis had been arousing a lot of interest since he captured the Coral UK title six months earlier, and was being tipped as a future world champion. Now was the chance for him to prove those tipsters right.

The man standing between Davis and his first title was the 1976 world amateur champion Doug Mountjoy, also appearing in his first professional world final.

Davis started as he often does, by winning the opening exchanges. But even he must have been surprised when he built up a 6–0 lead, a lead that was to prove too great a disadvantage for the Welshman to overcome.

Mountjoy salvaged some pride by winning the last three frames of the opening session, and compiled the session's highest break (76) in the eighth frame. This frame was uniquely replayed after the original frame was aborted at 49–48 in Davis's favour with only blue, pink and black left on the table. With the black in the jaws of the pocket and the blue getting closer to it all the time, safety play was at its best. In the end, referee John Williams called an end to the proceedings, and restarted the game.

Davis started the second session like the first and won the opening frame to go 7–3. Mountjoy then pulled two frames back before Davis restored his three-frame lead at 8–5. Mountjoy compiled the final's highest break, 129, in winning frame 14. Mountjoy had proved himself a fine break-builder in this championship, and in his semi-final against Ray Reardon he had a 145 clearance to establish a world championship best.

But big breaks don't win matches, only frames. Davis made it 9–6 but Mountjoy was now starting to string together his best snooker of the match. He made it 9–7 and should have reduced the arrears to one frame when he inexplicably went in-off after potting the green when in a frame-winning situation. Davis then fluked a blue to make it 10–7 when by rights it should have been 9–8. Mountjoy, however, won the final frame of the opening day and they went into the second day with Davis 10–8 ahead.

Once more Davis won the opening frame of the session, thanks to a break of 83. And then he restored his four-frame lead by taking the 20th frame. Again Mountjoy closed the gap by winning the next two. They then exchanged frames and with one session left there was still a two-frame margin in Davis's favour at 14–12.

The evening session started with Davis going in-off the red from the break – a shot that must have given Mountjoy heart. But how wrong he was. Davis put together an 84 to take the frame and a 119 break in the next opened up that four-frame gap again. Davis completed his run by taking the next two frames and thus reached the target required to give him his first world title. The winning margin was six frames; that was the lead Davis built up at the start of the match. In the end it proved too great a handicap for Mountjoy.

1982

After the euphoria of Steve Davis winning his first crown a year earlier, the 1982 final belonged to two well-established members of the snooker world: Ray Reardon and Alex Higgins. Reardon was looking for his seventh world title, whereas Higgins was hoping to make it title number two, and thus make up for the disappointment of losing to Cliff Thorburn two years earlier.

Higgins certainly had some testing matches leading up to the final. Doug Mountjoy pushed him to 13–12 in the second round, Willie Thorne made life tough in the quarter-finals and in the last four Alex had a great battle with Jimmy White, which the Irishman won 16–15.

The final was no different, and Reardon defied his years to produce snooker which had delighted crowds 10 years earlier.

The opening session was littered with errors: Reardon took a 5–3 lead by virtue of the fact that he made fewer than Higgins. The highlight of the opening session was a break of 118 by Higgins in the fourth frame to make it 2-all. In the first evening session Reardon led 6–4 and had a great chance to make it 7–4 but missed the pink. Higgins went on to win on the black and then take it to 6–6. Reardon regained the lead at 7–6 but that was the last time he was to hold the lead as Higgins went from 8–7 to 10–7 at the end of the first day.

A 95 break in the opening frame of day two reduced the Ulsterman's arrears, and when he won the next frame Higgins's lead was cut to one frame. Higgins restored the three-frame advantage by taking the next two. It was then Reardon's turn to win two, and again the lead was one frame at 12–11. They each won one further frame at the end of the penultimate session and the final session saw play resume with Higgins 13–12 in front.

Higgins soon went to 14–12 and a miss on an easy yellow by Reardon, with the colours ideally placed, allowed Higgins to extend his lead even further. But then it was Higgins's turn to miss when in a frame-winning position and it was back to 15–13. Nerves were visibly showing in Higgins's game and when Reardon potted a brilliant brown which brought the blue off the cushion in frame number 30 he made it 15-all with five to play.

Suddenly, Higgins's anxiety disappeared, and he regained his concentration. After making it 17–15 he won the match with a clearance of 135.

As Higgins clutched the trophy for the second time in his career he beckoned wife Lynn and daughter Lauren into the arena to share his moment of glory and emotion.

1983

The 1980 champion Cliff Thorburn walked into The Crucible arena for the 1983 final a tired man. His three previous matches, against Terry Griffiths, Kirk Stevens and Tony Knowles, had lasted a total of 17 hours 21 minutes and finished at 3.51 a.m., 2.12 a.m. and 12.45 a.m., respectively. Not surprisingly, he offered little challenge to Davis who comfortably won his second world crown.

In contrast to Thorburn's tough passage to the final, the only resistance Davis felt on his way was in the second round when Dennis Taylor held him to 13–11. But after that it was plain sailing.

Both players exchanged frames up to 2-all but then Davis took charge against the jaded Canadian. Davis ended the first session 6–2 in front and extended his sequence to seven consecutive frames at the start of the evening session to go to 9–2. The outcome of the final was never in doubt from this point on, although Thorburn staged a mini-revival in taking frames 12 and 13 to make it 9–4. A 92 by Davis in the next frame extended his lead and the first day ended with Davis 12–5 in front and needing just six more frames for the title.

A black-ball win in the first frame of session three made it 13–5 and Davis went on to win the next four frames, the 22nd was with the aid of a magnificent clearance of 131. Davis now led by 12 frames at 17–5. Thorburn had to win all 13 remaining frames to take the title. But the way he had been playing that was against all the odds. He did win the 23rd frame but in the next frame the end eventually came to one of The Crucible's most one-sided finals. Davis clinched the match on a re-spotted black as the first Crucible final to be concluded in three sessions mercifully ended for the Canadian.

1984

From the moment Jimmy White won his first major professional tournament, the Langs Scottish Masters in 1981, he had been talked about as a potential world champion. Now, in 1984, he was in his prime, and if he was going to dethrone Steve Davis, then this was his great chance.

Davis returned to the final with one barrier to beat; no man had successfully retained his world title at The Crucible. That gave an advantage to White. But White, on the other hand, had engaged in a classic semi-final with Kirk Stevens. Just how much it had mentally taken out of him remained to be seen.

The final turned out to be a classic, not that you would have thought so after the first nine frames when Davis led 8–1.

Davis, as always, played solid and steady snooker. And it was White who made the mistakes which, of course, Davis capitalized on. Davis raced into a 3–0 lead before White got on to the scoreboard. But the first session ended 6–1 in the Romford player's favour. He soon made it 8–1 with breaks of 47 and 44. But then White produced breaks of 61 and 76 in the 10th frame to give him a 137–0 victory, and the scoreboard read 8–2. But that was to be his only real glimpse of brilliance in the second session as Davis extended his lead to 12–4. The previous year, Davis led Thorburn 12–5 at this stage – surely it wasn't going to be another walkover? The answer was 'No', as day two told a completely different story.

White opened with a 119 break to make it 12–5, and with him winning the next two it was 12–7. Davis won frame 20 to go 13–7 in front but then White put together his best sequence to win four successive frames and go into the final session trailing by just two frames at 11–13.

Having lost seven of the eight afternoon frames, Davis was grateful to start the evening with a win after fluking a red. A break of 63 in the next frame put him back in front by four frames and White had it all to do again. But he had a go, and with breaks of 64 and 72 made it 16–14. A 53 break in the next frame took White to within one frame for the first time since the start of the match.

Both players missed frame-winning chances in the 32nd before Davis won on the black to make it 17–15. Trailing 60–0 in the next after a break of 51 by Davis, White produced a tremendous 65 clearance under such pressure to win on the black and reduce the deficit to one frame at 17–16. White looked like salvaging the 34th frame when, on a break of 40, he left the cue-ball virtually touching the pink and was forced to play away to safety. Davis took on a long red and sank it. Both players were feeling the pressure and made unforced errors. But it was Davis who ran out the winner by 77 points to 40, and by 18 frames to 16 at the conclusion of one of The Crucible's greatest-ever finals.

1985

Steve Davis had never lost in a ranking tournament final. And when he raced to a 7-0 first-session lead against Dennis Taylor he looked like holding on to that fine record. But 32 hours later as the clocks moved towards 1 a.m., 18.5 million television viewers, a record for a domestic sporting event in Britain, sat glued to their sets as the final came to a dramatic and nail-biting conclusion.

When Davis led 7-0 at the end of that first session Taylor must have cast his mind back to the 1981 Jameson final when he was 'whitewashed' 9-0 by the Londoner. Taylor had opened the match with a break of 50. But it wasn't good enough, and Davis won frame after frame.

The Englishman started the second session with an impressive 121-0 victory to make it 8-0 but then relief came for the Ulsterman as he got a frame on the scoreboard. Davis added another to make it 9-1 but then Taylor started a remarkable run which saw him win the next six frames and he went to bed only two frames in arrears at 7-9. Taylor's first winning frame took 50 minutes; his second took 48 minutes. But once he had started winning frames his confidence returned. Breaks of 61, 98 and 70 in the 12th, 13th and 14th frames confirmed that. He wound up the session with breaks of 56, 44 and 40.

Taylor continued his run, making it seven consecutive frames, by winning the first frame of the second day but then Davis won the next two to go 11-8 in front. Taylor then pulled back to 11-all and was all square for the first time since the start of the match. Any hopes he had of taking the lead were dented by Davis winning the last two frames of the afternoon session, both on black balls.

Davis made it 14-11 by taking the first frame of what was to be an exhilarating evening's play.

The two men were level again at 15-all but Davis went two up with three to play at 17-15. A great battle emerged in frame 33 and Davis should have clinched the title but snookered himself on the brown. Taylor then sank the brown and snookered himself behind the pink but he got away with it and reduced the deficit to 16-17. Taylor made sure of levelling it with a break of 57 and so it was all down to the 35th and final frame which was to take a dramatic 68 minutes to conclude.

Davis fluked the green to take a 62-44 lead. Davis missed a long brown. Taylor was also left with a long brown. He took it on and made the pot. That made it 62-48 to Davis. Taylor then sank blue and pink to make it 62-59. Taylor wasn't on the black but he went for the double. It missed, but fortunately for him the black ran safe

on to the top cushion. The two men exchanged safety shots, then Davis made a mistake when the two balls kissed. Taylor had a long pot on the black but missed. The ensuing result was that Davis had a cut into the top corner pocket. To everybody's amazement he missed. Ninety-nine times out of a hundred he would have made that shot. But this was the 35th and last frame of the world championship at The Crucible.

Davis left the black over the same pocket and up stepped Taylor to sink the black at the seventh attempt to become champion of the world for the first time.

1986

Anybody who fancied backing a long shot to win the 1985 world championship could have done worse than backed Joe Johnson at 250-1. A professional since 1979, Johnson was a grossly underrated player. And at Sheffield in 1986 he came out of his shell to take the snooker world by storm.

He came of age when he beat Terry Griffiths 13-12 in the quarter-final, and by comparison his semi-final win over Tony Knowles was a lot easier. But the final against Steve Davis, in his favourite arena – The Crucible Theatre – was a daunting task even for Joe, who approached the match in a relaxed fashion.

Davis took the opening frame but the Yorkshireman made it 1-1 with a 48 break. Successive century breaks of 108 and 107 saw Davis stamp his authority on the game and take a 3-1 lead. But Johnson, playing with a 'nothing to lose' attitude, surprised many by winning the last three frames of the opening session to lead 4-3. But then the game took on an amazing series of turnarounds.

Davis won the first four frames of the evening session to lead 7-4. Johnson then won four in succession to retake the lead at 8-7 before Davis put together an 81 break to level the scores at 8-all at the end of the first day.

Johnson certainly had the better of any luck that was on offer in the opening four frames of the third session and increased his lead to 12-8. Davis seemed to pull himself together after the mid-session break and won the next two frames. Johnson made it 13-10 after putting Davis in a position of needing three snookers. But then the three-times champion compiled his third century break of the match (100) to make it 13-11 in the last frame of the session.

Davis missed an easy red at the start of the final session to let Johnson go 14-11 in front. He then fluked a red in the next to make it 14-12. Breaks of 40, 54, 46 and 64 were all frame-winning ones for Johnson as the likeable

Yorkshireman won the next four frames to clinch the title 18–12 and become The Crucible's happy-go-lucky champion. For Davis it was a rare taste of defeat in his fourth successive final.

1987

The Crucible had never witnessed a repeat world final. Indeed there had never been a repeat world championship final since the Walter Donaldson–Fred Davis meeting in 1951. But what odds would one have given against Davis and Johnson meeting for the second successive season?

Johnson had a disastrous 12 months after winning the title. He was, however, starting to show signs of improvement in the second half of the season, a Joe Johnson trademark, but even he could not have imagined he would reach the final again, particularly after he had scraped home 10–9 against Eugene Hughes in the first round. But after that win his confidence grew and after beating the widely-tipped finalist Stephen Hendry in the quarter-final, a second final looked a probability for Joe.

Steve was in no mood to be runner-up again.

● ● ● ● ● ● ● ● ● ● ● ● ● ● ● ●

DENNIS TAYLOR

Born: 19 January 1949, Coalisland, N. Ireland

A professional since 1972, Dennis Taylor had to wait 12 years for his first major title. But in 1984–5 the wait was worth it because the likeable Irishman enjoyed a memorable season.

Runner-up in *Pot Black* in 1975 and 1976 he also came second in the 1979 world final when beaten 24–16 by Terry Griffiths. Other second places included an embarrassing 9–0 'whitewash' by Steve Davis in the 1981 Jameson final. But all that was forgotten in 1984 when he beat his old friend Cliff Thorburn 10–2 to win his first major title, the Rothmans Grand Prix.

The success did not end there. Before the season was out, Taylor was world champion after beating Steve Davis 18–17 in one of the game's great finals.

Shortly after that success Dennis teamed up with Davis in the Matchroom team and in 1986 climbed to number three in the rankings behind Davis and Thorburn.

Although he has not won a major honour since the 1988 Benson and Hedges Masters at Wembley he is still among the elite of professional snooker and remains one of its most popular characters.

● ● ● ● ● ● ● ● ● ● ● ● ● ● ● ●

He didn't like losing, and two successive defeats in The Crucible final was enough for any man, let alone the best in the world. He came at Johnson like a greyhound after a hare and opened with a 127 break in the first frame. It was Davis's first and only century of the championship. But what a moment to achieve it – in the first frame of the final!

Undeterred, Johnson employed his 'nothing-to-lose' approach again and won the next three frames. Davis levelled it at 3–3 before Johnson won the final frame to take the end-of-session lead just as he had done 12 months earlier.

Davis took the first three frames in the evening to go 6–4 up but then Joe scored a 101 in frame 11. Davis extended his lead from one to three frames by taking the next two. Again Johnson won one frame and Davis two before the final frame of the night went to Johnson and the overnight score stood at 9–7 in Davis's favour.

Johnson took the first frame on day two but then Davis won four successive frames to open up a five-frame lead at 13–8. Suddenly it was looking grim for the Yorkshireman. He managed to win two of the remaining three frames of the session but went into the final evening trailing 14–10.

Successive breaks of 52, 62 and 42 gave Johnson the first three frames of the final session and suddenly he was back in it. Was there going to be a repeat of the 1986 shock? A third successive Davis defeat was being talked about as a possibility. A few hours earlier, his victory was almost assured.

A mistake at a long pot by Johnson in the 28th frame allowed Davis to take the frame and build a two-frame lead at 15–13; a crucial lead at such a stage. Davis won the next two and went 17–13 ahead and needed just one of the last remaining five frames. Johnson won frame number 31 but that was to be his final moment of glory as Davis finished with a 78 to win the last frame 78–0 and for the seventh time in the match, beat Johnson to nil.

Joe Johnson surprised the snooker world by reaching his second consecutive final, and how close he came to toppling Steve Davis again. In the end it was Steve Davis who became world champion for the fourth time.

1988

As Steve Davis reached his sixth successive final in 1988 the pre-tournament speculation had Stephen Hendry or Jimmy White as Davis's likely final opponent. But in the end it was Steve's Matchroom team-mate Terry Griffiths who reached his second final.

The Welshman was the shock winner in 1979.

Nine years later he was a surprise finalist, not that his skills have ever rendered it impossible for him to reach the final. Despite not winning as many titles as his more illustrious opponent, the consistency of Terry Griffiths helped to keep him as one of the world's top players since winning the world title nine years earlier.

Griffiths took the first frame and should have made it 2–0 but missed an easy blue with the final red. Instead Davis made it 1–1 and capitalized on the error by going to 5–1 before Griffiths won the last frame of the opening session. He won the first frame of the evening session to bring Davis back to 5–3, but breaks of 83 and 81 took Davis back into a four-frame lead.

A four-frame winning run saw Griffiths level it at 7-all. Each player won one more frame before the end of the day's play and it was Griffiths who went to bed feeling the more confident, having won six of the nine evening frames.

Davis missed two easy blacks and a yellow in the first frame of the third session. But Griffiths failed to take advantage and Davis eventually won on the black. Griffiths, having missed a great chance to take the lead for the first time since the opening frame, seemed to be unsettled by that frame, and Davis won the next two to go 11–8 in front.

Both players were missing some easy pots; Davis particularly was missing an unusually high amount. And when he missed an easy blue in the next frame, Griffiths took advantage with a break of 46 and reduced the lead to two frames at 11–9.

Davis won two of the final three frames of the session and it was only in the last frame that he put together a sizeable break, 92, as he increased his lead to 14–10.

Despite leading 32–0 in the first frame of the last session, Griffiths lost the frame to a break of 46, and suddenly any chance the Welshman had of winning the title seemed to have disappeared. A 118 break in frame 26, followed by a 123 two frames later, put Davis into a 17–11 lead, and in the next a 66 left Griffiths needing two snookers to salvage the title. He didn't achieve this and Davis was champion for the fifth time.

1989

Steve Davis arrived at Sheffield for the 1989 world championship with the rare record of not winning a tournament in the four and a half months since the beginning of the year. It was certainly not the right credential for a man bidding to win his third consecutive world title. But Davis, as always, prepared impeccably for the championship and spent many hours practising with his father Bill.

With John Parrott elevating himself to number two on the provisional world ranking list, it was a good bet that the 1989 final would be a Davis–Parrott affair, as indeed it was. But the cloud Parrott had to play under in the early days of the championship would have left nobody surprised if he had been eliminated at the first hurdle.

A proud Liverpudlian, and a keen Liverpool FC fan, John had to play his opening match at The Crucible little more than 24 hours after the Hillsborough disaster in the same city. He desperately wanted to lift the world title in memory of those fans who lost their lives.

As the championship progressed, so Parrott's confidence increased, and he started showing the skill which had seen him dramatically move up the rankings. On the other hand, the hours of practice for Davis were paying off and he was playing some of the finest snooker of his career. When it came to the final, Davis produced snooker that even he didn't think he was capable of and, quite simply, he destroyed the Liverpudlian with the finest display of potting and safety play ever seen.

There is little to tell of the match itself, it was so one-sided with Davis running out the 18–3 winner; the biggest margin in Crucible history.

After three frames the score was 2–1 in Davis's favour. But he then advanced to 5–1 before Parrott closed the first session with his second frame. Davis came out for the evening session and knocked in breaks of 42, 37, 112 and 55 to go to 9–2. In those opening four frames Parrott could manage only 15 points.

After trailing by 44 points in the next frame, Davis stunned Parrott with a break of 60 to make it 10–2 and the break-building continued as a 59 helped Davis to move into an invincible 11–2 lead. A 68 break by Parrott reduced the arrears by

Despite losing heavily to Steve Davis in the 1989 world championship final, John Parrott emerged as a serious threat to Davis' no. 1 position.

one frame, but it was to be the Merseysider's last success of the match.

Breaks of 80 and 68 by Davis in the last two frames of the first day put him in a commanding position at 13–3 and just five frames away from his sixth title.

Davis started the second day where he had left off and five breaks in excess of 30 saw him win the required five frames in just over an hour and a half as the final ended with a session to spare.

Don't let the scoreline lead you to believe that Parrott did not do justice to the occasion. But simply, no man could have lived with Davis the way he played at The Crucible in 1989.

World Championship Records (1927–89)

Wins
15	Joe Davis
6	Steve Davis, Ray Reardon
3	Fred Davis, John Spencer
2	Walter Donaldson, Alex Higgins
1	Terry Griffiths, Joe Johnson, Horace Lindrum, Dennis Taylor, Cliff Thorburn

Finals
15	Joe Davis
8	Steve Davis
7	Ray Reardon
6	Fred Davis
5	Walter Donaldson
4	Tom Dennis, Alex Higgins, Horace Lindrum, John Spencer
3	Cliff Thorburn
2	Eddie Charlton, Terry Griffiths, Joe Johnson, Clark McConachy, Sidney Smith, Willie Smith, Dennis Taylor
1	Fred Lawrence, Perrie Mans, Graham Miles, Doug Mountjoy, Tom Newman, Gary Owen, John Parrott, John Pulman, Warren Simpson, Jimmy White

Most finals without winning the title
4	Tom Dennis
2	Eddie Charlton, Clark McConachy, Sidney Smith, Willie Smith

Semi-finals (1969–89 only)
10	Ray Reardon
8	Eddie Charlton, Steve Davis
7	Alex Higgins
6	John Spencer, Cliff Thorburn
5	Dennis Taylor
4	Jimmy White
3	Fred Davis, Tony Knowles, Rex Williams
2	Terry Griffiths, Joe Johnson, Perrie Mans, Gary Owen, John Pulman, Kirk Stevens
1	Neal Foulds, Stephen Hendry, Tony Meo, Graham Miles, Doug Mountjoy, John Parrott, Warren Simpson, David Taylor, John Virgo

●　●　●　●　●　●　●　●　●　●　●　●　●

WALTER DONALDSON

Born: 2 February 1907, Coatbridge, Scotland
Died: 1973

Stephen Hendry is not the first great Scottish snooker professional as many people believe. That honour belonged to Walter Donaldson.

After Joe Davis's retirement from the world championship in 1946, Donaldson succeeded him as the champion when he beat Fred Davis in the 1947 final, thus preventing a family double.

However, Fred beat Donaldson in the 1948 final and the two men dominated the championship and the subsequent Professional World Match-Play championship which was inaugurated in 1952 as the world championship in all but name.

A professional since he was 16, Donaldson was a steady player and one of the first great long potters. The war years saw him away from the game for five years, which makes his early post-war championship successes even more remarkable.

After losing the world title to Fred Davis in 1948, Donaldson regained it in 1950. He retired from competitive play in 1954 and died at his Buckinghamshire home in 1973.

●　●　●　●　●　●　●　●　●　●　●　●　●

Most semi-finals without appearing in final
3	Fred Davis, Tony Knowles, Rex Williams
2	Kirk Stevens

(Above records exclude Professional Match-Play 1952–7 and Challenge Matches 1964–8)

Oldest champions
45 yr 6 mth	Ray Reardon	(1978)
45 yr 4 mth	John Pulman	(1968)
45 yr 0 mth	Joe Davis	(1946)
43 yr 2 mth	Walter Donaldson	(1950)

Davis Versus Higgins:
The 1983 Coral Final

(Right) Steve Davis and Alex Higgins renewed their rivalry at the 1988 Rothmans Grand Prix after the thrilling 1983 Corals match (below) when they battled in one of the game's most exciting finals.

Steve Davis–Alex Higgins clashes in the early-eighties always promised something special. Sadly, meetings in recent years have tended to be one-sided affairs in Davis's favour. But one match the Irishman will savour for a long time was the 1983 Coral UK final at Preston when he enjoyed a thrilling 16–15 win after staging one of the sport's most remarkable comebacks.

It was at Preston's Guildhall that Davis had won his first major professional title in 1980. He returned a year later successfully to defend his UK title and in 1983 was attempting to make it three wins in four years.

Higgins, on the other hand, arrived at Preston with his private life in turmoil. There had been talks of a divorce from wife Lynn but her presence at his opening match against Murdo Mcleod seemed to be the motivation he needed as he came from 4–0 down to progress to the next round. After that it was a fairly easy passage to the final.

Davis came out with all cylinders firing, whilst Alex was left spluttering at the start. Breaks of 78, 84, and 82 took Davis into a 3–0 lead which he increased to a staggering 7–0 margin at the end of the first session. Higgins was looking bewildered. All he could hope for was to salvage some pride and make the scoreline look respectable. But he won the opening frame of the evening session. He then won the next two to make the scoreline 3–7.

Davis won the next but Higgins wound up the session with four consecutive frames to end the first day just one in arrears at 7–8. At least there was to be no humiliation for Higgins. Could there even be a win after such an awful start?

Higgins won the first frame of the second day and thus Davis had won just one of the last nine frames. Davis changed matters by winning the next two and went 10–8 up. It then went to 10–9 and 11–9 before Higgins finished the session with three breaks in excess of 40 to level it at 11–all.

Higgins took the lead for the first time in the match when he won the opening frame of the evening and should have gone two up, but Davis cleared up with two reds left to make it 12–12. In an exciting finish Higgins won the next two to take the lead at 14–12. His 86 in the 26th frame was the highest of the match. Davis then won three in succession to lead 15–14 and once again the Ulsterman had his back to the wall as Davis needed one frame for victory.

Davis had a chance to win the match but a black stayed out of a top pocket. Higgins took advantage and levelled it at 15–all with one to play. Two visits to the table yielded breaks of 26 and 44 for Higgins and his 70-point advantage was too much for Davis.

Higgins played some of the best safety play of his career and it was rewarded with the 1983 Coral UK title. But what a different story it had looked at the end of the first session.

Four great world champions. From left to right: John Pulman, Fred Davis, Walter Donaldson and Joe Davis.

Youngest champions

23 yr 1 mth   Alex Higgins (1972)
23 yr 8 mth   Steve Davis (1981)

World championship venues

(Excludes Professional Match-Play 1952–7)
Camkin's Hall, Birmingham 1927–8
Lounge Billiard Hall, Nottingham 1929, 1931, 1934*
Thurston's Hall, London 1930, 1932, 1935–40
Joe Davis Billiards Centre, Chesterfield 1933
Central Hall, Kettering 1934*
Horticultural Hall, London 1946
Leicester Square Hall, London 1947–9
Tower Circus, Blackpool 1950–1
Houldsworth Hall, Manchester 1952
Burroughes Hall, London 1964 (twice), 1965†
South Africa (various venues) 1965 (Pulman v. Williams challenge match)
Johannesburg 1965 (Pulman v. Francisco challenge match)
St George's Hall, Liverpool 1966†
Co-op Hall, Bolton 1968†
Victoria Hall, London 1969–70

Sydney, Australia 1971 (held November 1970)
Selly Park British Legion, Birmingham 1972
City Exhibition Hall, Manchester 1973
Belle Vue, Manchester 1974
Nunawading Basketball Centre, Melbourne, Australia 1975
Wythenshawe Forum, Manchester 1976
Crucible Theatre, Sheffield 1977–89

* Shared venue
† Challenge match

Break record

(Since first century break)
110   Joe Davis, v. Tom Newman (semi-final 1935)
113   Fred Davis, v. Joe Davis (semi-final 1939)
133   Joe Davis, v. Horace Lindrum (final 1946)
136   Joe Davis, v. Horace Lindrum (final 1946)
142   Rex Williams, v. John Pulman (challenge 1965)
142   Bill Werbeniuk, v. John Virgo (quarter-final 1979)
145   Doug Mountjoy, v. Ray Reardon (semi-final 1981)
147   Cliff Thorburn, v. Terry Griffiths (2nd round 1983)

The highest break for any qualifying match
143   Darren Morgan, v. Alex Higgins (qualifying round 5, 1989)
(The previous day Tony Meo compiled a break of 142 which was a new record until beaten by Morgan's 143.)

Right: Steve Davis captured his sixth world crown in 1989. Only Joe Davis has won more titles.

The Crucible records

Prize money

	Total prize money £	First prize £
1977	17,000	6,000
1978	24,000	7,500
1979	35,000	10,000
1980	60,000	15,000
1981	75,000	20,000
1982	110,000	25,000
1983	130,000	30,000
1984	200,000	44,000
1985	300,000	60,000
1986	350,000	70,000
1987	400,000	80,000
1988	475,000	95,000
1989	525,000	105,000

Wins

6   Steve Davis
1   Terry Griffiths, Alex Higgins, Joe Johnson, Ray Reardon, John Spencer, Dennis Taylor, Cliff Thorburn

Finals

8   Steve Davis
3   Cliff Thorburn
2   Terry Griffiths, Alex Higgins, Joe Johnson, Ray Reardon, Dennis Taylor
1   Perrie Mans, Doug Mountjoy, John Parrott, John Spencer, Jimmy White

Semi-finals

8   Steve Davis
6   Cliff Thorburn
4   Ray Reardon, Dennis Taylor, Jimmy White
3   Eddie Charlton, Alex Higgins, Tony Knowles
2   Terry Griffiths, Joe Johnson, Kirk Stevens
1   Fred Davis, Neal Foulds, Stephen Hendry, Perrie Mans, Tony Meo, Doug Mountjoy, John Parrott, John Pulman, John Spencer, David Taylor, John Virgo

Breaks

The first century at The Crucible was 105 by Eddie Charlton, v. David Taylor (1st round), 1977.

The first 15-red/15-black clearance was by Alex Higgins v. Steve Davis (quarter-final) in 1980. Higgins's break ended at 122.

The number of centuries each year at The Crucible
1977 – 6; 1978 – 7; 1979 – 13; 1980 – 11; 1981 – 13; 1982 – 10; 1983 – 18; 1984 – 8; 1985 – 14; 1986 – 20; 1987 – 18; 1988 – 18; 1989 – 19

● ● ● ● ● ● ● ● ● ● ● ● ● ● ● ● ●

STEVE DAVIS

Born: 22 August 1957, Plumstead, London

Unquestionably the finest snooker player of the modern era, and probably of all time, Steve Davis is the ultimate professional and his list of honours pales his rivals into insignificance by comparison. He has won as many ranking tournaments as all other professionals put together.

The national under-19 billiards champion in 1976, he won the WMC & IU snooker title in 1978. That was one of his last amateur events because he turned professional in September 1978. He was by then managed by Barry Hearn who has since become boss of the strongest outfit in snooker, the Matchroom team.

Davis won his first major title at Preston in 1980 when he beat Alex Higgins 16–6 in the final to win the Coral UK title. That was the beginning of a successful career that has been unrivalled in professional snooker, and indeed, many other sports.

He won the first of six world titles in 1981 when he beat Doug Mountjoy in the final. A lapse in the 1st round a year later saw him beaten 10–1 by Tony Knowles, but in 1983 and 1984 Davis was back on the winning trail and became the first man successfully to defend his title at The Crucible.

Defeat by Dennis Taylor in the 1985 final was a bitter pill for Davis to swallow. And, inexplicably, he was beaten again in 1986 by Joe Johnson. But 1987 and 1988 saw his name engraved on the trophy for the 4th and 5th times. And in beating John Parrott 18–3 in 1989 he became the first man to win the title three years in succession at The Crucible.

It is not only in the world championship that Davis has proved to be invincible. He has won all the major tournaments and at Oldham in 1982 he compiled the first televised maximum break.

For his services to snooker Steve Davis was honoured with the MBE. In 1988–9 he became the first player to win more than £500,000 in one season and he collects in the region of £1½ million a year from endorsements, exhibitions, and the like to make him one of the world's highest-paid sportsmen.

● ● ● ● ● ● ● ● ● ● ● ● ● ● ● ● ●

Highest break each year

1977	135	John Spencer v. John Pulman (1st round)
1978	138	John Spencer v. Perrie Mans (1st round)
1979	142	Bill Werbeniuk v. John Virgo (2nd round)*
1980	136	Kirk Stevens v. Graham Miles (1st round)
	136	Steve Davis v. Alex Higgins (quarter-final)
1981	145	Doug Mountjoy v. Ray Reardon (semi-final)†
1982	143	Willie Thorne v. Alex Higgins (quarter-final)
1983	147	Cliff Thorburn v. Terry Griffiths (2nd round)†
1984	138	Rex Williams v. Jimmy White (1st round)
1985	143	Bill Werbeniuk v. Joe Johnson (1st round)
1986	134	Steve Davis v. Jimmy White (quarter-final)
1987	127	Steve Davis v. Joe Johnson (final)
1988	140	Steve James v. Rex Williams (1st round)
1989	141	Stephen Hendry v. Terry Griffiths (quarter-final)

* Equalled championship record
† New championship record

Progressive break record at The Crucible

(Since first century)

105	Eddie Charlton v. David Taylor (1st round 1977)
135	John Spencer v. John Pulman (semi-final 1977)
138	John Spencer v. Perrie Mans (1st round 1978)
142	Bill Werbeniuk v. John Virgo (2nd round 1979)
145	Doug Mountjoy v. Ray Reardon (semi-final 1981)
147	Cliff Thorburn v. Terry Griffiths (2nd round 1983)

The following players have **scored centuries in consecutive frames:**

Alex Higgins (105 and 112) v. Terry Griffiths (quarter-final 1979)

Ray Reardon (116 and 122) v. Tony Knowles (2nd round 1983)

Steve Davis (108 and 107) v. Joe Johnson (final 1986)

Centuries in most consecutive matches

5 matches – Steve Davis (1986 every round)

4 matches – Neal Foulds (1987 1st round, 2nd round, quarter-final, semi-final)

3 matches – John Spencer (1977 semi-final, final; 1978 1st round)

3 matches – Willie Thorne (1982 1st round, 2nd round, quarter-final)

3 matches – Jimmy White (1984 semi-final, final; 1985 1st round)

3 matches – Steve James (1988 1st round, 2nd round, quarter-final)

Most centuries in one match

4	Terry Griffiths (2) v. Alex Higgins (2) (quarter-final 1979)
2	Joe Johnson (2) v. Terry Griffiths (1) (quarter-final 1986)
3	Steve Davis (3) v. Joe Johnson (final 1986)
3	Neal Foulds (1) v. Mike Hallett (2) (quarter-final 1987)
3	Stephen Hendry (3) v. Jimmy White (2nd round 1988)
3	John Parrott (3) v. Steve James (1st round 1989)

Most centuries by one player in a single match

3	Steve Davis v. Joe Johnson (final 1986)
3	Stephen Hendry v. Jimmy White (2nd round 1988)
3	John Parrott v. Steve James (1st round 1989)
2	Cliff Thorburn v. Dennis Taylor (semi-final 1977)
2	John Spencer v. Perrie Mans (1st round 1978)
2	Terry Griffiths v. Alex Higgins (quarter-final 1979)
2	Alex Higgins v. Terry Griffiths (quarter-final 1979)
2	Steve Davis v. Jimmy White (1st round 1981)
2	Dennis Taylor v. Kirk Stevens (2nd round 1981)
2	Doug Mountjoy v. Ray Reardon (semi-final 1981)
2	Willie Thorne v. Alex Higgins (quarter-final 1982)
2	Alex Higgins v. Ray Reardon (final 1982)
2	Eddie Charlton v. Les Dodd (1st round 1983)
2	Ray Reardon v. Tony Knowles (2nd round 1983)
2	Kirk Stevens v. Perrie Mans (2nd round 1983)
2	Steve Davis v. David Taylor (2nd round 1985)
2	Steve Davis v. Jimmy White (quarter-final 1986)
2	Joe Johnson v. Terry Griffiths (quarter-final 1986)
2	Joe Johnson v. Eugene Hughes (1st round 1987)
2	Mike Hallett v. Neal Foulds (quarter-final 1987)
2	Silvino Francisco v. Eddie Charlton (1st round 1988)
2	Steve James v. Rex Williams (1st round 1988)
2	Steve Davis v. Terry Griffiths (final 1988)
2	Steve Davis v. Steve Newbury (1st round 1989)

Centuries in most consecutive championships

7 Jimmy White (1982–8), Steve Davis (1983–9)

4 John Spencer (1977–80)

Centuries in finals

1977	John Spencer (105) v. Cliff Thorburn
1978	Ray Reardon (100) v. Perrie Mans
1979	Terry Griffiths (120) v. Dennis Taylor
1980	Cliff Thorburn (119) v. Alex Higgins
1981	Doug Mountjoy (129) v. Steve Davis (119)
1982	Alex Higgins (118 and 135) v. Ray Reardon
1983	Steve Davis (131) v. Cliff Thorburn
1984	Jimmy White (119) v. Steve Davis
1985	None*
1986	Steve Davis (108, 107 and 100) v. Joe Johnson
1987	Joe Johnson (101) v. Steve Davis (127)
1988	Steve Davis (118 and 123) v. Terry Griffiths
1989	Steve Davis (112) v. John Parrott

* The highest break in the 1985 final was 98 by Dennis Taylor v. Steve Davis.

Most centuries at The Crucible

28	Steve Davis
11	Jimmy White
9	Terry Griffiths, Cliff Thorburn
8	Doug Mountjoy
7	Stephen Hendry, Alex Higgins, Joe Johnson, Ray Reardon, John Spencer, Dennis Taylor
6	Eddie Charlton, Neal Foulds, Tony Meo, Kirk Stevens, Willie Thorne
5	Tony Knowles, John Parrott

The Crucible's highest breaks

A total of 175 century breaks have been compiled at The Crucible. These are the leading ones:

147 Cliff Thorburn v. Terry Griffiths (2nd round 1983)
145 Doug Mountjoy v. Ray Reardon (semi-final 1981)
143 Willie Thorne v. Alex Higgins (quarter-final 1982)
143 Bill Werbeniuk v. Joe Johnson (1st round 1985)
142 Bill Werbeniuk v. John Virgo (2nd round 1979)
141 Stephen Hendry v. Terry Griffiths (quarter-final 1989)
140 Steve James v. Rex Williams (1st round 1988)
139 Kirk Stevens v. Perrie Mans (2nd round 1983)

139 Stephen Hendry v. Steve Davis (semi-final 1989)
138 John Spencer v. Perrie Mans (1st round 1978)
138 Rex Williams v. Jimmy White (1st round 1984)
137 Tony Knowles v. Jimmy White (quarter-final 1985)
136 Kirk Stevens v. Graham Miles (1st round 1980)
136 Steve Davis v. Alex Higgins (quarter-final 1980)
135 John Spencer v. John Pulman (1st round 1977)
135 Dennis Taylor v. Kirk Stevens (2nd round 1981)
135 Alex Higgins v. Ray Reardon (final 1982)
134 Tony Meo v. John Virgo (1st round 1981)
134 Steve Davis v. Jimmy White (quarter-final 1986)
133 Dennis Taylor v. Kirk Stevens (2nd round 1981)
133 Mike Hallett v. Steve Davis (quarter-final 1989)
131 Steve Davis v. Cliff Thorburn (final 1983)

Miscellaneous Crucible records

Most matches won

40 Steve Davis
24 Cliff Thorburn
20 Terry Griffiths, Ray Reardon
19 Jimmy White
18 Dennis Taylor
16 Eddie Charlton, Alex Higgins
14 Doug Mountjoy, Kirk Stevens
13 Tony Knowles
10 Joe Johnson, John Parrott

Most matches played

45 Steve Davis
36 Cliff Thorburn
30 Terry Griffiths, Ray Reardon, Dennis Taylor
28 Eddie Charlton, Jimmy White
27 Alex Higgins, Doug Mountjoy
24 Kirk Stevens
22 Tony Knowles

Most appearances

13 Doug Mountjoy (1977–89), Dennis Taylor (1977–89), Cliff Thorburn (1977–89)
12 Alex Higgins (1977–88), Eddie Charlton (1977–86, 1988–9), Willie Thorne (1977–8, 1980–9), John Virgo (1977, 1979–89)
11 Ray Reardon (1977–87), David Taylor (1977–87), Steve Davis (1979–89), Terry Griffiths (1979–89)

Most championships without winning a match at The Crucible

8 Rex Williams
7 Cliff Wilson
4 Ray Edmonds, Dave Martin
3 Warren King, Jim Meadowcroft

Oldest competitors

70 yr	8 mth	Fred Davis (1984)
59 yr	6 mth	Eddie Charlton (1989)
55 yr	0 mth	John Dunning (1982)
55 yr	0 mth	John Pulman (1980)
54 yr	11 mth	Cliff Wilson (1989)
54 yr	9 mth	Rex Williams (1988)
54 yr	6 mth	Ray Reardon (1987)
54 yr	0 mth	Jack Fitzmaurice (1982)
50 yr	7 mth	John Spencer (1986)

Oldest match winners at The Crucible

65 yr 8 mth	Fred Davis (1979)
59 yr 6 mth	Eddie Charlton (1989)
54 yr 6 mth	Ray Reardon (1987)

Oldest champions

45 yr 6 mth	Ray Reardon (1978)
41 yr 7 mth	John Spencer (1977)
36 yr 4 mth	Dennis Taylor (1985)

Oldest finalists

49 yr 6 mth	Ray Reardon (1982)
45 yr 6 mth	Ray Reardon (1978)
41 yr 7 mth	John Spencer (1977)
40 yr 6 mth	Terry Griffiths (1988)

Oldest debutants

63 yr	8 mth	Fred Davis (1977)
54 yr	0 mth	Jack Fitzmaurice (1982)
54 yr	0 mth	John Dunning (1981)
52 yr	0 mth	John Pulman (1977)
48 yr	6 mth	Pat Houlihan (1978)
47 yr	6 mth	Eddie Charlton (1977)
47 yr	3 mth	Mark Wildman (1983)
46 yr	11 mth	Eddie Sinclair (1984)
45 yr	11 mth	Cliff Wilson (1980)

Youngest competitors

17 yr	3 mth	Stephen Hendry (1986)
18 yr	11 mth	Jimmy White (1981)
19 yr	3 mth	Dean Reynolds (1982)
19 yr	11 mth	John Parrott (1984)
20 yr	6 mth	Tony Meo (1980)
20 yr	8 mth	Kirk Stevens (1979)
20 yr	9 mth	Neal Foulds (1984)

Youngest winners at The Crucible

18 yr	3 mth	Stephen Hendry (1987)
19 yr	3 mth	Dean Reynolds (1982)
19 yr	11 mth	Jimmy White (1982)
19 yr	11 mth	John Parrott (1984)
20 yr	9 mth	Neal Foulds (1984)

Youngest finalists

22 yr 0 mth Jimmy White (1984)
23 yr 8 mth Steve Davis (1981)
24 yr 11 mth John Parrott (1989)
25 yr 1 mth Steve Davis (1983)

Youngest champions

23 yr 8 mth Steve Davis (1981)
25 yr 8 mth Steve Davis (1983)
26 yr 8 mth Steve Davis (1984)
29 yr 8 mth Steve Davis (1987)
30 yr 8 mth Steve Davis (1988)
31 yr 6 mth Terry Griffiths (1979)

Most frequent meetings

6 Steve Davis (6) and Terry Griffiths (0) 1980–1, 1984–5, 1987–8
4 Terry Griffiths (4) and Alex Higgins (0) 1979, 1985–7
4 Steve Davis (4) and Jimmy White (0) 1981, 1984, 1986–7
4 Steve Davis (2) and Dennis Taylor (2) 1979, 1983–5
4 Steve Davis (4) and Cliff Thorburn (0) 1981, 1983, 1986, 1988

(Figures in parenthesis indicate number of wins)

Biggest winning margins

Margin (frames)	Match score	
15	18–3	Steve Davis beat John Parrott (final 1989)
12	18–6	Steve Davis beat Cliff Thorburn (final 1983)
12	13–1	Steve Davis beat Mike Hallett (2nd round 1988)
12	13–1	Neal Foulds beat Doug Mountjoy (2nd round 1988)
11	13–2	Cliff Thorburn beat Graham Miles (2nd round 1981)
11	16–5	Steve Davis beat Alex Higgins (semi-final 1983)
11	13–2	Kirk Stevens beat Ray Reardon (quarter-final 1984)
11	16–5	Steve Davis beat Ray Reardon (semi-final 1985)
11	16–5	Dennis Taylor beat Tony Knowles (semi-final 1985)
10	13–3	David Taylor beat Fred Davis (2nd round 1981)
10	13–3	Kirk Stevens beat Perrie Mans (2nd round 1983)
10	13–3	Cliff Thorburn beat Bill Werbeniuk (2nd round 1985)
10	13–3	Steve Davis beat Steve Duggan (2nd round 1989)
10	13–3	Dean Reynolds beat Wayne Jones (2nd round 1989)
10	13–3	Steve Davis beat Mike Hallett (quarter-final 1989)

(Note: There has never been a 'whitewash' at The Crucible)

'I don't believe it, she's all mine' . . . Dennis Taylor after his memorable black-ball win over Steve Davis in that classic 1985 world championship final.

Ranking positions of champions

1977	John Spencer	8th
1978	Ray Reardon	1st
1979	Terry Griffiths	Unranked
1980	Cliff Thorburn	5th
1981	Steve Davis	14th
1982	Alex Higgins	11th
1983	Steve Davis	4th
1984	Steve Davis	1st
1985	Dennis Taylor	11th
1986	Joe Johnson	16th
1987	Steve Davis	1st
1988	Steve Davis	1st
1989	Steve Davis	1st

Played through qualifying rounds

The following Crucible finalists have had to play through the qualifying rounds: Cliff Thorburn (1977), Perrie Mans (1978), Terry Griffiths (1979). Only Griffiths won the title.

The Maximum Men

Compiling snooker's maximum break of 147 is the equivalent of getting a hole-in-one at golf; except the hole-in-one happens more often than the 147.

It took a long time for the first maximum break to be compiled. But that was largely due to the lack of the cue-ball control which the modern players employ. In the 1920s snooker was seen purely as a potting game and breaks of 50 were regarded as outstanding. A 147 break was unheard of.

The first witnessed maximum break was made by New Zealander Murt O'Donoghue in Australia in 1934. But like the maximums subsequently made by Horace Lindrum, Leo Levitt and Clark McConachy, it was never ratified because it was not compiled on a standard table. Even today many 147s are not ratified because they are made in practice or exhibition conditions, or on a non-conforming table. Consequently, they do not qualify for record purposes.

The first official maximum was, perhaps predictably, made by Joe Davis in 1955 when he scored 147 against Willie Smith in an exhibition (exhibition match breaks qualified for record purposes in those days) at the Leicester Square Hall. However, the break was not ratified by the BA & CC until two years later.

It was ten years before the next official 147 break was recorded. It was by Rex Williams against Mannie Francisco (Silvino's brother) in Cape Town in December 1965. John Spencer compiled a maximum in the 1979 Holsten Lager Tournament at Slough. But there were two pieces of bad news for the former world champion. Firstly, the break was not ratified because the pockets were oversized. And, secondly, the television cameras which were covering the event missed the break because cameramen were at lunch. Consequently, the honour of compiling the first televised maximum, and the first official 147 in tournament play, fell to Steve Davis in the Lada Classic at the Oldham Civic Centre in 1982.

Since then Cliff Thorburn has compiled the first maximum in the world championship (after fluking the first red) in 1983. At Wembley in

In 1989 Canada's Cliff Thorburn became the first man to compile two official maximum breaks.

'CT phone home' . . . Cliff Thorburn phoning home to Canada after compiling his memorable 147 break in the 1983 world championship at Sheffield.

1984 his fellow Canadian Kirk Stevens compiled a maximum in the Benson and Hedges Masters.

Willie Thorne is the champion when it comes to making 147 breaks and in practice and exhibition matches has over 100 to his credit. But he has compiled just one in tournament play, against Tommy Murphy in the 1987 Tennents UK Open. Thorne's team-mate Tony Meo, at one time the youngest person to compile a maximum, made an official 147 against Stephen Hendry in the Matchroom League in 1988.

The Canadians seem to make a habit of putting together 147s. New professional Alain Robidoux did so in the qualifying tournament for the European Open in September 1988. Within three weeks of each other in 1989 John Rea compiled a maximum on his way to winning the Scottish Professional Championship and then Cliff Thorburn became the first man to compile two official maximums when he cleared the table against Jimmy White in the Matchroom League at Crawley.

It took 80 years for Joe Davis to compile the first maximum, but since 1982 the feat has been achieved no less than eight times. Technically it is possible to compile a 155 break. Now that the 147 goal is no longer as outrageous as it was in the days of Joe Davis, then the 155 has got to be the next target for today's record-breaker.

Willie Thorne is the top man when it comes to maximums. He has more than one hundred to his credit, but only one was in tournament play.

Official Maximum Breaks

Date	Made by v. (Opponent)	Tournament	Venue
22 Jan 1955	Joe Davis (v. Willie Smith)	Exhibition	Leicester Sq. Hall, London
22 Dec 1965	Rex Williams (v. Mannie Francisco)	Exhibition	Prince's Hotel, Newlands, S. Africa
11 Jan 1982*	Steve Davis (v. John Spencer)	Lada Classic	Civic Centre, Oldham
23 Apr 1983*	Cliff Thorburn (v. Terry Griffiths)	Embassy World Championship	Crucible Theatre, Sheffield
28 Jan 1984*	Kirk Stevens (v. Jimmy White)	Benson and Hedges Masters	Wembley Conference Centre, London
17 Nov 1987	Willie Thorne (v. Tommy Murphy)	Tennents UK Championship	Guildhall, Preston
20 Feb 1988	Tony Meo (v. Stephen Hendry)	Matchroom League	Winding Wheel Centre, Chesterfield
24 Sep 1988	Alain Robidoux (v. Jim Meadowcroft)	European Open (qualifying)	Norbreck Castle Hotel, Blackpool
18 Feb 1989	John Rea (v. Ian Black)	Scottish Professional Championship	Marco's Leisure Centre, Glasgow
8 Mar 1989	Cliff Thorburn (v. Jimmy White)	Matchroom League	Hawth Theatre, Crawley

* Televised

All smiles before the start of the 1989 world championship. Three sessions later John Parrott's smile was not so broad; Steve Davis had beaten him 18-3, the biggest winning margin in The Crucible's history.

● ● ● ● ● ● ● ● ● ● ● ● ● ● ● ●

JOHN PARROTT

Born: 11 May 1964, Liverpool

It is terrible for any sportsman to be labelled the 'nearly man'. But sadly for John Parrott he had to live with that tag for a couple of years until he shook it off in 1989 when he won his first ranking tournament, the ICI European Open by beating Terry Griffiths 9–8 at Deauville.

Parrott had a great record as an amateur and won the Pontins Junior, Pontins Open, and Junior *Pot Black* (twice) titles. He was also runner-up to Tony Jones in the 1983 English amateur championship.

He turned professional in 1983 and made an immediate impact by beating Tony Knowles and Alex Higgins in the Lada Classic before losing 5–4 to Steve Davis.

At the end of his first season he had jumped to 20th in the rankings. By 1987 he was in the top-16 and in 1988–9 he challenged Steve Davis for the number one position. But that first title seemed to elude him.

He lost to Steve Davis in the finals of the Mercantile Credit Classic and Everest World Match-Play championship in 1988, and to Stephen Hendry in the 1989 Benson and Hedges Masters. But then it all came good at Deauville. At the end of the season he reached his first world final but the reigning champion Steve Davis produced some of the finest snooker of his career and Parrott had to be content with the runner-up position again, but surely his day will come.

● ● ● ● ● ● ● ● ● ● ● ● ● ● ● ●

All-time Crucible career records

A total of 72 different players have played at The Crucible.
This is the career record of each of them:

	P	W	L	Frames For	Against	Highest break
Andrewartha, Roy (Eng)	1	0	1	4	10	52 v. Eddie Charlton, 1984
Bear, John (Can)	1	0	1	7	10	44 v. Bill Werbeniuk, 1982
Bennett, Mark (Wal)	1	0	1	4	10	47 v. Dennis Taylor, 1987
Black, Ian (Sco)	1	0	1	3	10	63 v. Perrie Mans, 1983
Browne, Paddy (RoI)	1	0	1	5	10	77 v. Willie Thorne, 1989
Campbell, John (Aus)	6	1	5	33	61	96 v. Silvino Francisco, 1987
Chaperon, Bob (Can)	2	0	2	8	20	55 v. Terry Griffiths, 1989
Charlton, Eddie (Aus)	28	16	12	300	289	118 v. Les Dodd, 1983
Davis, Fred (Eng)	10	3	7	90	117	110 v. Eddie Charlton, 1979
Davis, Steve (Eng)	45	40	5	597	354	136 v. Alex Higgins, 1980
Dodd, Les (Eng)	1	0	1	7	10	47 v. Eddie Charlton, 1983
Donnelly, Jim (Sco)	1	0	1	5	10	70 v. Ray Reardon, 1982
Drago, Tony (Mal)	3	2	1	27	20	72 v. Dennis Taylor, 1988
Duggan, Steve (Eng)	2	1	1	14	16	84 v. Steve Davis, 1989
Dunning, John (Eng)	2	0	2	8	20	55 v. Kirk Stevens, 1981
Edmonds, Ray (Eng)	4	0	4	24	40	73 v. John Spencer, 1981
Fagan, Patsy (RoI)	8	3	5	72	89	105 v. Fred Davis, 1978
Fisher, Mick (Eng)	1	0	1	2	10	37 v. Kirk Stevens, 1983
Fitzmaurice, Jack (Eng)	1	0	1	4	10	45 v. Kirk Stevens, 1982
Foulds, Neal (Eng)	12	6	6	119	112	109 v. Joe Johnson, 1987
Fowler, Danny (Eng)	2	0	2	9	20	46 v. Tony Knowles, 1988
Francisco, Peter (SAf)	2	0	2	13	20	68 v. Dean Reynolds, 1989
Francisco, Silvino (SAf)	14	6	8	125	128	109 v. Eddie Charlton, 1988
Gauvreau, Marcel (Can)	1	0	1	5	10	66 v. David Taylor, 1984
Griffiths, Terry (Wal)	30	20	10	345	289	121 v. Alex Higgins, 1979
Hallett, Mike (Eng)	14	6	8	108	135	133 v. Steve Davis, 1989
Hendry, Stephen (Sco)	10	6	4	110	90	141 v. Terry Griffiths, 1989
Higgins, Alex (Ire)	27	16	11	306	284	135 v. Ray Reardon, 1982
Houlihan, Pat (Eng)	1	0	1	8	13	83 v. Cliff Thorburn, 1978
Hughes, Eugene (RoI)	6	1	5	44	60	99 v. Cliff Thorburn, 1986
James, Steve (Eng)	4	2	2	43	38	140 v. Rex Williams, 1988
Johnson, Joe (Eng)	15	10	5	169	146	110 v. Mike Hallett, 1986
						110 v. Terry Griffiths, 1986
Jones, Tony (Eng)	1	0	1	8	10	46 v. Tony Knowles, 1985
Jones, Wayne (Wal)	4	1	3	24	42	86 v. Jimmy White, 1985
King, Warren (Aus)	3	0	3	14	30	71 v. John Parrott, 1988
Knowles, Tony (Eng)	22	13	9	226	212	137 v. Jimmy White, 1985
Longworth, Steve (Eng)	3	1	2	18	27	103 v. Stephen Hendry, 1987
Macleod, Murdo (Sco)	3	1	2	22	28	66 v. Rex Williams, 1987
Mans, Perrie (SAf)	13	5	8	124	155	85 v. Alex Higgins, 1980
Martin, Dave (Eng)	4	0	4	16	40	68 v. Joe Johnson, 1986
Meadowcroft, Jim (Eng)	3	0	3	9	30	75 v. Alex Higgins, 1982
Meo, Tony (Eng)	16	7	9	146	158	134 v. John Virgo, 1981
Mifsud, Paul (Mal)	1	0	1	2	10	46 v. Terry Griffiths, 1984
Miles, Graham (Eng)	12	4	8	89	122	75 v. John Pulman, 1977
Morgan, Darren (Wal)	1	0	1	4	10	49 v. John Virgo, 1989
Morra, Mario (Can)	1	0	1	3	10	48 v. Cliff Thorburn, 1984
Mountjoy, Doug (Wal)	27	14	13	261	254	145 v. Ray Reardon, 1981
Newbury, Steve (Wal)	1	0	1	5	10	53 v. Steve Davis, 1989

continued over

All-time Crucible career records – continued

	P	W	L	Frames For	Against	Highest break
O'Boye, Joe (Eng)	1	0	1	6	10	59 v. Silvino Francisco, 1989
O'Kane, Dene (NZ)	5	2	3	38	43	127 v. Jimmy White, 1989
Parrott, John (Eng)	16	10	6	170	148	114 v. Ray Reardon, 1985
Pulman, John (Eng)	5	2	3	51	63	76 v. Graham Miles, 1977
Reardon, Ray (Wal)	30	20	10	346	316	122 v. Tony Knowles, 1983
Reynolds, Dean (Eng)	10	3	7	79	93	115 v. Kirk Stevens, 1986
Roe, David (Eng)	2	1	1	22	19	69 v. Mike Hallett, 1989
Sinclair, Eddie (Sco)	1	0	1	1	10	45 v. Kirk Stevens, 1984
Spencer, John (Eng)	17	8	9	178	186	138 v. Perrie Mans, 1978
Stevens, Kirk (Can)	24	14	10	253	207	139 v. Perrie Mans, 1983
Taylor, David (Eng)	19	8	11	167	176	94 v. Fred Davis, 1980
Taylor, Dennis (Ire)	30	18	12	347	312	135 v. Kirk Stevens, 1981
Thorburn, Cliff (Can)	36	24	12	423	375	147 v. Terry Griffiths, 1983
Thorne, Willie (Eng)	20	8	12	178	195	143 v. Alex Higgins, 1982
Virgo, John (Eng)	17	5	12	152	170	112 v. Jimmy White, 1986
Werbeniuk, Bill (Can)	20	10	10	180	190	143 v. Joe Johnson, 1985
West, Barry (Eng)	2	0	2	11	20	65 v. Ray Reardon, 1987
White, Jimmy (Eng)	28	19	9	320	272	126 v. Kirk Stevens, 1982
Wildman, Mark (Eng)	1	0	1	8	10	87 v. Terry Griffiths, 1983
Wilkinson, Gary (Eng)	1	0	1	9	10	78 v. Stephen Hendry, 1989
Williams, Rex (Eng)	8	0	8	37	83	138 v. Jimmy White, 1984
Wilson, Cliff (Wal)	7	0	7	33	70	66 v. Doug Mountjoy, 1980
Wright, Jon (Eng)	1	0	1	6	10	59 v. Alex Higgins, 1987
Wych, Jim (Can)	5	2	3	40	48	87 v. Ray Reardon, 1984

Representation of countries

38 England; 8 Canada, Wales; 4 Scotland; 3 Australia, Republic of Ireland, South Africa; 2 Malta, Northern Ireland; 1 New Zealand.

CHAPTER THREE

The Ranking Tournaments 1982-9

The following are all the tournaments, other than the Embassy World Championship, that have carried ranking points since 1982-3 when the Jameson International (now Fidelity Unit Trusts International) and Professional Players' Tournament (now Rothmans Grand Prix) were both accorded ranking status.

All results are for those matches which had ranking points at stake. For a full explanation of the ranking system see Chapter 6.

Fidelity Unit Trusts International

Traditionally the first ranking tournament of the season. It started life as the Jameson International and was the first tournament to be accorded ranking status after the Embassy World Professional Championship.

Year	Tournament name	Venue	First prize £
1982	Jameson International	Assembly Rooms, Derby	22,000
1983	Jameson International	Eldon Square Recreation Centre, Newcastle upon Tyne	24,000
1984	Jameson International	Eldon Square Recreation Centre, Newcastle upon Tyne	30,000
1985	Goya Matchroom Trophy	Trentham Gardens, Stoke-on-Trent	35,000
1986	BCE International	Trentham Gardens, Stoke-on-Trent	35,000
1987	Fidelity Unit Trusts International	Trentham Gardens, Stoke-on-Trent	40,000
1988	Fidelity Unit Trusts International	Trentham Gardens, Stoke-on-Trent	45,000

Devonian John Street was the first secretary of the professional Referees' Association in 1979.

1982

Round two Steve Davis beat Dean Reynolds 5-0; David Taylor beat Bill Werbeniuk 5-2; Kirk Stevens beat Perrie Mans 5-2; Terry Griffiths beat Alex Higgins 5-2; Dennis Taylor beat Cliff Thorburn 5-2; Cliff Wilson beat Jimmy White 5-2; John Virgo beat John Spencer 5-4; Tony Knowles beat Ray Reardon 5-2

Quarter-finals John Virgo beat Dennis Taylor 5-3; David Taylor beat Steve Davis 5-3; Tony Knowles beat Cliff Wilson 5-4; Kirk Stevens beat Terry Griffiths 5-3

Semi-finals Tony Knowles beat Kirk Stevens 9-3; David Taylor beat John Virgo 9-5

Final Tony Knowles beat David Taylor 9-6

This was David Taylor's one and only ranking final. After eliminating Steve Davis and then holding Knowles to 2-all in the final he must have been confident of his first major title. But Knowles then raced away to a 5-2 lead. Taylor pulled back to 5–3 at the interval, but the next frame saw Knowles restore his three-frame lead. It was in this frame that Knowles compiled the highest break of the tournament, 114, which deprived Taylor of the £1200 break prize he was holding for his 101 against Bill Werbeniuk.

Taylor pulled back to 5–6 but three of the next four frames, including a 76 in the last frame, were enough to take Knowles to his first major title.

1983

Round two Terry Griffiths beat George Scott 5–0; John Spencer beat Tony Knowles 5–4; Cliff Thorburn beat Dennis Taylor 5–3; Doug Mountjoy beat Dave Martin 5–0; Eddie Charlton beat Mario Morra 5–3; Willie Thorne beat Ray Reardon 5–0; Silvino Francisco beat Jim Donnelly 5–1; Steve Davis beat Mike Watterson 5–0

Quarter-finals Terry Griffiths beat John Spencer 5–4; Cliff Thorburn beat Doug Mountjoy 5–2; Eddie Charlton beat Willie Thorne 5–0; Steve Davis beat Silvino Francisco 5–1

Semi-finals Cliff Thorburn beat Terry Griffiths 9–8; Steve Davis beat Eddie Charlton 9–2

Final Steve Davis beat Cliff Thorburn 9–4

Davis opened with consecutive clearances of 74 to take an early 2–0 lead. It was soon extended to 4–0 before Thorburn got his act together and reduced the arrears to two frames. Trailing 5–2 going into the last frame of the first session the Canadian had a great chance to make it 5–3 but left the black in the jaws of the pocket for Davis to snatch victory and take a 6–2 lead.

They shared the first four frames of the evening session and with Davis within one of the title he had no difficulty in securing a 9–4 win.

1984

Round two Steve Davis beat David Taylor 5–1; Alex Higgins beat Terry Griffiths 5–4; Eugene Hughes beat Ray Reardon 5–1; Willie Thorne beat Marcel Gauvreau 5–3; Silvino Francisco beat John Virgo 5–2; Jimmy White beat Tony Meo 5–1; Dennis Taylor beat Joe Johnson 5–2; Tony Knowles beat Steve Newbury 5–4

Quarter-finals Steve Davis beat Alex Higgins 5–1; Eugene Hughes beat Willie Thorne 5–2; Silvino Francisco beat Dennis Taylor w.o.; Tony Knowles beat Jimmy White 5–4

Semi-finals Steve Davis beat Eugene Hughes 9–3; Tony Knowles beat Silvino Francisco 9–6

Final Steve Davis beat Tony Knowles 9–2

Once more Tony Knowles failed to reproduce the form that took him to a 10–1 win over Davis in the 1982 Embassy World Championship. He lost the opening frame on the black and soon slipped to 4–1 down. At the end of the first session Davis led 5–2 and steady break-building was to carry him through.

A run of four consecutive frames in the evening saw Davis conclude proceedings earlier than anticipated as Knowles, the 1982 champion, went down 9–2.

1985

Round four Steve Davis beat John Virgo 5–1; Murdo Macleod beat Bob Chaperon 5–4; Dean Reynolds beat Matt Gibson 5–0; Jimmy White beat Warren King 5–2; Cliff Wilson beat Tony Chappel 5–0; Joe Johnson beat Malcolm Bradley 5–2; David Taylor beat Bill Werbeniuk 5–4; Neal Foulds beat Tony Knowles 5–3; Cliff Thorburn beat David Martin 5–3; John Campbell beat Doug Mountjoy 5–1; Willie Thorne beat George Scott 5–1; Steve Duggan beat Ian Black 5–1; Terry Griffiths beat John Spencer 5–1; John Parrott beat Tony Meo 5–4; Alex Higgins beat Tommy Murphy 5–2; Dennis Taylor beat Bob Harris 5–3

Round five Steve Davis beat Murdo Macleod 5–1; Jimmy White beat Dean Reynolds 5–1; Joe Johnson beat Cliff Wilson 5–1; Neal Foulds beat David Taylor 5–4; Cliff Thorburn beat John Campbell 5–0; Steve Duggan beat Willie Thorne 5–4; John Parrott beat Terry Griffiths 5–1; Dennis Taylor beat Alex Higgins 5–1

Quarter-finals Jimmy White beat Steve Davis 5–3; Neal Foulds beat Joe Johnson 5–2; Cliff Thorburn beat Steve Duggan 5–2; Dennis Taylor beat John Parrott 5–1

Semi-finals Jimmy White beat Neal Foulds 9–5; Cliff Thorburn beat Dennis Taylor 9–5

Final Cliff Thorburn beat Jimmy White 12–10

After retaining the Canadian Masters and winning the Langs Scottish Masters, Cliff Thorburn started the final full of confidence, but matches with Jimmy White are always guaranteed to be tough. White ran away to a 7–0 lead at the end of the first session and it looked as though Thorburn's good run was at an end.

The first session had lasted just 1 hour 44 minutes as White made light work of the Canadian. But then came one of the game's greatest recoveries.

White led 74–0 in the first frame of the second session but Thorburn got the required snookers to win an amazing frame on the black. That was the boost the Canadian needed and he took the next three frames as well to close the gap to 7–4. White made it 8–4 before Thorburn won the last two frames of the day, to go to bed 8–6 down, which was a big improvement on the scoreline at the start of the evening.

White started the next day with another win to go 9–6, but a 113 clearance by Thorburn started a run of five frames for the Canadian which took him into an 11–9 lead, needing just one for the title. White made it 11–10 but Thorburn won the next frame to clinch the match and complete one of the greatest recoveries ever seen in a major final.

1986

Round four Cliff Thorburn beat Jim Wych 5–3; Terry Griffiths beat Barry West 5–1; Cliff Wilson beat Roger Bales 5–1; Tony Knowles beat Eddie Charlton 5–1; Peter Francisco beat Alex Higgins 5–4; Marcel Gauvreau beat Ray Reardon 5–2; Silvino Francisco beat John Virgo 5–0; Dennis Taylor beat Stephen Hendry 5–3; Steve Davis beat Warren King 5–4; Rex Williams beat Steve Duggan 5–4; Eugene Hughes beat Pat Houlihan 5–1; Bob Chaperon beat Tony Drago 5–1; Ken Owers beat Dene O'Kane 5–0; Neal Foulds beat Geoff Foulds 5–0; Dean Reynolds beat Doug Mountjoy 5–2; David Taylor beat Joe Johnson 5–3

Round five Cliff Thorburn beat Terry Griffiths 5–4; Cliff Wilson beat Tony Knowles 5–4; Peter Francisco beat Marcel Gauvreau 5–2; Silvino Francisco beat Dennis Taylor 5–0; Steve Davis beat Rex Williams 5–4; Eugene Hughes beat Bob Chaperon 5–0; Neal Foulds beat Ken Owers 5–1; Dean Reynolds beat David Taylor 5–1

Quarter-finals Cliff Thorburn beat Cliff Wilson 5–1; Peter Francisco beat Silvino Francisco 5–3; Eugene Hughes beat Steve Davis 5–4; Neal Foulds beat Dean Reynolds 5–2

Semi-finals Cliff Thorburn beat Peter Francisco 9–7; Neal Foulds beat Eugene Hughes 9–8

Final Neal Foulds beat Cliff Thorburn 12–9

Of the 14 frames played on the first day, each player won seven and at no stage was there a gap of more than one frame between the two men. Of the seven frames won by Thorburn, five were on the black and one on the pink. The only one he won comfortably was the second frame of the day when he compiled a break of 102 to level the match at 1–1.

Foulds won the first two frames of the second day to open up a 9–7 lead. Thorburn started to lose touch and a change of tip did little to alter his fortunes as Foulds completed the match with a 71 break to beat the defending champion and in doing so win his first ranking tournament.

1987

Round four Stephen Hendry beat Neal Foulds 5–2; Dave Gilbert beat Cliff Wilson 5–1; Joe O'Boye beat Robbie Foldvari 5–4; Martin Clark beat Dennis Taylor 5–0; Eugene Hughes beat Jim Wych 5–4; Silvino Francisco beat Bill Werbeniuk 5–3; Steve James beat David Roe 5–3; Cliff Thorburn beat Steve Newbury 5–3; Jimmy White beat Steve Longworth 5–1; Mike Hallett beat John Spencer 5–2; Nigel Gilbert beat Wayne Jones 5–4; Eddie Charlton beat Terry Griffiths 5–2; Tony Knowles beat David Taylor 5–2; John Virgo beat Willie Thorne 5–4; John Parrott beat Bob Chaperon 5–1; Steve Davis beat Tony Meo 5–3

Found five Stephen Hendry beat Dave Gilbert 5–0; Joe O'Boye beat Martin Clark 5–2; Eugene Hughes beat Silvino Francisco 5–4; Cliff Thorburn beat Steve James 5–0; Mike Hallett beat Jimmy White 5–4; Eddie Charlton beat Nigel Gil-

bert 5–0; John Virgo beat Tony Knowles 5–2; Steve Davis beat John Parrott 5–2

Quarter-finals Stephen Hendry beat Joe O'Boye 5–2; Cliff Thorburn beat Eugene Hughes 5–1; Mike Hallett beat Eddie Charlton 5–4; Steve Davis beat John Virgo 5–2

Semi-finals Cliff Thorburn beat Stephen Hendry 9–1; Steve Davis beat Mike Hallet 9–3

Final Steve Davis beat Cliff Thorburn 12–5

Thorburn was appearing in his third consecutive final at Trentham Gardens. But 1987 went the same way as 1986; with defeat. After winning the opening frame on the black Davis went to 5–1 at the end of the first session and for Thorburn it was reminiscent of his start against Jimmy White in 1985. But this time there was to be no fairy-tale recovery.

Davis opened the second session with a championship record equalling break of 140. That signalled the start of an evening session littered with big breaks by both players. Every frame contained a break of at least 50 as Davis wound up the session 8–5 in the lead.

The Canadian wasn't to win another frame as Davis won four in succession to take the title by 12 frames to five.

1988

Round four Steve Davis beat Alain Robidoux 5–4; David Taylor beat John Rea 5–4; Dennis Taylor beat John Campbell 5–4; Jim Wych beat Dene O'Kane 5–4; Tony Meo beat Mike Hallett 5–3; Bob Chaperon beat Silvino Francisco 5–2; Steve James beat Murdo Macleod 5–2; Stephen Hendry beat Steve Longworth 5–3; Dean Reynolds beat Neal Foulds 5–3; John Spencer beat John Virgo 5–1; Joe Johnson beat Doug Mountjoy 5–4; Steve Newbury beat Tony Knowles 5–4; Barry West beat Les Dodd 5–3; Rex Williams beat Steve Duggan 5–4; Willie Thorne beat Tony Drago 5–2; Jimmy White beat Eugene Hughes 5–1

Round five Steve Davis beat David Taylor 5–1; Dennis Taylor beat Jim Wych 5–2; Joe Johnson beat Steve Newbury 5–2; Dean Reynolds beat John Spencer 5–2; Tony Meo beat Bob Chaperon 5–4; Steve James beat Stephen Hendry 5–2; Barry West beat Rex Williams 5–4; Jimmy White beat Willie Thorne 5–4

Quarter-finals Steve Davis beat Dennis Taylor 5–2; Steve James beat Tony Meo 5–1; Dean Reynolds beat Joe Johnson 5–1; Jimmy White beat Barry West 5–2

Semi-finals Steve Davis beat Steve James 9–1; Jimmy White beat Dean Reynolds 9–5

Final Steve Davis beat Jimmy White 12–6

Steve Davis has played some brilliant snooker over the years but his performance in the final of the 1988 Fidelity was, by his own admission, 'the best of his life'.

His constant high standard of break-building was a major feature of one of the most one-sided matches between these two talented players.

Davis led 6–1 at the end of the opening session and in the sixth frame put together a break of 121, one of four centuries the crowd was to witness.

White immediately started to reduce Davis's lead in the second session but then Davis compiled centuries (108, 101 and 104) in consecutive frames for the first time in his career (either in tournament play or practice) to go 9–2 up. In all three frames White failed to reply.

Davis started the second day with a lead of 10–4 and while the 'Whirlwind' won the first two frames it was too late and Davis won the next two to retain his title in convincing style.

Rothmans Grand Prix

The Rothmans Grand Prix started as the Professional Players' Tournament in 1982 and was the first tournament promoted by the WPBSA's own promotions company. It was one of the two new ranking tournaments in 1982–3 (along with the Jameson International).

Not a televised event initially, it received full coverage in 1984 when Rothmans began its sponsorship of the event.

Year	Tournament name	Venue	First prize £
1982	Professional Players' Tournament	La Reserve, Sutton Coldfield/ International SC, Birmingham	5,000
1983	Professional Players' Tournament	Redwood Lodge, Bristol	12,500
1984	Rothmans Grand Prix	Hexagon Theatre, Reading	45,000
1985	Rothmans Grand Prix	Hexagon Theatre, Reading	50,000
1986	Rothmans Grand Prix	Hexagon Theatre, Reading	55,000
1987	Rothmans Grand Prix	Hexagon Theatre, Reading	60,000
1988	Rothmans Grand Prix	Hexagon Theatre, Reading	65,000

1982

Round three Bill Werbeniuk beat Cliff Thorburn 5–2; Joe Johnson beat Mark Wildman 5–4; Dean Reynolds beat Cliff Wilson 5–1; John Virgo beat John Spencer 5–1; Eddie Charlton beat Tony Meo 5–3; Jimmy White beat Dennis Taylor 5–3; Terry Griffiths beat Eddie Sinclair 5–3; Ray Reardon beat Murdo Macleod 5–2

Quarter-finals Jimmy White beat Terry Griffiths 5–2; John Virgo beat Joe Johnson 5–1; Ray Reardon beat Bill Werbeniuk 5–3; Eddie Charlton beat Dean Reynolds 5–2

Semi-finals Jimmy White beat John Virgo 10–4; Ray Reardon beat Eddie Charlton 10–7

Final Ray Reardon beat Jimmy White 10–5

Apart from success in the Embassy World Championship, this was the only ranking final contested by Ray Reardon. It was also the first final for Jimmy White.

The early exchanges belonged to Jimmy White who opened up a 2–0 lead. Reardon levelled it at 2-all and then took the lead after a clearance of 132. Reardon held on to his one frame lead at 5–4 at the half-way stage and from a lead of 6–5 won four consecutive frames to take the title by 10 frames to five.

1983

Round three Willie Thorne beat Ray Reardon 5–3; Cliff Thorburn beat Cliff Wilson 5–3; Eugene Hughes beat Terry Griffiths 5–2; Joe Johnson beat Eddie Charlton 5–0; Kirk Stevens beat Mark Wildman 5–0; John Campbell beat Dave Martin 5–0; Tony Knowles beat Silvino Francisco 5–0; Tony Meo beat Mike Hallett 5–3

Quarter-finals Joe Johnson beat Cliff Thorburn 5–1; Willie Thorne beat Eugene Hughes 5–1; Tony Meo beat Kirk Stevens 5–3; Tony Knowles beat John Campbell 5–3

Semi-finals Tony Knowles beat Willie Thorne 9–7; Joe Johnson beat Tony Meo 9–6

Final Tony Knowles beat Joe Johnson 9–8

Joe Johnson reached his first major final after four years as a professional. In the past, Johnson seemed to have problems playing in front of the television cameras, and the fact that this tournament was untelevised added fuel to that argument.

However, the way Knowles started, it made little difference whether cameras were there or not. He won six of the first seven frames before Johnson displayed the skill he was truly capable of. He started a great run with a 135 total clearance. That made it 6–2 to Knowles at the interval.

Johnson then won three of the next four frames to trail 5–7. At 8–5 however, and with Knowles needing one more frame for the title, all seemed lost for the Yorkshireman but three consecutive frames made it 8-all with one to play. Knowles built up a big lead in the final frame. But once more Johnson came back at him with a 33 break. However, Lancastrian Knowles won his second ranking tournament when he took the final red and cleared the colours to the pink.

1984

Round three Tony Knowles beat Ian Williamson 5–2; Neal Foulds beat Willie Thorne 5–1; Dennis Taylor beat Ray Reardon 5–3; Kirk Stevens beat Mike Hallett 5–3; Cliff Thorburn beat Tony Meo 5–4; Doug Mountjoy beat Eddie

Charlton 5-4; Dean Reynolds beat Silvino Francisco 5-1; Steve Davis beat David Taylor 5-1

Quarter-finals Neal Foulds beat Tony Knowles 5-2; Dennis Taylor beat Kirk Stevens 5-2; Cliff Thorburn beat Doug Mountjoy 5-3; Steve Davis beat Dean Reynolds 5-0

Semi-finals Dennis Taylor beat Neal Foulds 9-3; Cliff Thorburn beat Steve Davis 9-7

Final Dennis Taylor beat Cliff Thorburn 10-2

After 12 years as a professional, one of snooker's nice guys at last got his just rewards. For Dennis Taylor, victory in the first event under Rothmans' sponsorship started the dawn of a new era that was to take him to the world title before the season was out.

Victory over Cliff Thorburn at The Hexagon Theatre came easier than many expected. After being held at 2-all, the Irishman won the last four frames of the first session, concluding with a 112 break.

From 6-2 he compiled breaks of 47, 49, 79 and 65 to win the first four frames of the evening session which took him to his first major title.

1985

Round four Dennis Taylor beat Rex Williams 5-2; Tony Meo beat Eugene Hughes 5-3; Tony Drago beat Eddie Charlton 5-3; Cliff Wilson beat George Scott 5-3; Kirk Stevens beat Graham Miles 5-2; Steve Longworth beat David Taylor 5-1; John Campbell beat Doug Mountjoy 5-2; Tony Knowles beat Ray Edmonds 5-3; Cliff Thorburn beat Mark Wildman 5-2; Joe Jonhson beat Mike Hallet 5-4; Peter Francisco beat Wayne Jones 5-3; Terry Griffiths beat Bob Harris 5-3; Jimmy White beat Joe O'Boye 5-4; Silvino Francisco beat Dave Martin 5-3; Alex Higgins beat Neal Foulds 5-3; Steve Davis beat Danny Fowler 5-1

Round five Dennis Taylor beat Tony Meo 5-3; Cliff Wilson beat Tony Drago 5-2; Kirk Stevens beat Steve Longworth 5-3; Tony Knowles beat John Campbell 5-2; Cliff Thorburn beat Joe Johnson 5-1; Terry Griffiths beat Peter Francisco 5-2; Silvino Francisco beat Jimmy White 5-4; Steve Davis beat Alex Higgins 5-0

Quarter-finals Dennis Taylor beat Cliff Wilson 5-2; Tony Knowles beat Kirk Stevens 5-4; Cliff Thorburn beat Terry Griffiths 5-1; Steve Davis beat Silvino Francisco 5-2

Semi-finals Dennis Taylor beat Tony Knowles 9-6; Steve Davis beat Cliff Thorburn 9-5

Final Steve Davis beat Dennis Taylor 10-9

Six months earlier, Taylor came from 8-0 behind in the Embassy World Championship to clinch a dramatic win over Davis at The Crucible. Now, at the Hexagon Theatre, Taylor again found himself in arrears to Davis after the first session; this time he trailed 6-1.

Anxious to hold on to the Rothmans title, Taylor won the first frame of the evening session scheduled for 12 frames. Davis won the next to

make it 7-2 but then the Ulsterman rattled off six consecutive frames to take the lead at 8-7 and stage another comeback reminiscent of the world championship. Davis made it 8-all and regained the lead after a 17th frame which lasted 51 minutes.

Davis had a chance to take the match in the next frame but played the white off the table when attempting a deep screw on the pink. At 9-all the time was beyond 1.30 a.m. and yet another Davis-Taylor encounter was proving to be a thriller. In the end the honours went to the Londoner this time as he put paid to Taylor's brave challenge at nearly 2.15 in the morning.

1986

Round four Steve Davis beat Tony Drago 5-1; Terry Griffiths beat John Campbell 5-1; Rex Williams beat Mark Wildman 5-1; Alex Higgins beat Dave Martin 5-2; Willie Thorne beat Warren King 5-2; Neal Foulds beat Cliff Wilson 5-0; Tony Meo beat John Parrott 5-3; Dennis Taylor beat John Virgo 5-3; Steve Newbury beat Joe O'Boye 5-2; Silvino Francisco beat Wayne Jones 5-4; Doug Mountjoy beat Jim Wych 5-1; Tony Knowles beat Peter Francisco 5-3; Jimmy White beat Jack McLaughlin 5-2; Mike Hallett beat Les Dodd 5-2; Stephen Hendry beat Bob Chaperon 5-2; Paddy Browne beat Mark Bennett 5-0

Round five Steve Davis beat Terry Griffiths 5-2; Rex Williams beat Alex Higgins 5-1; Neal Foulds beat Willie Thorne 5-3; Tony Meo beat Dennis Taylor 5-2; Silvino Francisco beat Steve Newbury 5-2; Tony Knowles beat Doug Mountjoy 5-1; Jimmy White beat Mike Hallett 5-3; Stephen Hendry beat Paddy Browne 5-3

Quarter-finals Rex Williams beat Steve Davis 5-1; Neal Foulds beat Tony Meo 5-3; Silvino Francisco beat Tony Knowles 5-2; Jimmy White beat Stephen Hendry 5-4

Semi-finals Rex Williams beat Neal Foulds 9-8; Jimmy White beat Silvino Francisco 9-6

Final Jimmy White beat Rex Williams 10-6

A professional since 1951, Rex Williams was making his first appearance in a major professional snooker final at the age of 55. And after beating Steve Davis 5-1 on the way to the final, there were few who would back against him winning his first major title. But the younger Jimmy White proved too good when it mattered.

Williams won the first frame but White went 2-1 up with a great 101 clearance. But then Williams produced some vintage snooker to take a 5-2 lead. In the seventh frame he compiled a break of 125.

Having won the final frame of the afternoon, White won the first of the evening to close the gap to 5-4. Williams won the tenth but that proved to be his last success of the match. White won the next six (the last two in 16 minutes) to win 10-6.

The start of a great career – Stephen Hendry holds aloft the Rothmans Grand Prix trophy after winning his first ranking event.

STEPHEN HENDRY

Born: 13 January 1969, Edinburgh

Like Scotland's first great snooker player, Walter Donaldson, Stephen Hendry hails from the Edinburgh area. However, Hendry has had a more immediate impact on the professional game than his predecessor.

Winner of the national under-16 championship in 1983 he was the youngest-ever Scottish amateur champion a year later when only 15. He retained the title in 1985 before turning professional. He captured the 1986 Scottish professional title when still only 17, and the following year he retained the title, won the Winfield Masters and then became the youngest winner of a ranking tournament when he beat Dennis Taylor 10-7 to win the Rothmans Grand Prix.

A further win that season in the MIM Britannia British Open helped elevate him from 23 to number four in the world rankings.

Although he was without a ranking win in 1988-9 he managed to lift some titles, notably the Benson and Hedges Masters at Wembley where he beat John Parrott. However, defeats by Doug Mountjoy in the Tennents UK Open final and by Alex Higgins in the Benson and Hedges Irish Masters final were setbacks for the youngster. He has still managed to maintain his position near the top of the rankings and at the age of 20 still has a chance to overtake Alex Higgins as the youngest-ever world champion.

1987

Round four Tony Drago beat Jimmy White 5-3; Willie Thorne beat Roger Bales 5-2; Graham Cripsey beat Paul Gibson 5-4; Peter Francisco beat Joe Johnson 5-2; Dennis Taylor beat Bill Werbeniuk 5-3; Cliff Wilson beat John Virgo 5-3; Gary Wilkinson beat Silvino Francisco 5-3; Steve Newbury beat Cliff Thorburn 5-0; Mick Fisher beat Martin Clark 5-4; Bob Chaperon beat Pat Houlihan 5-0; John Parrott beat Kirk Stevens 5-0; Terry Griffiths beat Tony Chappel 5-3; Tony Knowles beat David Roe 5-2; Eddie Charlton beat Ray Edmonds 5-3; Stephen Hendry beat Jim Chambers 5-1; Steve Davis beat Jim Wych 5-1

Round five Willie Thorne beat Tony Drago 5-2; Peter Francisco beat Graham Cripsey 5-1; Bob Chaperon beat Mick Fisher 5-2; John Parrott beat Terry Griffiths 5-4; Dennis Taylor beat Cliff Wilson 5-2; Steve Newbury beat Gary Wilkinson 5-3; Tony Knowles beat Eddie Charlton 5-0; Stephen Hendry beat Steve Davis 5-2

Quarter-finals Peter Francisco beat Willie Thorne 5-3; Dennis Taylor beat Steve Newbury 5-2; John Parrott beat Bob Chaperon 5-2; Stephen Hendry beat Tony Knowles 5-2

Semi-finals Dennis Taylor beat Peter Francisco 9-4; Stephen Hendry beat John Parrott 9-7

Final Stephen Hendry beat Dennis Taylor 10-7

From the moment Stephen Hendry first appeared on the professional scene in 1985 he had been talked about as a potential champion. At the Hexagon Theatre he had a chance to prove those tipsters right as he matched up against Dennis Taylor in his first ranking final.

He did not disappoint, and at 18 years of age became the youngest winner of a ranking tournament.

The final was not a spectacular one. Taylor took a 3-0 lead and led by three again at 4-1 before Hendry won seven consecutive frames to lead 8–4. A 98 by the Scot in the 12th frame was the highest of the match. At 5–9 and Hendry one frame away from victory, Taylor staged a mini-revival to win two frames. But Hendry then clinched it with a 49 break to win his first ranking event.

1988

Round four Doug Mountjoy beat Stephen Hendry 5–1; Alain Robidoux beat Tony Meo 5–0; Nigel Gilbert beat Eddie Charlton 5–0; Tony Knowles beat Dean Reynolds 5–3; Ray Edmonds beat John Parrott 5–3; Rex Williams beat Gary Wilkinson 5–2; Alex Higgins beat Dene O'Kane 5–0; Neal Foulds beat Steve Duggan 5–4; Jimmy White beat Wayne Jones 5–1; Jack McLaughlin beat John Spencer 5–3; Dennis Taylor beat Bob Chaperon 5–4; Mike Hallett beat Steve James 5–2; Terry Griffiths beat Barry West 5–1; Eugene Hughes beat Joe Johnson 5–2; Cliff Wilson beat Tony Drago 5–4; Steve Davis beat Steve Newbury 5–1

Round five Alain Robidoux beat Doug Mountjoy 5–4; Nigel Gilbert beat Tony Knowles 5–4; Rex Williams beat Ray Edmonds 5–3; Alex Higgins beat Neal Foulds 5–3; Jimmy White beat Jack McLaughlin 5–2; Dennis Taylor beat Mike Hallet 5–2; Terry Griffiths beat Eugene Hughes 5–2; Steve Davis beat Cliff Wilson 5–1

Quarter-finals Alain Robidoux beat Nigel Gilbert 5–4; Alex Higgins beat Rex Williams 5–4; Dennis Taylor beat Jimmy White 5–2; Steve Davis beat Terry Griffiths 5–3

Semi-finals Alex Higgins beat Alain Robidoux 9–7; Steve Davis beat Dennis Taylor 9–1

Final Steve Davis beat Alex Higgins 10–6

Steve Davis versus Alex Higgins has always had a ring about it. Their meetings in the early eighties were legendary. The 1988 Rothmans pitched them together in a ranking final for the first time since the 1984 Coral and it was nice to see Higgins back in a major final.

Davis was the clear favourite and a 137 total clearance in the first frame did nothing to help Alex's confidence and he soon found himself trailing 3–0. Higgins won two of the next three frames and compiled an 82 in the sixth frame but he ended the session 6–2 down.

Davis immediately went to 7–2 at the start and was three frames away from the 19th ranking success of his career. Higgins got to within three frames of the Englishman, but that was as close as he got as Davis kept matching Higgins every time he won a frame. And in the end title number 19 was won by 10 frames to six.

What a remarkable season Doug Mountjoy had in 1988-89. After beating Stephen Hendry to win the Tennents UK Open he followed that up in the very next tournament by beating fellow Welshman Wayne Jones (right). Snooker guru and Mountjoy's 'mentor', Frank Callan, is in the middle.

Pot Black and Its Contribution to Snooker

There is no denying the magnitude of *Pot Black*'s contribution to the growth of snooker. It was immense.

With the advent of colour television in the late 1960s, BBC television sought new programmes that would fit nicely into the new technology. Naturally sport was an area tailormade for colour television, and there were few more colourful sports than snooker.

Snooker had been tried on black-and-white television, but without any great success. Now, producer Phillip Lewis was given the task of arousing interest a second time around. He sought the advice and help of commentator Ted Lowe who went away and came up with the idea of an eight-man tournament which he called *Pot Black*. Lowe could not have recruited more than eight professionals—there weren't any more at the time.

The first programme was recorded at the BBC's Costa Green studio in Birmingham and the series of single-frame matches was very popular with viewers. The programme's theme music, '*Black and White Rag*' by Winifred Atwell became as synonymous with snooker as it did with the programme itself.

However, one major problem that had to be overcome was that of lighting. It had to be right for the cameras, but it also had to be right for the players and it was not easy at first getting the blend right to please both parties. Blown bulbs on to the playing area was not an uncommon sight in the early days of televised snooker. However, this problem was overcome.

Thanks to *Pot Black*, the likes of Ray Reardon and John Spencer

Pot Black's long serving referee, Sydney Lee.

became household names as the clean-cut image of the snooker player was projected into millions of homes. Suddenly these players became sporting heroes and they became sought-after celebrities for exhibition matches and as resident professionals at holiday camps around the country. The snooker boom was on its way.

The success that stemmed from *Pot Black* is there for all to see today. More tournaments were organized to meet the demands of both the public and the ever-increasing number of professional players.

Despite the sport's growth, *Pot Black* remained, and was as popular as ever, even though it became less

popular with the players who were not keen on single-frame matches. In 1986 the final black was potted when Jimmy White won the last competition.

Pot Black may have now left the snooker calendar but it will never be forgotten.

● ——————————

The first eight competitors in *Pot Black* were:
Fred Davis, Kingsley Kennerley, Gary Owen, John Pulman, Jackie Rea, Ray Reardon, John Spencer, and Rex Williams.
—————————— ●

The man behind the microphone on Pot Black *was 'Whispering' Ted Lowe.*

Mercantile Credit Classic

The Mercantile Credit Classic fills the spot on the calendar previously held by the Wilsons Classic, and later the Lada Classic. It was as the Lada that the event first became a ranking tournament in 1984. It became the Mercantile Credit Classic in 1985.

Year	Tournament Name	Venue	First prize £
1984	Lada Classic	Spectrum Arena, Warrington	18,000
1985	Mercantile Credit Classic	Spectrum Arena, Warrington	40,000
1986	Mercantile Credit Classic	Spectrum Arena, Warrington	45,000
1987	Mercantile Credit Classic	Norbreck Castle, Blackpool	50,000
1988	Mercantile Credit Classic	Norbreck Castle, Blackpool	50,000
1989	Mercantile Credit Classic	Norbreck Castle, Blackpool	55,000

1984

Round two Steve Davis beat John Spencer 5–1; Eddie Charlton beat Jimmy White 5–3; Mark Wildman beat Silvino Francisco 5–1; Tony Knowles beat Mike Hallett 5–3; Kirk Stevens beat Murdo Macleod 5–1; Terry Griffiths beat Colin Roscoe 5–2; Tony Meo beat Rex Williams 5–3; John Parrott beat Alex Higgins 5–2

Quarter-finals Mark Wildman beat Eddie Charlton 5–4; Steve Davis beat Terry Griffiths 5–4; Tony Meo beat Kirk Stevens 5–2; John Parrott beat Tony Knowles 5–1

Semi-finals Tony Meo beat Mark Wildman 5–3; Steve Davis beat John Parrott 5–4

Final Steve Davis beat Tony Meo 9–8

Tony Meo was looking for his first major individual title, and how close he came. Only a member of the audience deprived him of a great victory in a close and tense final.

Davis tried to intimidate Meo with a 98 in the opening frame. He won a scrappy second frame but Meo then won four in succession to lead 4–2 before Davis closed the session with a 122 clearance.

Davis built on that and won the next four frames to take a 7–4 lead and needed just two of the remaining six frames. But once more Meo staged a recovery to take the lead at 8–7 and he needed just one frame with two to play. An 84 by Davis in a 101–0 win levelled it at 8-all and so it was down to the last frame.

Meo came from behind to get himself into a championship-winning position. He needed all the colours to the pink to secure victory. All were on their spots and as he was about to play the yellow a cry of: 'Come on Tony' bellowed from the audience. Meo missed the yellow and with it lost the title.

1985

Round two Ray Reardon beat Eugene Hughes 5–1; Steve Davis beat Alex Higgins 5–2; John Virgo beat Murdo Macleod 5–0; Willie Thorne beat Kirk Stevens 5–1; Cliff Thorburn beat Steve Longworth 5–3; Terry Griffiths beat Rex Williams 5–3; Joe Johnson beat Cliff Wilson 5–0; Warren King beat Jimmy White 5–2

Quarter-finals Steve Davis beat Ray Reardon 5–1; Cliff Thorburn beat Terry Griffiths 5–4; Joe Johnson beat Warren King 5–3; Willie Thorne beat John Virgo 5–1

Semi-finals Willie Thorne beat Steve Davis 9–8; Cliff Thorburn beat Joe Johnson 9–2

Final Willie Thorne beat Cliff Thorburn 13–8

The first event under Mercantile's sponsorship coincided with Willie Thorne's first major title after nearly ten years as a professional.

Thorne's opponent was his good friend Cliff Thorburn. But friendship went by the wayside as he destroyed Thorburn on the second day to secure a 13–8 victory.

A break of 72 gave Thorne the first frame. But Thorburn bettered that in taking the second frame with a 77. The Canadian then edged 2–1 ahead and kept his nose in front throughout the session to lead 4–3. Thorne took the first frame in the evening with a break of 105. He then won the next two to lead at 6–4. Breaks of 75 and 48 in frame 11 gave victory to Thorburn. But Thorne's second century (118) restored his lead to two frames. Both men continued to compile big breaks and the session ended with Thorburn compiling a 100 to trail the day at 7–8.

He levelled it at 8-all in the first frame of day two but Thorne won five consecutive frames to clinch the match at 13–8.

1986

Round four Bill Werbeniuk beat Tony Jones 5–3; Doug Mountjoy beat Dene O'Kane 5–3; Neal Foulds beat Stephen Hendry 5–4; John Campbell beat Bernie Mikkelsen 5–2; Eugene Hughes beat Fred Davis 5–3; Joe Johnson beat Perrie Mans 5–2; Tony Meo beat Barry West 5–1; Cliff Thorburn beat Mike Hallett 5–3; Steve Davis beat Jimmy van Rensburg 5–1; Peter Francisco beat Dave Martin 5–2; Marcel Gauvreau beat Paddy Browne 5–3; Jimmy White beat John Virgo 5–2; Tony Knowles beat Murdo Macleod 5–4; Rex Williams beat Vic Harris 5–1; Alex Higgins beat Graham Cripsey 5–2; Dennis Taylor beat Dean Reynolds 5–4

Round five Doug Mountjoy beat Bill Werbeniuk 5–3; Neal Foulds beat John Campbell 5–1; Joe Johnson beat Eugene Hughes 5–1; Cliff Thorburn beat Tony Meo 5–1; Steve Davis beat Peter Francisco 5–0; Jimmy White beat Marcel

Gauvreau 5-2; Rex Williams beat Tony Knowles 5-2; Alex Higgins beat Dennis Taylor 5-4

Quarter-finals Doug Mountjoy beat Neal Foulds 5-3; Cliff Thorburn beat Joe Johnson 5-4; Jimmy White beat Steve Davis 5-2; Rex Williams beat Alex Higgins 5-2

Semi-finals Cliff Thorburn beat Doug Mountjoy 9-6; Jimmy White beat Rex Williams 9-7

Final Jimmy White beat Cliff Thorburn 13-12

For the second successive year Cliff Thorburn lost in the Mercantile final. But this time it was a closer battle against Londoner Jimmy White.

Steady break-building, after a nervous opening frame, saw White take a 4-0 lead. But Thorburn won the last three of the session to remind White of how the Canadian eroded his 7-0 lead in the Goya at the start of the season.

White forfeited the first frame of the evening session for being late arriving. It was the first time since the 1979 Coral UK final between John Virgo and Terry Griffiths that a player forfeited a frame for this reason.

The delay did White no good and he soon found himself 4-6 in arrears. Thorburn had a 107 clearance in the 12th when restoring his two-frame lead. He made it 8-5 before White reduced the arrears by winning the last two frames of the session with breaks of 40 and 63.

Thorburn extended his lead to 9-7 with a break of 87 but White drew level at 9-all. White then extended his run to four consecutive frames and a 117 in the 20th frame made it 11-9 to White who needed two frames for victory. Thorburn then won the next two frames to level at 11-11. White made it 12-11 and again Thorburn drew level. So, with one frame left, it was 12-all and everything to play for.

Thorburn built up a 49-point lead in the last frame. White reduced the lead with a 28 but missed a difficult yellow. After an intense tactical battle, White was left needing a snooker which he got with only pink and black on the table. Thorburn gave away the points White had been seeking and the Englishman then sank the last two colours for a great win.

1987

Round four Jimmy White beat Malcolm Bradley 5-0; Steve Duggan beat Bill Werbeniuk 5-0; Terry Griffiths beat Dave Martin 5-4; John Campbell beat John Spencer 5-3; Wayne Jones beat Tony Kearney 5-1; Cliff Wilson beat Les Dodd 5-4; Barry West beat Kirk Stevens 5-3; Dean Reynolds beat Cliff Thorburn 5-4; Steve Davis beat John Virgo 5-2; Tony Meo beat Steve Longworth 5-0; Eddie Charlton beat Rex Williams 5-4; John Parrott beat Alex Higgins 5-2; Danny Fowler beat Mike Hallett 5-4; Stephen Hendry beat Jon Wright 5-1; Silvino Francisco beat Bob Harris 5-3; Peter Francisco beat Joe Johnson 5-3

Round five Jimmy White beat Steve Duggan 5-2; Terry Griffiths beat John Campbell 5-3; Cliff Wilson beat Wayne Jones 5-3; Dean Reynolds beat Barry West 5-3; Steve Davis beat Tony Meo 5-2; John Parrott beat Eddie Charlton 5-4; Stephen Hendry beat Danny Fowler 5-4; Silvino Francisco beat Peter Francisco 5-1

Quarter-finals Dean Reynolds beat Cliff Wilson 5-1; Jimmy White beat Terry Griffiths 5-3; Stephen Hendry beat Silvino Francisco 5-0; Steve Davis beat John Parrott 5-4

Semi-finals Jimmy White beat Dean Reynolds 9-8; Steve Davis beat Stephen Hendry 9-3

Final Steve Davis beat Jimmy White 13-12

The Mercantile had certainly gained a reputation for producing good finals and the 1987 encounter between Steve Davis and Jimmy White was no exception.

Throughout the 25-frame final neither player led by more than two frames. The first honours fell to White who took the opening two frames. Davis made it 2-all but the remainder of the session saw the two men exchange frames before Davis ended with a slight advantage at 4-3.

The second session followed a similar pattern with frames being exchanged. A 119 break by Davis in the 11th frame put him in front again at 6-5 and he turned that lead into a two-frame advantage when he won the next frame. Two successive frames for the left-hander made it 7-all before Davis won the last frame of the first day thanks to a fluked pink.

Davis kept himself a couple of frames in front at 9-7, 10-8 and 11-9 with breaks of 72, 53 and 61, but White drew level at 11-all. Davis edged in front again before White made it 12-12 and for the second successive year the final went the full distance.

White built up a 35-0 lead but made an error when he split the pack after missing a long red. This let Davis in, and two visits yielded breaks of 36 and 33 which were enough for him to win another memorable Mercantile final.

1988

Round four Steve Davis beat Jim Donnelly 5-0; Alex Higgins beat Tony Meo 5-3; Silvino Francisco beat Steve Longworth 5-2; Stephen Hendry beat Joe Johnson 5-3; Terry Griffiths beat Cliff Wilson 5-2; Barry West beat Willie Thorne 5-2; Martin Clark beat Mark Bennett 5-2; Steve Newbury beat Cliff Thorburn 5-3; John Virgo beat Neal Foulds 5-3; John Parrott beat David Taylor 5-0; Peter Francisco beat Ken Owers 5-0; Dennis Taylor beat Tony Drago 5-0; Tony Knowles beat Colin Roscoe 5-0; Tommy Murphy beat Dean Reynolds 5-4; Dave Martin beat Doug Mountjoy 5-4; Jimmy White beat John Spencer 5-1

Round five Steve Davis beat Alex Higgins 5-0; Stephen Hendry beat Silvino Francisco 5-3; Terry Griffiths beat Barry West 5-2; Steve Newbury beat Martin Clark 5-2; John Parrott beat John Virgo 5-0; Dennis Taylor beat Peter

Francisco 5–3; Tony Knowles beat Tommy Murphy 5–3; Dave Martin beat Jimmy White 5–2

Quarter-finals Steve Davis beat Stephen Hendry 5–3; Steve Newbury beat Terry Griffiths 5–4; John Parrott beat Dennis Taylor 5–1; Tony Knowles beat Dave Martin 5–1

Semi-finals Steve Davis beat Steve Newbury 9–2; John Parrott beat Tony Knowles 9–4

Final Steve Davis beat John Parrott 13–11

The 1988 Mercantile final didn't quite go the distance, but it was as memorable and exciting as the previous two finals.

Even in defeat John Parrott showed himself capable of mixing with the best in the world, and indicated that he would be a champion one day.

Davis scored 99 with his first visit to the table. Many men would have crumbled under such intimidation, but not Parrott. He went on to win the next three frames. Davis came back to level it at 3-all but Parrott wound up the first session with a slight lead at 4–3. The second session belonged to Davis as he won the first six of the scheduled seven frames. Parrott found some reserve to win the last frame of the day when a seventh successive loss seemed the inevitable outcome.

Parrott opened the second day with a 103 clearance to make it 6–9. Davis moved into a 10–6 lead but then Parrott started playing with great confidence and won the next five frames to lead 11–10 and suddenly the finishing post was in his sights.

Davis struck with an 83 to make it 11–11. A 68 break by Davis in the next saw Parrott concede with four reds left, and in the next frame Davis inflicted the killer blow with a 99 and finished the match just as he had started.

1989

Round four Tony Chappel beat Anthony Harris 5–1; Paddy Browne beat Steve James 5–4; Doug Mountjoy beat Nick Terry 5–4; Tony Knowles beat Dean Reynolds 5–4; Cliff Thorburn beat Graham Cripsey 5–1; John Virgo beat Bob Chaperon 5–1; Steve Newbury beat Dennis Taylor 5–4; Stephen Hendry beat Ray Reardon 5–4; Martin Clark beat Neal Foulds 5–4; Joe Johnson beat Alex Higgins 5–0; Willie Thorne beat Dene O'Kane 5–3; Terry Griffiths beat Tony Drago 5–0; John Parrott beat Jon Wright 5–2; Silvino Francisco beat Tony Meo 5–1; David Taylor beat Cliff Wilson 5–3; Wayne Jones beat Eugene Hughes 5–1

Round five Paddy Browne beat Tony Chappel 5–1; Doug Mountjoy beat Tony Knowles 5–4; Cliff Thorburn beat John Virgo 5–3; Stephen Hendry beat Steve Newbury 5–1; Martin Clark beat Joe Johnson 5–3; Willie Thorne beat Terry Griffiths 5–1; John Parrott beat Silvino Francisco 5–1; Wayne Jones beat David Taylor 5–3

Quarter-finals Doug Mountjoy beat Paddy Browne 5–3; Cliff Thorburn beat Stephen Hendry 5–4; Willie Thorne beat Martin Clark 5–4; Wayne Jones beat John Parrott 5–4

● ● ● ● ● ● ● ● ● ● ● ● ● ● ● ●

DOUG MOUNTJOY

Born: 8 June 1942, Tir-y-Berth, Glamorgan, Wales

The 1988–9 season was certainly one for reviving former glories: Alex Higgins was back in a ranking final for the first time since 1984. Tony Meo won his first-ever ranking title, and Doug Mountjoy won two ranking tournaments in one of the most amazing comebacks in snooker history.

The winner of the Welsh amateur title in 1968, he next won the title eight years later, and the same year, 1976, he captured the world amateur crown. He turned professional immediately afterwards and in his first professional event, the 1977 Benson and Hedges Masters, went all the way to the final where he beat fellow Welshman Ray Reardon. But even that fairy-tale was bettered in 1988.

The runner-up in the world professional championship in 1981, Doug had not won a major title since capturing the 1978 Coral UK Championship. Ten years later, however, a revitalized Mountjoy took centre-stage in the same tournament, which was now renamed the Tennents UK Open. In the final he met the up-and-coming Stephen Hendry but the experienced Welshman ran out the 18–14 winner.

To add to that success Mountjoy won the next ranking event, the Mercantile Credit Classic, where he beat his former practice partner Wayne Jones in the final. Only Steve Davis had previously won back-to-back ranking tournaments.

● ● ● ● ● ● ● ● ● ● ● ● ● ● ●

Semi-finals Doug Mountjoy beat Cliff Thorburn 9–5; Wayne Jones beat Willie Thorne 9–4

Final Doug Mountjoy beat Wayne Jones 13–11

Once more, the Mercantile provided a tense and close final. And who would have believed that Doug Mountjoy, who came out of the wilderness to win the season's previous ranking tournament, the Tennents, would make it back-to-back wins; something only Steve Davis had previously done.

If Mountjoy's presence in his second successive final was a shock, then the appearance of his opponent Wayne Jones was an equally big surprise.

Ranked 24 and 34 in the world, respectively, the two men used to be playing partners at the Abertysswg WMC in South Wales.

What a comeback Doug Mountjoy had in 1988-89. He won two ranking tournaments and was fifth on the money list with £181,934.

Only one break over 50 was seen in the opening session as Jones led at 4–3. A 96 by Mountjoy in the evening session was the only break of note as the two men, who knew each other's game so well, ended the day all square at seven frames each.

Things warmed up on the second day and it was only towards the end of the match that the two men showed their break-building skills.

Mountjoy levelled it at 9–9 with a 74, but breaks of 39 and 75 took Jones nearer the finishing line. But the mental barrier suddenly became a big obstacle and Mountjoy with breaks of 54, 60, 35, 67 and 38 took the last four frames for a remarkable second consecutive title.

United Kingdom Open

A ranking tournament since 1984, the Open is one of the oldest tournaments still on the professional calendar. It started life as the Super Crystalate UK Championship in 1977 before becoming the Coral UK Championship in 1979. It changed its style to the Coral United Kingdom Open in 1984 after being accorded ranking status. Since 1986 it has been known as the Tennents UK Open, but they withdrew their sponsorship after the 1988 event.

Year	Tournament Name	Venue	First Prize £
1984	Coral UK Open	Guildhall, Preston	20,000
1985	Coral UK Open	Guildhall, Preston	24,000
1986	Tennents UK Open	Guildhall, Preston	60,000
1987	Tennents UK Open	Guildhall, Preston	70,000
1988	Tennents UK Open	Guildhall, Preston	80,000

1984

Round two Willie Thorne beat Eddie Charlton 9–7; Jimmy White beat Doug Mountjoy 9–2; Alex Higgins beat Rex Williams 9–7; Kirk Stevens beat Joe Johnson 9–2; Ray Reardon beat David Taylor 9–4; Tony Knowles beat Dennis Taylor 9–2; Cliff Thorburn beat Cliff Wilson 9–3; Steve Davis beat Tony Meo 9–7

Quarter-finals Alex Higgins beat Willie Thorne 9–5; Steve Davis beat Jimmy White 9–4; Cliff Thorburn beat Ray Reardon 9–8; Kirk Stevens beat Tony Knowles 9–7

Semi-finals Alex Higgins beat Cliff Thorburn 9–7; Steve Davis beat Kirk Stevens 9–2

Final Steve Davis beat Alex Higgins 16–8

Victory over Alex Higgins started a remarkable run of four consecutive UK Open titles for Steve Davis.

Davis lost 16–15 to Higgins in a memorable final in 1983 when the event was non-ranking, but this latest episode in the Davis versus Higgins saga was a more one-sided affair.

The Englishman was 5–0 up before Higgins got on the scoreboard and Davis's 6–1 first session lead contained some big breaks; notably of 69, 73, 95, 71 and a 106. After allowing Higgins to win the first frame of the second session Davis compiled breaks of 120 and 61 to go 8–2 in front.

A 124 by Higgins in the 12th frame was his most significant contribution to the evening's play which saw Davis end the day 9–5 in front.

Higgins started the second day by taking the first three frames and making the score respectable at 8–9. But that was to be the Ulsterman's last chance. Davis won the last four frames of the afternoon and then proceeded to win the first three in the evening to win 16–8.

1985

Round four Steve Davis beat Tony Drago 9–2; Tony Meo beat Danny Fowler 9–2; Barry West beat Doug Mountjoy 9–4; Murdo Macleod beat Ray Reardon 9–5; Jimmy White beat Tony Chappel 9–5; Alex Higgins beat Fred Davis 9–2; David Taylor beat John Campbell 9–4; Tony Knowles beat John Spencer 9–7; Cliff Thorburn beat John Parrott 9–6; Willie Thorne beat John Virgo 9–8; Silvino Francisco beat Dave Martin 9–6; Terry Griffiths beat Dean Reynolds 9–7; Kirk Stevens beat Mike Hallett 9–5; Rex Williams beat Peter Francisco 9–7; Neal Foulds beat Joe Johnson 9–8; Dennis Taylor beat Graham Cripsey 9–2

Round five Steve Davis beat Tony Meo 9–5; Barry West beat Murdo Macleod 9–4; Jimmy White beat Alex Higgins 9–6;

Steve Davis and Matchroom minder 'Robbo' with the Coral UK trophy after Steve had beaten Willie Thorne in the 1985 final.

Tony Knowles beat David Taylor 9–7; Willie Thorne beat Cliff Thorburn 9–7; Terry Griffiths beat Silvino Francisco 9–5; Kirk Stevens beat Rex Williams 9–7; Dennis Taylor beat Neal Foulds 9–5

Quarter-finals Steve Davis beat Barry West 9–1; Jimmy White beat Tony Knowles 9–4; Willie Thorne beat Terry Griffiths 9–7; Dennis Taylor beat Kirk Stevens 9–1

Semi-finals Steve Davis beat Jimmy White 9–5; Willie Thorne beat Dennis Taylor 9–7

Final Steve Davis beat Willie Thorne 16–14

Break-building was a feature of this final and the pattern was set in frame two when Thorne cleared with a 112. By the end of the session, with Thorne leading 4–3, no fewer than seven breaks in excess of 40 had been compiled.

The second session was even more prolific in terms of big breaks. Davis opened with a 48 to level the match. But then it was a 121 for Thorne in frame nine and a 104 for Davis a frame later. Thorne took a two-frame lead at 7–5 with breaks of 87, 66 and 35. Despite making a 67 in frame 13 Thorne still lost, but won the final session of the evening, with another big break of 63 to lead 8–6.

Thorne still led at the end of the second afternoon's play and went from 8–6 to 12–6 after winning the first four frames of the day. He compiled his third century of the final, and seventh of the tournament, in frame 17 when he had a 115 clearance. At the end of the session Thorne led 13–8 and needed three of the last ten frames for victory; Davis needed eight.

Davis won the first frame of the last session on the black and Thorne, still believing he had victory in his grasp, allowed Davis to win frame after frame. Suddenly it was 13–13. Thorne took the next with a 96 but Davis levelled it again and it was his experience that took him safely through the next two frames to retain his title.

1986

Round four Steve Davis beat Eddie Charlton 9–6; Dean Reynolds beat Silvino Francisco 9–8; Tony Drago beat John Virgo 9–6; Willie Thorne beat Robbie Grace 9–1; Alex Higgins beat Dave Martin 9–6; Mike Hallett beat Tony Meo 9–4; Eugene Hughes beat Ray Reardon 9–5; Wayne Jones beat Dennis Taylor 9–2; Cliff Thorburn beat David Taylor 9–4; John Spencer beat Kirk Stevens 9–4; Neal Foulds beat Jim Wych 9–3; Jimmy White beat Peter Francisco 9–5; Tony Knowles beat Tony Jones 9–2; Terry Griffiths beat Dene O'Kane 9–0; Steve Longworth beat Doug Mountjoy 9–1; John Parrott beat Joe Johnson 9–1

Round five Steve Davis beat Dean Reynolds 9–5; Tony Drago beat Willie Thorne 9–5; Alex Higgins beat Mike Hallett 9–7; Wayne Jones beat Eugene Hughes 9–5; Cliff Thorburn beat John Spencer 9–2; Neal Foulds beat Jimmy White 9–7; Tony Knowles beat Terry Griffiths 9–6; John Parrott beat Steve Longworth 9–6

Quarter-finals Steve Davis beat Tony Drago 9–8; Alex Higgins beat Wayne Jones 9–5; Neal Foulds beat Cliff Thorburn 9–2; John Parrott beat Tony Knowles 9–4

Semi-finals Steve Davis beat Alex Higgins 9–3; Neal Foulds beat John Parrott 9–3

Final Steve Davis beat Neal Foulds 16–7

This was Davis's first ranking final of the season; remarkably, it was his opponent's second. But for Neal Foulds it was not to be his second win of the season.

Foulds opened with confidence and took the first two frames with breaks of 63 and 53. But the experience of Davis kept his young predator at bay. Davis won the next four frames before allowing the youngster to take the last frame of the afternoon.

Davis won six of the seven evening frames after opening the session with a 104. Another century (110) in frame 17 took Davis to 12–5 and he then went to 14–7 at the end of the third session. With ten frames to play, Davis needed just two and he won them straight away in the evening with breaks of 124 and 66.

Davis's triumph was a personal landmark because it took his career winnings past the £1 million barrier.

1987

Round four Steve Davis beat Peter Francisco 9–6; Alex Higgins beat David Taylor 9–6; John Parrott beat Jim Wych 9–6; Tony Knowles beat Kirk Stevens 9–8; Dene O'Kane beat Dennis Taylor 9–7; Willie Thorne beat Tommy Murphy 9–4; John Campbell beat Martin Smith 9–8; Cliff Thorburn beat John Virgo 9–6; Danny Fowler beat Graham Miles 9–4; Mike Hallett beat Tony Meo 9–5; Tony Chappel beat Steve Longworth 9–6; Joe Johnson beat Barry West 9–6; Terry Griffiths beat Ray Edmonds 9–5; Silvino Francisco beat Cliff Wilson 9–1; David Roe beat Vic Harris 9–5; Jimmy White beat Eugene Hughes 9–4

Round five Steve Davis beat Alex Higgins 9–2; John Parrott beat Tony Knowles 9–4; Willie Thorne beat Dene O'Kane 9–7; Cliff Thorburn beat John Campbell 9–4; Mike Hallett beat Danny Fowler 9–4; Joe Johnson beat Tony Chappel 9–4; Terry Griffiths beat Silvino Francisco 9–3; Jimmy White beat David Roe 9–5

Quarter-finals Steve Davis beat John Parrott 9–5; Willie Thorne beat Cliff Thorburn 9–8; Joe Johnson beat Mike Hallett 9–7; Jimmy White beat Terry Griffiths 9–7

Semi-finals Steve Davis beat Willie Thorne 9–2; Jimmy White beat Joe Johnson 9–4

Final Steve Davis beat Jimmy White 16–14

Steve Davis-Jimmy White matches have produced some of the sport's outstanding matches over the years. The 1987 Tennents final was one of those occasions as both men played to the highest of standards. It was sad there had to be a loser.

The first two frames saw Davis open with a break of 106 which White countered in frame two with a 91. White went 2–1 up and then 3–1 with a brilliant 139 and the highest break of the televised stage of the competition. White won two of the last three frames of the session to lead 5–2. Davis pulled back to 4–5 before White took the next with a 90. Another Davis century (107) made it 5–6 and he levelled it at 6-all with a 98 break. Two half-century breaks by White in frame 13 restored his lead. But, at the end of an exhilarating day's play, Davis made it 7-all with a 75.

Vandals damaged the cloth during the night and a replacement kept the big breaks at bay for a while at the start of the next day's play. White won the first two frames, but Davis won the next four before White won the final frame of the session to trail 10–11

White went back into the lead by quickly taking the opening frames of the final evening. Davis levelled it at 12-all with his third century (100) in frame 24. Davis retook the lead in a black-ball game. White made it 13–13 and then Davis compiled his fourth century (110) to go back in front. White came from behind once more to draw level before Davis compiled his fifth century, a 108, to get in front again. This time White could not pull level after Davis had laid a good snooker and Davis ran out the 16–14 winner in one of the finest displays of all-round snooker. In all there were six century breaks and 34 breaks of 30 or more.

1988

Round four Steve Davis beat Gary Wilkinson 9–3; Danny Fowler beat Martin Clark 9–6; Dennis Taylor beat Joe O'Boye 9–4; John Parrott beat Nigel Gilbert 9–8; Cliff Thorburn beat Steve James 9–6; David Roe beat Peter Francisco 9–7; Willie Thorne beat Kirk Stevens 9–3; Stephen Hendry beat Colin Roscoe 9–3; Doug Mountjoy beat Neal Foulds 9–4; Joe Johnson beat Rex Williams 9–7; John Virgo beat Dene O'Kane 9–8; Tony Knowles beat Alex Higgins 9–6; Terry Griffiths beat Steve Duggan 9–2; Dean Reynolds beat Cliff Wilson 9–3; Barry West beat Silvino Francisco 9–4; Mark Bennett beat Jimmy White 9–6

Round five Steve Davis beat Danny Fowler 9–6; John Parrott beat Dennis Taylor 9–4; Cliff Thorburn beat David Roe 9–8; Stephen Hendry beat Willie Thorne 9–4; Doug Mountjoy beat Joe Johnson 9–5; John Virgo beat Tony Knowles 9–3; Terry Griffiths beat Dean Reynolds 9–6; Barry West beat Mark Bennett 9–4

Quarter-finals Steve Davis beat John Parrott 9–4; Stephen Hendry beat Cliff Thorburn 9–2; Doug Mountjoy beat John Virgo 9–8; Terry Griffiths beat Barry West 9–5

Semi-finals Stephen Hendry beat Steve Davis 9–3; Doug Mountjoy beat Terry Griffiths 9–4

Final Doug Mountjoy beat Stephen Hendry 16–12

For the first time since the UK Open became a ranking tournament in 1984 Steve Davis was not the champion. That honour belonged to Doug Mountjoy who won his first major title for ten years and at the same time thwarted a slide down the rankings.

Not only did the Welshman cause an upset by reaching the final, but his win over the much-fancied Scot Stephen Hendry was also one of the game's biggest surprises. But Mountjoy had to work for the title.

He led 5–2 at the first interval, but Hendry had displayed some awesome skill in compiling breaks of 103 and 113 in the two frames he won. Mountjoy made it 6–2 after a 98, but the next, a black-ball game, signalled the start of a Hendry revival which took him to 6-all. Mountjoy retook the lead but Hendry, with a 129 break, levelled it at 7-all at the end of day one.

After two scrappy opening frames which Mountjoy won, the Welshman then produced the finest snooker of his illustrious career to extend his winning sequence to seven frames and end the next session 14–7 in front. Frame-winning breaks of 81, 72, and 32 were followed by consecutive centuries and his 131 in frame 20 was to overtake Hendry's 129 as the highest break of the televised stage of the tournament.

The first frame of the final session saw Mountjoy emulate Steve Davis and score a century in three consecutive frames in a major final. His 124 took him to 15–7 and within one of the title. But he then allowed Hendry to win the next five frames and suddenly defeat looked a possibility for Mountjoy as his lead was cut to three frames at 15–12. But an error by Hendry allowed the Welshman to compile a break of 39 and that was enough to set up a great victory for a man back from the wilderness.

British Open

The British Open, originally called the Dulux British Open, replaced the Yamaha Organs Trophy, which had previously replaced the shortlived British Gold Cup. All three tournaments were played at Derby's Assembly Rooms.

ICI sponsored the event for the first time in 1985 and used their Dulux brand name. That same year it was granted ranking status. Anglian Windows sponsored the event for the first and only time in 1989.

Year	Tournament Name	Venue	First Prize £
1985	Dulux British Open	Assembly Rooms, Derby	50,000
1986	Dulux British Open	Assembly Rooms, Derby	55,000

Year	Tournament Name	Venue	First Prize £
1987	Dulux British Open	Assembly Rooms, Derby	60,000
1988	MIM Britannia British Open	Assembly Rooms, Derby	60,000
1989	Anglian British Open	Assembly Rooms, Derby	70,000

1985

Round three Tony Meo beat Tony Knowles 5–2; Steve Davis beat Malcolm Bradley 5–2; Dene O'Kane beat Dave Martin 5–4; Silvino Francisco beat Bob Chaperon 5–2; Dennis Taylor beat Steve Newbury 5–3; Eugene Hughes beat Murdo Macleod 5–2; Kirk Stevens beat Graham Miles 5–2; Alex Higgins beat Cliff Thorburn 5–2

Quarter-finals Kirk Stevens beat Dennis Taylor 5–2; Steve Davis beat Dene O'Kane 5–1; Silvino Francisco beat Tony Meo 5–4; Alex Higgins beat Eugene Hughes 5–2

Semi-finals Kirk Stevens beat Steve Davis 9–7; Silvino Francisco beat Alex Higgins 9–6

Final Silvino Francisco beat Kirk Stevens 12–9

The first Dulux final was notable on two counts. It was the first ranking final not to contain a British competitor, and it was the first final to offer a £50,000 first prize.

Kirk Stevens, by virtue of his semi-final win over Steve Davis, was favourite to take the title, but Francisco knocked in breaks in excess of 40 in each of the first five frames to take a 5–0 lead. He had a 41 break in frame six but Stevens's 60 was enough to get him on the scoreboard. He won the next to trail 2–5 at the end of the first session.

The opening frame of the evening session lasted over an hour which Francisco won after a fluked pink. Neither player was playing to his full capacity and the highlight of the evening session was in the final frame when Stevens compiled a break of 108. But he still trailed 5–9 at the end of the first day.

The Canadian took the opening three frames of the second day to pull within one frame of Francisco. But then luck helped the South African as a couple of flukes helped to take him to 11–8 and needing one frame for victory. Two frames later Silvino Francisco was the inaugural British Open Champion.

South African Silvino Francisco won his first major title in 1985 when he beat Kirk Stevens of Canada in the final of the Dulux British Open. The Dulux dog is sharing Francisco's moment of glory.

Mike Watterson – Snooker's Forgotten Man

Mike Watterson started the 1988–9 season ranked 107th in the world. He never made a great impact on the world of professional snooker—as a player that is. But the contribution he made to the game as a promoter in the mid-1970s should never be forgotten.

Born in Chesterfield, home of Joe and Fred Davis, Watterson started his working career as a tea boy for a building company. In his spare time he played golf and at the age of 17 was playing off a handicap of 2. Surprisingly, he didn't take up

Mike Watterson did so much for snooker but is now in the wilderness . . .

snooker until he was 27. But within ten years he was the British CIU champion, and had represented England in the Home International Championship. But it was as a promoter that he attracted the most attention.

In 1972 he promoted a match between Alex Higgins and Ray Reardon at nearby Staveley. That was his first venture into snooker promotions which eventually resulted in him taking the world championships to The Crucible Theatre.

The 1976 world championships were the first to be sponsored under the Embassy banner but the organization left a lot to be desired

and Embassy pulled out. Mike guaranteed the WPBSA £17,000 in prize money for the 1977 championship and his persuasive powers convinced Embassy's Peter Dyke that they should give it one more try. A couple of months before the commencement of the tournament Embassy came back into the sport.

Mike's first task was to find suitable premises. Thankfully his wife Carol had been to see a play at Sheffield's Crucible Theatre, and she recommended it as a possible world championship venue. The rest is history as Embassy and The Crucible have become synonymous with snooker.

After that success, Watterson created the United Kingdom Professional Championship, World Team Cup, British Open and Jameson International. He also promoted the inaugural Embassy World Professional Darts Championship at Nottingham in 1978 and he was responsible for the first UK Indoor Bowls Championship at Preston's Guildhall.

Watterson also played 'host' to many professionals, and the Canadian trio of Bill Werbeniuk, Kirk Stevens and Cliff Thorburn all lived with him when they first arrived in Britain to pursue their snooker careers.

The chance for Watterson to continue his activities of promoting professional snooker at the highest level went in 1983 when the WPBSA set up their own promotions company to look after such matters, and took a large proportion of Mike's staff to run the new company! Watterson was on the WPBSA board for another two years. He had, by then, turned his attentions to soccer and become chairman of Derby County and then chairman of his home-town team, Chesterfield, before resigning in the 1986–7 season.

Today, Watterson is involved with snooker as proprietor of seven snooker clubs and banqueting and leisure complexes in the Chesterfield, South Yorkshire and Nottinghamshire

Mike Watterson (second from right) stood behind Patsy Fagan the first winner of the Super Crystalate UK Championship, just one of Mike's 'brainchilds'.

areas. He still plays snooker but his interest in the game has waned in recent years and that has coincided with a slide down the rankings for the forgotten man of snooker.

1986

Round four Murdo Macleod beat Silvino Francisco 5–1; Terry Griffiths beat Neal Foulds 5–3; Willie Thorne beat Perrie Mans 5–1; Kirk Stevens beat Cliff Wilson 5–0; John Virgo beat John Rea 5–0; Eddie Charlton beat Paddy Browne 5–1; Tony Meo beat Steve Newbury 5–0; Cliff Thorburn beat Mark Wildman 5–1; Steve Davis beat Dave Martin 5–1; John Campbell beat Paul Medati 5–4; John Parrott beat Patsy Fagan 5–0; Jim Wych beat Tony Knowles 5–4; Peter Francisco beat Steve Longworth 5–2; Alex Higgins beat Mike Hallett 5–1; Bill Werbeniuk beat Joe Johnson 5–3; Rex Williams beat Roger Bales 5–4

Round five Terry Griffiths beat Murdo Macleod 5–2; Willie Thorne beat Kirk Stevens 5–4; John Virgo beat Eddie Charlton 5–4; Tony Meo beat Cliff Thorburn 5–3; Steve Davis beat John Campbell 5–0; Jim Wych beat John Parrott 5–4; Alex Higgins beat Peter Francisco 5–2; Bill Werbeniuk beat Rex Williams 5–3

Quarter-finals Willie Thorne beat Terry Griffiths 5–4; John Virgo beat Tony Meo 5–3; Steve Davis beat Jim Wych 5–2; Alex Higgins beat Bill Werbeniuk 5–1

Semi-finals Willie Thorne beat John Virgo 9–4; Steve Davis beat Alex Higgins 9–3

Final Steve Davis beat Willie Thorne 12–7

Willie Thorne opened by taking the first frame; something not many people have managed against Steve Davis in a major final. But Davis came back with six consecutive frames to end the first session 6–1 in front. Breaks of 77 and 127 then took Davis to 8–1 in the best-of-23 frame match. Thorne, however, won four of the five remaining frames of the session to trail 5–9 at the end of the first day.

Thorne reduced the deficit by one more frame by winning the opening frame of the final session on the black. Davis won the next frame before Thorne made it 7–10 after compiling his highest break of the match, 81. Davis then ran in breaks of 93 and 85 to secure a 12–7 victory and gain his 10th ranking tournament success.

1987

Round four John Virgo beat Steve Davis 5–4; Cliff Wilson beat Silvino Francisco 5–4; Neal Foulds beat Warren King 5–4; Willie Thorne beat Steve Duggan 5–2; Tony Knowles beat Dean Reynolds 5–0; Tommy Murphy beat Ray Reardon 5–4; Terry Griffiths beat Tony Jones 5–3; Dennis Taylor beat Eddie Charlton 5–1; Cliff Thorburn beat Graham Cripsey 5–2; Doug Mountjoy beat Peter Francisco 5–3; Kirk Stevens beat Barry West 5–4; David Taylor beat Jack McLaughlin 5–2; Jimmy White beat Mike Hallett 5–2; Rex Williams beat Steve James 5–2; John Spencer beat Dave Martin 5–2; Joe Johnson beat Eugene Hughes 5–3

Round five John Virgo beat Cliff Wilson 5–2; Neal Foulds beat Willie Thorne 5–2; Tony Knowles beat Tommy Murphy 5–3; Dennis Taylor beat Terry Griffiths 5–4; Cliff Thorburn beat Doug Mountjoy 5–4; David Taylor beat Kirk Stevens

5–2; Jimmy White beat Rex Williams 5–0; John Spencer beat Joe Johnson 5–3

Quarter-finals Neal Foulds beat John Virgo 5–3; Tony Knowles beat Dennis Taylor 5–4; Cliff Thorburn beat David Taylor 5–3; Jimmy White beat John Spencer 5–3

Semi-finals Neal Foulds beat Tony Knowles 9–2; Jimmy White beat Cliff Thorburn 9–5

Final Jimmy White beat Neal Foulds 13–9

This was White's second ranking final of the season. But for the fast-rising Foulds it was his third final. Both men were looking for the second triumph of the season. And it looked as though that honour would go to Foulds as he raced into a 4–0 lead in little over an hour. Breaks of 58, 105, 51 and 52 helped secure his lead.

However, White came back to win the last three frames of the session to trail 3–4. It was neck-and-neck in the evening session although Foulds briefly held a two-frame lead at 8–6 before White won the last frame of the evening session.

From 7–8 down, White went to 12–8 by winning the first five frames of the second day. Foulds stopped the sequence with a 58 break in the 21st frame but a 61 from White in the next frame assured him of his second ranking tournament of the season.

1988

Round four Jimmy White beat Steve James 5–1; Gary Wilkinson beat Silvino Francisco 5–3; Tony Jones beat Bob Chaperon 5–4; Stephen Hendry beat Terry Griffiths 5–1; John Spencer beat Dennis Taylor 5–0; Rex Williams beat Barry West 5–0; Willie Thorne beat Cliff Wilson 5–3; Cliff Thorburn beat Paul Medati 5–2; Neal Foulds beat Peter Francisco 5–3; John Parrott beat John Virgo 5–1; Dene O'Kane beat Paddy Browne 5–2; Joe Johnson beat Brian Rowswell 5–2; Murdo Macleod beat Tony Knowles 5–4; Mike Hallett beat Graham Cripsey 5–2; Joe O'Boye beat John Campbell 5–1; David Roe beat Ray Reardon 5–2

Round five Jimmy White beat Gary Wilkinson 5–1; Rex Williams beat John Spencer 5–4; John Parrott beat Neal Foulds 5–0; Dene O'Kane beat Joe Johnson 5–2; Cliff Thorburn beat Willie Thorne 5–2; Joe O'Boye beat David Roe 5–1; Stephen Hendry beat Tony Jones 5–3; Mike Hallett beat Murdo Macleod 5–2

Quarter-finals Stephen Hendry beat Jimmy White 5–4; Cliff Thorburn beat Rex Williams 5–2; John Parrott beat Dene O'Kane 5–2; Mike Hallett beat Joe O'Boye 5–4

Semi-finals Stephen Hendry beat Cliff Thorburn 9–5; Mike Hallett beat John Parrott 9–8

Final Stephen Hendry beat Mike Hallett 13–2

For Mike Hallett it was his second final of the season. But sadly, like the first, when he was given a 9–0 drubbing by Steve Davis, he was no match for Stephen Hendry at the Assembly

● ● ● ● ● ● ● ● ● ● ● ● ● ● ● ●

TONY MEO

Born: 4 October 1959, Hampstead, London

Tony Meo's standing as one of snooker's elite seemed to have disappeared in recent years and a slide down the rankings to number 31 in 1988 looked like being even greater the next season. But, suddenly, Meo returned from the wilderness to win his first ranking title, the 1989 Anglian British Open at Derby, when he beat Dean Reynolds in the final.

A professional since 1979, Tony was the second member of the Barry Hearn stable after Steve Davis. But his only successes had been either with Steve in the Hofmeister World Doubles or in the World Cup.

He was runner-up to Steve in the 1984 Lada Classic. He could well have been the champion had a member of the audience not shouted 'Come on Tony' just before a crucial shot.

Tony did have two moments of personal glory in winning the English professional championship in 1986 and 1987 when he beat Neal Foulds and Les Dodd respectively. But they were non-ranking events and could not prevent his slide down the rankings. That slide has now been arrested thanks to his great win in the British Open. And his first world championship semi-final appearance in 1989 saw him return to the top-16.

● ● ● ● ● ● ● ● ● ● ● ● ● ● ● ●

The downward slide of Tony Meo was stopped in 1989 when he beat Dean Reynolds to win the Anglian Windows British Open at Derby.

Rooms where the Scot ran out the convincing 13–2 victor to take his second title of the season.

Hallett got on to the scoreboard when trailing 3–0 but Hendry then went from 3–1 to 6–1. From there he went to 11–1 before Hallett took another frame. The first day ended at 12–2 and Hendry sealed the fate of his team-mate and world doubles partner by winning the first frame of the second day.

Hendry's highest breaks in the most one-sided ranking final were 78, 75 and 70, while the best Hallett could offer was a 40 in his first winning frame.

1989

Round four Stephen Hendry beat Dene O'Kane 5–2; Tony Meo beat Colin Roscoe 5–3; Peter Francisco beat David Roe 5–3; Barry West beat Tony Knowles 5–0; Cliff Thorburn beat Darren Morgan 5–4; Mike Hallett beat Roger Bales 5–0; Martin Clark beat John Virgo 5–1; Neal Foulds beat Alain Robidoux 5–1; Dean Reynolds beat Jimmy White w.o.; Cliff Wilson beat Tony Chappel 5–3; Joe Johnson beat Tony Drago 5–3; Mark Johnston-Allen beat Eugene Hughes 5–2; John Parrott beat Steve Longworth 5–1; Doug Mountjoy beat Murdo Macleod 5–0; Willie Thorne beat Robert Marshall 5–1; Steve Davis beat Alex Higgins 5–0

Round five Tony Meo beat Stephen Hendry 5–3; Peter Francisco beat Barry West 5–1; Mike Hallett beat Cliff Thorburn 5–4; Martin Clark beat Neal Foulds 5–4; Dean Reynolds beat Cliff Wilson 5–0; Joe Johnson beat Mark Johnston-Allen 5–2; John Parrott beat Doug Mountjoy 5–2; Steve Davis beat Willie Thorne 5–0

Quarter-finals Tony Meo beat Peter Francisco 5–3; Mike Hallett beat Martin Clark 5–3; Dean Reynolds beat Joe Johnson 5–4; John Parrott beat Steve Davis 5–1

Semi-finals Tony Meo beat Mike Hallett 9–8; Dean Reynolds beat John Parrott 9–8

Final Tony Meo beat Dean Reynolds 13–6

Tony Meo returned from two years in the wilderness to capture his first major title since the 1987 English professional title. But in capturing the Anglian British Open he won his first ever ranking tournament after nearly ten years as a professional.

After enjoying a great win over Stephen Hendry, Meo came back from a near-impossible position to beat Mike Hallett in the semi-final.

The final was a more one-sided affair which saw Meo play controlled snooker as he kept the challenge from Dean Reynolds in check. The first ranking final between two left-handed players, it was not a game of high breaks; Meo's 84 being the highest.

Meo had his nose in front right from the start and led 5–2 at the end of the first session. He also won the second session by the same score to lead 10–4 overnight. Reynolds took the first two frames of the second day to reduce the gap to four frames. But then Meo won the next three to take him to his first ranking tournament success.

BCE Canadian Masters

The Canadian Masters was inaugurated in 1985 but did not become a ranking event until 1988–9 when it was the first ranking tournament to be staged outside Britain, and indeed the only one outside Europe.

Year	Tournament Name	Venue	First Prize £
1988	BCE Canadian Masters	Minkler Auditorium, Toronto	40,000

It looks more like a WANTED poster. But in Jimmy's case it should read: WANTED, ONE WORLD TITLE. His talent certainly deserves to have seen the world championship trophy on his sideboard.

1988

Round four Steve Davis beat George Scott 5–1; Steve James beat Joe Johnson 5–4;.Doug Mountjoy beat Willie Thorne 5–4; Terry Griffiths beat Ray Reardon 5–2; Cliff Thorburn beat John Spencer 5–2; Ian Graham beat Eddie Charlton 5–2; Cliff Wilson beat Dean Reynolds 5–4; Stephen Hendry beat Danny Fowler 5–2; Warren King beat Steve Duggan 5–4; Mike Hallett beat Marcel Gauvreau 5–3; John Virgo beat Steve Newbury 5–2; John Parrott beat Darren Morgan 5–3; David Taylor beat Colin Roscoe 5–1; Dennis Taylor beat Martin Clark 5–4; Steve Longworth beat Murdo Macleod 5–3; Jimmy White beat Mark Bennett 5–3

Round five Steve Davis beat Steve James 5–0; Terry Griffiths beat Doug Mountjoy 5–4; Cliff Thorburn beat Ian Graham 5–4; Stephen Hendry beat Cliff Wilson 5–1; Mike Hallett beat Warren King 5–2; John Parrott beat John Virgo 5–4; Dennis Taylor beat David Taylor 5–2; Jimmy White beat Steve Longworth 5–0

Quarter-finals Steve Davis beat Terry Griffiths 5–3; Stephen Hendry beat Cliff Thorburn 5–4; Mike Hallett beat John Parrott 5–3; Jimmy White beat Dennis Taylor 5–3

● ● ● ● ● ● ● ● ● ● ● ● ● ● ● ●

JIMMY WHITE

Born: 2 May 1962, Tooting, London

In terms of ranking tournament successes Jimmy White is second only to Steve Davis.

The youngest winner of the English amateur title in 1979 he then became the youngest world amateur champion a year later. He turned professional in 1980 and when he beat Cliff Thorburn to win the Langs Scottish Masters in 1981 he was the then youngest winner of a professional tournament.

Since then, left-hander White has become one of the biggest box-office draws in snooker.

He has been in the top-16 since 1982 and was the biggest threat to Steve Davis in the mid-1980s. Winner of four ranking titles, the first was the 1986 Mercantile Credit Classic when he beat Cliff Thorburn 13–12 in a great final. He won two titles in the 1986–7 season when he beat Rex Williams to capture the Rothmans Grand Prix and Neal Foulds to win the Dulux British Open.

Since that last success he lost to Steve Davis in the final of the 1987 Tennents and 1988 Fidelity, but in the BCE Canadian Masters, two tournaments later, he became the first person to beat Davis in a ranking final (other than the world championship) when he beat him 9–4.

In addition to the above tournaments, White has won the Benson and Hedges Masters, Benson and Hedges Irish Masters, Carlsberg Challenge and Northern Ireland Classic, amongst others.

● ● ● ● ● ● ● ● ● ● ● ● ● ● ●

Semi-finals Steve Davis beat Stephen Hendry 9–5; Jimmy White beat Mike Hallett 9–2

Final Jimmy White beat Steve Davis 9–4

Apart from defeats by Dennis Taylor and Joe Johnson in the world championships in 1985 and 1986, this was Steve Davis's first defeat in a ranking final. It was also Davis's first defeat in a ranking tournament since he lost to Ray Reardon in the MIM Britannia Open earlier in the year.

It was not a classic final considering the two finalists were ranked number one and two in the world. White opened with a break of 75. He went two up before Davis won the next two; a break of 97 in the fourth being the highlight.

Davis was not playing to his best and made uncharacteristic errors and the first session ended with White leading 5–2.

Two frames each at the start of the next session saw White still leading by three at 7–4 but he then won the match by taking the next two frames to win 9–4. White was well below par; fortunately for him, so was Davis.

ICI European Open

The second ranking tournament after the BCE Canadian Masters to be played outside Britain, the European Open was staged at the Deauville Casino in France. It was, however, poorly attended. The event was unsponsored until ICI stepped in during the competition and from the quarter-final stage it was known as the ICI European Open. John Parrott, after several years of near-misses, eventually won his first ranking tournament.

Year	Tournament Name	Venue	First Prize £
1989	ICI European Open	Deauville, France	40,000

1989

Round four Eddie Charlton beat Jim Chambers 5–2; John Virgo beat Craig Edwards 5–3; John Campbell beat Mark Bennett 5–3; John Parrott beat Gary Wilkinson 5–2; Danny Fowler beat Tony Wilson 5–2; Jim Wych beat Mark Johnston-Allen 5–4; Mike Hallett beat Paddy Browne 5–4; Stephen Hendry beat Steve Longworth 5–0; Martin Clark beat Eugene Hughes 5–1; Joe Johnson beat David Roe 5–2; Alain Robidoux beat Cliff Wilson 5–0; Terry Griffiths beat Tony Chappel 5–2; Cliff Thorburn beat Murdo Macleod 5–1; Doug Mountjoy beat Dennis Taylor 5–3; Willie Thorne beat Alex Higgins 5–1; Jimmy White beat Rex Williams 5–2

Round five Eddie Charlton beat John Virgo 5–4; John Parrott beat John Campbell 5–0; Jim Wych beat Danny Fowler 5–4; Mike Hallett beat Stephen Hendry 5–3; Martin Clark beat Joe Johnson 5–4; Terry Griffiths beat Alain Robidoux 5–3; Cliff Thorburn beat Doug Mountjoy 5–0; Jimmy White beat Willie Thorne 5–3

Alex Higgins during the Tennents UK Open, formerly the Coral UK Open.

Quarter-finals John Parrott beat Eddie Charlton 5–1; Mike Hallett beat Jim Wych 5–3; Terry Griffiths beat Martin Clark 5–1; Jimmy White beat Cliff Thorburn 5–3

Semi-finals John Parrott beat Mike Hallett 5–4; Terry Griffiths beat Jimmy White 5–4

Final John Parrott beat Terry Griffiths 9–8

After so many near-misses, Liverpudlian John Parrott eventually lifted his first ranking tournament when he beat Terry Griffiths 9–8 in a close final.

Griffiths, appearing in his first ranking final other than the 1979 and 1988 world champion-ships, took a 3–0 lead and at 4–1 should have extended his lead but made an error in his safety play. That allowed Parrott to get in, and breaks of 58, 42 and 62 enabled him to level at 4-all.

The evening session saw the advantage fluctuate between the two players. From 5–5 Parrott won the next two to lead 7–5. Griffiths won the next three, including a black-ball win in frame 15 to lead at 8–7. He was just one frame away from his first ranking title. But Parrott made a great 106 in levelling at 8-all and in the final frame the Liverpudlian won a great tactical battle to win his first ranking event.

Records

1982–9 Ranking Finals in Chronological Order (including Embassy World Professional Championship)

Figures in square brackets [] indicate that season's ranking position.

1982–3
Jameson International
    Tony Knowles [15]   9–6   David Taylor [8]
Professional Players' Tournament
    Ray Reardon [1]   10–5   Jimmy White [10]
Embassy World Championship
    Steve Davis [4]   18–6   Cliff Thorburn [3]

1983–4
Jameson International
    Steve Davis [1]   9–4   Cliff Thorburn [3]
Professional Players' Tournament
    Tony Knowles [4]   9–8   Joe Johnson [23]
Lada Classic
    Steve Davis [1]   9–8   Tony Meo [15]
Embassy World Championship
    Steve Davis [1]   18–16   Jimmy White [11]

1984–5
Jameson International
    Steve Davis [1]   9–2   Tony Knowles [2]
Rothmans Grand Prix
    Dennis Taylor [11]   10–2   Cliff Thorburn [3]
Coral UK Open
    Steve Davis [1]   16–8   Alex Higgins [9]
Mercantile Credit Classic
    Willie Thorne [12]   13–8   Cliff Thorburn [3]
Dulux British Open
    Silvino Francisco [17]   12–9   Kirk Stevens [4]
Embassy World Championship
    Dennis Taylor [11]   18–17   Steve Davis [1]

1985–6
Goya Matchroom Trophy
    Cliff Thorburn [2]   12–10   Jimmy White [7]
Rothmans Grand Prix
    Steve Davis [1]   10–9   Dennis Taylor [4]
Coral UK Open
    Steve Davis [1]   16–14   Willie Thorne [11]
Mercantile Credit Classic
    Jimmy White [7]   13–12   Cliff Thorburn [2]
Dulux British Open
    Steve Davis [1]   12–7   Willie Thorne [11]
Embassy World Championship
    Joe Johnson [16]   18–12   Steve Davis [1]

1986–7
BCE International
    Neal Foulds [13]   12–9   Cliff Thorburn [2]
Rothmans Grand Prix
    Jimmy White [5]   10–6   Rex Williams [16]
Tennents UK Open
    Steve Davis [1]   16–7   Neal Foulds [13]
Mercantile Credit Classic
    Steve Davis [1]   13–12   Jimmy White [5]
Dulux British Open
    Jimmy White [5]   13–9   Neal Foulds [13]
Embassy World Championship
    Steve Davis [1]   18–14   Joe Johnson [8]

1987–8
Fidelity Unit Trusts International
    Steve Davis [1]   12–5   Cliff Thorburn [4]
Rothmans Grand Prix
    Stephen Hendry [23]   10–7   Dennis Taylor [8]
Tennents UK Open
    Steve Davis [1]   16–14   Jimmy White [2]
Mercantile Credit Classic
    Steve Davis [1]   13–11   John Parrott [13]
MIM Britannia British Open
    Stephen Hendry [23]   13–2   Mike Hallett [16]
Embassy World Championship
    Steve Davis [1]   18–11   Terry Griffiths [6]

1988-9

Fidelity Unit Trusts International
    Steve Davis [1]   12–6   Jimmy White [2]
Rothmans Grand Prix
    Steve Davis [1]   10–6   Alex Higgins [17]
BCE Canadian Masters
    Jimmy White [2]   9–4   Steve Davis [1]
Tennents UK Open
    Doug Mountjoy [24]   16–12   Stephen Hendry [4]
Mercantile Credit Classic
    Doug Mountjoy [24]   13–11   Wayne Jones [34]
ICI European Open
    John Parrott [7]   9–8   Terry Griffiths [5]
Anglian British Open
    Tony Meo [31]   13–6   Dean Reynolds [22]
Embassy World Championship
    Steve Davis [1]   18–3   John Parrott [7]

Lowest ranked winners

Position	Winner	Tournament
31	Tony Meo	1989 Anglian British Open
24	Doug Mountjoy	1988 Tennents UK Open
		1989 Mercantile Credit Classic
23	Stephen Hendry	1987 Rothmans Grand Prix
		1988 MIM Britannia British Open
17	Silvino Francisco	1985 Dulux British Open

Lowest ranked finalists

34	Wayne Jones	1989 Mercantile Credit Classic
31	Tony Meo*	1989 Anglian British Open
24	Doug Mountjoy*	1988 Tennents UK Open
		1989 Mercantile Credit Classic
23	Joe Johnson	1983 Professional Players' Tournament
23	Stephen Hendry*	1987 Rothmans Grand Prix
		1988 MIM Britannia British Open
22	Dean Reynolds	1989 Anglian British Open
17	Alex Higgins	1988 Rothmans Grand Prix

* winner

Finals involving nos 1 and 2 ranked players

1984 Jameson International
    Steve Davis [1] beat Tony Knowles [2]
1987 Tennents UK Open
    Steve Davis [1] beat Jimmy White [2]
1988 Fidelity Unit Trusts International
    Steve Davis [1] beat Jimmy White [2]
1988 BCE Canadian Masters
    Jimmy White [2] beat Steve Davis [1]

Finals involving lowly-ranked players
(Aggregate ranking 20 or higher)
1989 Mercantile Credit Classic
    Doug Mountjoy [24] beat Wayne Jones [34]
1989 Anglian British Open
    Tony Meo [31] beat Dean Reynolds [22]
1988 MIM Britannia British Open
    Stephen Hendry [23] beat Mike Hallett [16]
1987 Rothmans Grand Prix
    Stephen Hendry [23] beat Dennis Taylor [8]
1988 Tennents UK Open
    Doug Mountjoy [24] beat Stephen Hendry [4]
1983 Professional Players' Tournament
    Tony Knowles [4] beat Joe Johnson [23]
1982 Jameson International
    Tony Knowles [15] beat David Taylor [8]

1985 Dulux British Open
    Silvino Francisco [17] beat Kirk Stevens [4]
1986 Rothmans Grand Prix
    Jimmy White [5] beat Rex Williams [16]

The following records are for all ranking tournaments, but excluding the Embassy World Championship. Those records can be found on pp. 43–56.

Wins

14	Steve Davis
4	Jimmy White
2	Stephen Hendry, Tony Knowles, Doug Mountjoy
1	Neal Foulds, Silvino Francisco, Tony Meo, John Parrott, Ray Reardon, Dennis Taylor, Cliff Thorburn, Willie Thorne

Finals

15	Steve Davis
9	Jimmy White
7	Cliff Thorburn
3	Neal Foulds, Stephen Hendry, Tony Knowles, Dennis Taylor, Willie Thorne
2	Alex Higgins, Tony Meo, Doug Mountjoy, John Parrott
1	Silvino Francisco, Terry Griffiths, Mike Hallett, Joe Johnson, Wayne Jones, Ray Reardon, Dean Reynolds, Kirk Stevens, David Taylor, Rex Williams

Semi-finals

19	Steve Davis
12	Cliff Thorburn
11	Jimmy White
7	John Parrott
6	Neal Foulds, Stephen Hendry, Tony Knowles, Dennis Taylor, Willie Thorne
5	Mike Hallett, Alex Higgins
3	Silvino Francisco, Terry Griffiths, Joe Johnson, Tony Meo, Doug Mountjoy, Dean Reynolds, Kirk Stevens, John Virgo
2	Eddie Charlton, Peter Francisco, Eugene Hughes, Rex Williams
1	Steve James, Wayne Jones, Steve Newbury, Ray Reardon, Alain Robidoux, David Taylor, Mark Wildman

Breaks

The highest break in every ranking tournament has been (* indicates set in final):

Fidelity Unit Trusts International
(formerly Jameson International, Goya Matchroom Trophy, BCE International)

1982	Tony Knowles	114*
1983	Kirk Stevens	120
1984	Neal Foulds	140
1985	Dennis Taylor	134
1986	Cliff Thorburn	134
1987	Steve Davis	140*
1988	Dean Reynolds	136

(contd over)

Rothmans Grand Prix
(formerly Professional Players' Tournament)

1982	Willie Thorne	135
1983	Joe Johnson	135*
1984	Steve Davis	130
1985	John Virgo	130
1986	Jimmy White	138
1987	John Parrott	130
1988	Dean Reynolds	139

Mercantile Credit Classic
(formerly Lada Classic)

1984	Rex Williams	143

1985	Terry Griffiths	137
1986	Jimmy White	135
1987	Cliff Thorburn	140
1988	Dennis Taylor	132
1989	Nigel Gilbert	143

Tennents UK Open
(formerly Coral UK Open)

1984	Jack McLaughlin	135
1985	Willie Thorne	140
1986	Jimmy White	144
1987	Willie Thorne	147
1988	David Roe	139

Anglian British Open
(formerly Dulux British Open, MIM Britannia British Open)

1985	Alex Higgins	142
1986	Dave Martin	145
1987	Neal Foulds	140
1988	Stephen Hendry	118
1989	Mark Johnston-Allen	140

BCE Canadian Masters

1988	Dennis Taylor	132

ICI European Open

1989	Alain Robidoux	147

Whitewashes

Because most qualifying tournaments are over the best-of-nine frames, the 'whitewash' is not an uncommon result. However, there have been only three instances of a 'whitewash' in the quarter-final stage of a ranking tournament as follows:

1983 Jameson International
     Eddie Charlton beat Willie Thorne 5–0
1984 Rothmans Grand Prix
     Steve Davis beat Dean Reynolds 5–0
1987 Mercantile Credit Classic
     Stephen Hendry beat Silvino Francisco 5–0

Winning margins

When Stephen Hendry beat Mike Hallett 13–2 in the final of the 1988 MIM Britannia British Open it was the **biggest winning margin** in any match in a ranking tournament. It is also the only winning margin by 10 frames or more. There have been 15 instances of 9–0 scorelines in the Tennents UK Open (formerly Coral UK Open) which is played over the best-of-17 frames. The only time this scoreline has been achieved as late as the 4th round (last 32) was in 1986 when Terry Griffiths beat Dene O'Kane.

Finalists

The first final without a British player was the 1985 Dulux British Open between Silvino Francisco (SAf) and Kirk Stevens (Can).

The following finals have not figured an English player

1984 Rothmans Grand Prix
     Dennis Taylor (Ire) v. Cliff Thorburn (Can)
1985 Dulux British Open
     Silvino Francisco (SAf) v. Kirk Stevens (Can)
1987 Rothmans Grand Prix
     Stephen Hendry (Sco) v. Dennis Taylor (Ire)
1988 Tennents UK Open
     Doug Mountjoy (Wal) v. Stephen Hendry (Sco)
1989 Mercantile Credit Classic
     Doug Mountjoy (Wal) v. Wayne Jones (Wal)

The only all-Welsh final was the Mountjoy-Jones meeting in the 1989 Mercantile Credit Classic as above.

The only final involving two left-handed players was the 1989 Anglian British Open between Tony Meo (Eng) and Dean Reynolds (Eng). (Jimmy White is the only other left-hander to have appeared in a ranking final.)

Oldest winners

50 yr 0 mth	Ray Reardon	1982 Professional Players' Tournament
46 yr 7 mth	Doug Mountjoy	1989 Mercantile Credit Classic
46 yr 5 mth	Doug Mountjoy	1988 Tennents UK Open
38 yr 9 mth	Silvino Francisco	1985 Dulux British Open
37 yr 8 mth	Cliff Thorburn	1985 Goya Matchroom Trophy
35 yr 9 mth	Dennis Taylor	1984 Rothmans Grand Prix

Oldest finalists

53 yr 3 mth	Rex Williams	1986 Rothmans Grand Prix
50 yr 0 mth	Ray Reardon	1982 Professional Players' Tournament
46 yr 7 mth	Doug Mountjoy	1989 Mercantile Credit Classic
46 yr 5 mth	Doug Mountjoy	1988 Tennents UK Open
41 yr 4 mth	Terry Griffiths	1989 ICI European Open
39 yr 8 mth	Cliff Thorburn	1987 Fidelity Unit Trusts International
39 yr 7 mth	Alex Higgins	1988 Rothmans Grand Prix
39 yr 2 mth	David Taylor	1982 Jameson International

Youngest tournament winners

18 yr 9 mth	Stephen Hendry	1987 Rothmans Grand Prix
19 yr 1 mth	Stephen Hendry	1988 MIM Britannia British Open
23 yr 2 mth	Neal Foulds	1986 BCE International
23 yr 8 mth	Jimmy White	1986 Mercantile Credit Classic
24 yr 5 mth	Jimmy White	1986 Rothmans Grand Prix
24 yr 9 mth	Jimmy White	1987 Dulux British Open
24 yr 9 mth	John Parrott	1989 ICI European Open

Youngest finalists

18 yr 9 mth	Stephen Hendry	1987 Rothmans Grand Prix
19 yr 1 mth	Stephen Hendry	1988 MIM Britannia British Open
19 yr 10 mth	Stephen Hendry	1988 Tennents UK Open
20 yr 5 mth	Jimmy White	1982 Professional Players' Tournament

Ranking points

The following players have **gained points in all ranking tournaments in one season** (including Embassy World Championship) since the number of ranking events was increased to six:

Steve Davis	1984–5; 1985–6; 1986–7
Tony Knowles	1985–6; 1987–8
Cliff Thorburn	1985–6; 1987–8
Terry Griffiths	1986–7; 1987–8
John Virgo	1986–7; 1987–8
John Campbell	1985–6
Neal Foulds	1985–6
Alex Higgins	1985–6
Joe Johnson	1985–6
Dave Martin	1985–6
Silvino Francisco	1986–7
John Parrott	1987–8
Dennis Taylor	1987–8
Willie Thorne	1987–8
Jimmy White	1987–8
Cliff Wilson	1987–8
Doug Mountjoy	1988–9
Stephen Hendry	1988–9

One of snooker's nicest characters, Dennis Taylor.

The Welsh Invasion

The Welsh are a proud nation, but when it comes to playing sport there is no nation with bigger hearts. And snooker has had its fair share of big-hearted Welshmen over the years.

It is not only in the professional game that they have shown their Red Dragon tenacity, but also in the amateur game. Doug Mountjoy was the first Welsh winner of the world amateur title in 1976 and he started a run that was to see three other compatriots win the title in the ten years between 1978 and 1988.

Cliff Wilson beat Joe Johnson 11–5 to win the title in Malta in 1978 and in Calgary, Canada, four years later, Terry Parson, one of the finest Welshmen never to turn professional, lifted the crown. He nearly retained it in Dublin two years later, losing to the Indian O. B. Agrawal. Dilwyn John was the beaten finalist in 1985, Kerry Jones lost in the 1986 final, but it was another Welsh winner in 1987 when current professional Darren Morgan beat Joe Grech of Malta in the final.

Cliff Wilson and Doug Mountjoy have, of course, made their mark on the professional game, and Darren Morgan is on the verge of making his breakthrough having joined the professional ranks in 1988. But the two most outstanding Welsh professionals have been Ray Reardon and Terry Griffiths.

Reardon won the world championship six times between 1970 and 1978, including a modern-day record four in succession between 1973–6. A great ambassador for the sport he still remains popular even though the glory days are behind him. As for Griffiths, he has only once won the world title, in 1979, but confirmed his standing as one of the game's most consistent players in 1988 when he reached his second world final, before losing to Steve Davis. Griffiths has been ranked in the top-ten in the world every year since 1983.

But the Welsh domination doesn't end there, Steve Newbury has shown in recent years that he is capable of pushing the best players. And in reaching the semi-final of the 1988 Mercantile Credit Classic he beat Eugene Hughes, Cliff Thorburn, Marlin Clark and Terry Griffiths before losing to Steve Davis. But the next in the long line of Welshmen to make an impact did so in the same event a year later when Wayne Jones beat Jimmy White, John Parrott and then Willie Thorne before setting up the first all-Welsh final before losing to the revitalized Doug Mountjoy.

With Tony Chappel, Mark Bennett and Colin Roscoe making up the complement of Welsh tournament-playing professionals there is certainly plenty of up-and-coming talent ready to cause a few surprises in the snooker world.

Right: *Another fine player from Wales, the underrated Steve Newbury.*

Right, below: *One of the game's great characters, Cliff Wilson.*

Below: *Doug Mountjoy (with trophy) and former Abertysswg team-mate Wayne Jones after the two had contested the 1989 Mercantile Credit final.*

CHAPTER FOUR

Non-Ranking Tournaments Past and Present

In the early days of professional snooker there were very few tournaments other than the world championship which, as we have already seen, was a season-long affair. The three major tournaments in the pre-boom days were the *Daily Mail* Gold Cup, *News of the World* Tournament and Professional Match-Play Championship, and they were often week-long matches.

These tournaments can be found on the following pages, together with the other leading tournaments that have subsequently appeared and, in many cases, disappeared, since the success of *Pot Black* in 1969. All tournaments are listed in chronological order according to when they first appeared.

Daily Mail Gold Cup

Having spent two seasons sponsoring a billiards tournament the *Daily Mail* switched its allegiance to snooker in the 1936–37 season. This gave a tremendous boost to the sport and many regarded the 15-week tournaments as more prestigious than the world championship.

Players were handicapped, with Joe Davis playing off scratch and having to concede as many as 45 points per frame. The players travelled Britain and played in a round-robin series of matches. A major feature of the event was a sealed handicap indicating how many frame advantage the 'inferior' player should receive. This envelope was not opened until *after* the match.

The tournament did not offer any cash prize but the winner received the magnificent gold cup and a range of household goods which were offered as prizes.

It was during the inaugural Gold Cup that Sidney Smith compiled the first ever official total clearance in making his record break of 133.

Year	Winner	Runner-up
1936-7	Joe Davis	Horace Lindrum
1937-8	Joe Davis	Willie Smith
1938-9	Alec Brown	Sidney Smith
1939-40	Alec Brown	Sydney Lee

Highest break
138 Joe Davis (1937–8)

Sunday Empire News Tournament

A season-long event, the *Empire News* tournament was held just once, in 1948–9. Eight professionals took part and were given an open handicap before each frame. However, in addition there was a sealed handicap which was opened at the end of each match. The final game between Joe and Fred Davis was effectively the final of the tournament. Whoever won claimed the title.

Fred beat Joe 36–35 and for the first time had beaten his famous brother on level terms in tournament play. However, when the sealed handicaps were opened Joe, astonishingly, received a two-frame advantage and thus won 37–36.

Final standings
1st	Joe Davis	8 pts
2nd	John Pulman	6 pts
3rd	Fred Davis	4 pts
4th	Walter Donaldson	2 pts
5th	Sidney Smith	0 pts

Highest break
138 Fred Davis

News of the World Tournament

One of the leading post-war tournaments the *News of the World* was, like other events of the day, a handicapped competition and the top seed, Joe Davis, had to concede anything from 7 to 20 points per frame.

Played at the Leicester Square Hall, London,

Alec Brown (right) one of the leading professionals of the early post-war days.

Leicester Square Hall, scene of many of the early post-war tournaments.

the competition was organized on a round-robin basis. In his match with Albert Brown in 1954–5 Joe Davis equalled the world record with a break of 146. Big breaks were a major feature of the tournaments and the following breaks were recorded: 143 Joe Davis (1951); 141 Walter Donaldson (1958); 140 Albert Brown (1952); 135 Fred Davis (1954); 132 Joe Davis (1953).

It was during the last playing of the *News of the World* tournament in 1959 that Joe Davis introduced the game of Snooker Plus.

Year	Winner	Runner-up
1949–50	Joe Davis	Sidney Smith
1950–1	Alec Brown	John Pulman
1951–2	Sidney Smith	Albert Brown
1952–3	Joe Davis	Jackie Rea
1953–4	John Pulman	Joe Davis
1954–5	Jackie Rea	Joe Davis
1955–6	Joe Davis	Fred Davis
1956–7	John Pulman	Fred Davis
1957–8	Fred Davis	John Pulman
1958–9	Fred Davis	Joe Davis

Highest break
146 Joe Davis (1954–5)

Joe Davis (right), the first winner of the *News of the World* tournament, and brother Fred, the last winner of the title in 1959.

Professional Match-Play Championship

Following the dispute between the B A & C C and the professional players in 1952 the latter formed their own governing body and organized their own 'world championship' known as the Professional Match-Play Championship. Because only two leading players, Horace Lindrum and Clark McConachy, contested the official world championship in 1952, many regard that year's Match-Play Championship, and those until its demise in 1957, as the world championship. The standard of the fields was certainly of world championship quality even if the competition's title did not carry that billing.

Year	Winner	Runner-up	Score
1952	Fred Davis	Walter Donaldson	38–35
1953	Fred Davis	Walter Donaldson	37–34
1954	Fred Davis	Walter Donaldson	39–21
1955	Fred Davis	John Pulman	37–34
1956	Fred Davis	John Pulman	38–35
1957	John Pulman	Jackie Rea	39–34

Highest break
141 Rex Williams (1956)

Pot Black

This was the tournament that 'started it all'. Following the success of *Pot Black*'s single-frame format, snooker received a tremendous boost. The contribution of *Pot Black* to snooker can be found on p. 64 as a separate feature.

The first tournament consisted of eight professionals who played in a straight knockout. The number of entrants was later increased to 16. After the inaugural competition the event was organized on a round-robin basis with the top players from each group meeting in either a final or semi-final, depending upon the number of competitors. It reverted to a knockout event in 1984.

Following the programme's success, a *Junior Pot Black* event (under-19 years) was organized in 1981 and ran for three years. The senior event was last held in 1986, and when Jimmy White potted the very last black it completed a break of 106, only the third century in the tournament's long history.

Year	Winner	Runner-up	Score
1969	Ray Reardon	John Spencer	88–29*
1970	John Spencer	Ray Reardon	88–27*
1971	John Spencer	Fred Davis	61–40*
1972	Eddie Charlton	Ray Reardon	75–43*
1973	Eddie Charlton	Rex Williams	93–33*

Eddie Charlton, three times a winner of *Pot Black*.

The talented Humbersider Dean Reynolds is one of a few top class left-handed players in snooker.

Year	Winner	Runner-up	Score
1974	Graham Miles	John Spencer	147–86**
1975	Graham Miles	Dennis Taylor	81–27*
1976	John Spencer	Dennis Taylor	69–42*
1977	Perrie Mans	Doug Mountjoy	90–21*
1978	Doug Mountjoy	Graham Miles	2–1†
1979	Ray Reardon	Doug Mountjoy	2–1†
1980	Eddie Charlton	Ray Reardon	2–1†
1981	Cliff Thorburn	Jim Wych	2–0†
1982	Steve Davis	Eddie Charlton	2–0†
1983	Steve Davis	Ray Reardon	2–0†
1984	Terry Griffiths	John Spencer	2–1†
1985	Doug Mountjoy	Jimmy White	2–0†
1986	Jimmy White	Kirk Stevens	2–0†

* Single frame score
** Aggregate score over two frames
† Best of three frames

Most wins
3 Eddie Charlton, John Spencer
2 Steve Davis, Graham Miles, Doug Mountjoy, Ray Reardon

Highest break
110 Eddie Charlton (1973)

Junior *Pot Black*

1981   Dean Reynolds beat Dene O'Kane
1982   John Parrott beat John Keers
1983   John Parrott beat Steve Ventham

Highest break
97 John Parrott (1981)

DEAN REYNOLDS

Born: 11 January 1963, Grimsby, Humberside

It is not only good Rugby League and baseball teams that come from Humberside, but it is also home to several good snooker players, and Dean Reynolds is one of them.

A former under-19 champion and the first winner of the Junior *Pot Black* title in 1981, he turned professional that same year. He reached The Crucible stage of the world championship in his first professional season, and at 19 was one of The Crucible's youngest-ever competitors.

A talented left-hander he made his way into the top-16 in 1987 after reaching the semi-final of the Mercantile Credit Classic. Hopes of reaching his first professional final were thwarted by Jimmy White who won 9–8.

The following year Reynolds did reach his first major final when he went on to beat Neal Foulds 9–5 and capture the English professional title.

After a mixed season in 1988–9, which saw him reach the semi-final of the Fidelity, Dean then went all the way to the final of the Anglian Open, the last ranking event before the world championship. But it was defeat at the hands of the rejuvenated Tony Meo.

Park Drive 2000

A four-man invitation event. The four players travelled the country and played each other three times in a round-robin tournament. The top two then played each other for the first prize of £750. The event lasted only two years before Gallahers, using their Park Drive brand name, sponsored the world championship. There were two Park Drive 2000's each year: one at the beginning of the year and one in the autumn.

Year		Winner	Runner-up	Score
1971	(1)	John Spencer	Rex Williams	4-1
	(2)	Ray Reardon	John Spencer	4-3
1972	(1)	John Spencer	Alex Higgins	4-3
	(2)	John Spencer	Alex Higgins	5-3

Highest break
146 Ray Reardon (1972 (2))

Norwich Union Open

An invitation event open to professionals and amateurs. The first event was held at London's Piccadilly Hotel and consisted of a field of 24. This was reduced to 16 in the second year. It was the last time Norwich Union sponsored an event until the Norwich Union Grand Prix in 1988 (see p. 112). The only amateur to gain a win over a professional was Sid Hood who beat Jackie Rea 4-0 in the first round in 1973.

Year	Winner	Runner-up	Score
1973	John Spencer	John Pulman	8-7
1974	John Spencer	Ray Reardon	10-9

Highest break
74 John Spencer (1973)

Pontins Championships

In the days after the birth of *Pot Black* many professionals, like Ray Reardon and John Spencer, worked during the summer months entertaining holidaymakers at Pontins and Butlins holiday camps. As early as 1974 Pontins organized a Snooker Festival each spring, and in 1976 launched their Autumn Festival. The Spring Festival at Prestatyn remains the most popular of the two and the main events are the Professional and Open competitions. In the Open, professionals concede points per frame to the non-professional players.

Open

Year	Winner	Runner-up	Score
1974	Doug Mountjoy*	John Spencer	7-4
1975	Ray Reardon	John Virgo*	7-1
1976	Doug Mountjoy*	Lance Pibworth*	7-1
1977	Alex Higgins	Terry Griffiths*	7-4
1978	Steve Davis*	Tony Meo*	7-6
1979	Steve Davis	Jimmy White*	7-3
1980	Willie Thorne	Cliff Wilson	7-3
1981	John Hargreaves*	Cliff Wilson	7-2
1982	John Parrott*	Ray Reardon	7-4
1983	Terry Griffiths	Ray Reardon	7-3
1984	Neal Foulds	Doug Mountjoy	7-4
1985	Jim Chambers*	John Parrott	7-6
1986	John Parrott	Tony Putnam*	7-6
1987	Stefan Mazrocis*	Barry Pinches*	7-2
1988	Ken Doherty*	Colin Morton*	7-5
1989	Peter Ebdon*	Ken Doherty	7-4

* non-professional

Most wins
2 Steve Davis, Doug Mountjoy, John Parrott

Most finals
3 Doug Mountjoy, John Parrott, Ray Reardon
2 Steve Davis, Terry Griffiths, Cliff Wilson

Highest break
144 Willie Thorne (1987)

Professional

Year	Winner	Runner-up	Score
1974	Ray Reardon	John Spencer	10-9
1975	Ray Reardon	John Spencer	10-4
1976	Ray Reardon	Fred Davis	10-9
1977	John Spencer	John Pulman	7-5
1978	Ray Reardon	John Spencer	7-2
1979	Doug Mountjoy	Graham Miles	8-4
1980	John Virgo	Ray Reardon	9-6
1981	Terry Griffiths	Willie Thorne	9-8
1982	Steve Davis	Ray Reardon	9-4
1983	Doug Mountjoy	Ray Reardon	9-7
1984	Willie Thorne	John Spencer	9-7
1985	Terry Griffiths	John Spencer	9-7
1986	Terry Griffiths	Willie Thorne	9-6
1987	Neal Foulds	Willie Thorne	9-6
1988	John Parrott	Mike Hallett	9-1
1989	Darren Morgan	Tony Drago	9-2

Most wins
4 Ray Reardon
3 Terry Griffiths
2 Doug Mountjoy

Most finals
7 Ray Reardon
6 John Spencer
4 Willie Thorne
3 Terry Griffiths
2 Doug Mountjoy

Highest break
134 Willie Thorne (1987 – twice)

Canadian Open

First held in 1974 it was organized to coincide with the Canadian National Exhibition week in Toronto. Held seven times, Alex Higgins reached every semi-final and appeared in three consecutive finals 1975–7. The 1975 Open was notable for the fact that more than 20 century breaks were made, including a 142 by Cliff Thorburn.

The 1980 event, which happened to be the last, changed its name to the Canadian National Exhibition Open. It was the first snooker event to be covered by an outside television broadcast in Canada. However, with the season in England getting longer all the time the Canadian Open was removed from the calendar.

Year	Winner	Runner-up	Score
1974	Cliff Thorburn	Dennis Taylor	8–6
1975	Alex Higgins	John Pulman	15–7
1976	John Spencer	Alex Higgins	17–9
1977	Alex Higgins	John Spencer	17–14
1978	Cliff Thorburn	Tony Meo	17–15
1979	Cliff Thorburn	Terry Griffiths	17–16
1980	Cliff Thorburn	Terry Griffiths	17–10

Most wins
4 Cliff Thorburn
2 Alex Higgins

Highest break
146 John Spencer (1977)

Many snooker players are quite useful at golf as well. Stephen Hendry is no exception.

Benson and Hedges Masters

Unquestionably, the Benson and Hedges Masters is the most prestigious non-ranking event and is regarded by many players as the second-best tournament after the Embassy World Championship. (The history of the Masters can be found as one of the special features on p. 16.)

John Spencer was the first Benson and Hedges champion in 1975 and collected a cheque for £2000. The 1989 winner, Stephen Hendry, pocketed £68,000 for his triumph.

The event has always been an invitation-only event, and, today, entry is generally restricted to players in the top-16.

Over the years the Benson and Hedges Masters, held at the imposing Wembley Conference Centre, has been the scene of many great matches. It has also been the scene of the biggest attendances ever seen at snooker matches. The first-round match between Alex Higgins and Bill Werbeniuk in 1983 drew a crowd of 2876. This is a record for any match in Britain.

One feature of the tournament over the years has been the high standard of break-building. Alex Higgins compiled a tournament best of 132 in his 1979 quarter-final against Eddie Charlton. The following year, against Higgins in the final, Welshman Terry Griffiths came within one of that record. But in the following year's final, which was another Griffiths-Higgins affair, the Welshman established a new championship best with a 136. Griffiths continued his excellent record of compiling big breaks with a 128 in 1983 but even he was overshadowed a year later by the Canadian Kirk Stevens.

In his semi-final clash with Jimmy White, Stevens compiled a memorable 147 maximum, only the fifth man to do so, and only the third in tournament play.

The 1986 quarter-final clash between Steve Davis and Willie Thorne was an outstanding match which Davis won 5–4. But Thorne had a 138 clearance (the tournament's second highest break) to level at 2-all. Davis responded with a 132 clearance, and Thorne completed the hat-trick of centuries with a 110.

Year	Winner	Runner-up	Score
1975	John Spencer	Ray Reardon	9-8
1976	Ray Reardon	Graham Miles	7-3
1977	Doug Mountjoy	Ray Reardon	7-6
1978	Alex Higgins	Cliff Thorburn	7-5
1979	Perrie Mans	Alex Higgins	8-4
1980	Terry Griffiths	Alex Higgins	9-5
1981	Alex Higgins	Terry Griffiths	9-6
1982	Steve Davis	Terry Griffiths	9-5
1983	Cliff Thorburn	Ray Reardon	9-7
1984	Jimmy White	Terry Griffiths	9-5
1985	Cliff Thorburn	Doug Mountjoy	9-6
1986	Cliff Thorburn	Jimmy White	9-5
1987	Dennis Taylor	Alex Higgins	9-8
1988	Steve Davis	Mike Hallett	9-0
1989	Stephen Hendry	John Parrott	9-6

Most wins
3 Cliff Thorburn
2 Steve Davis, Alex Higgins

Most finals
5 Alex Higgins
4 Terry Griffiths, Ray Reardon, Cliff Thorburn
2 Steve Davis, Doug Mountjoy, Jimmy White

Highest break
147 Kirk Stevens (1984)

World Professional Match-Play

Held just once, in 1976, the event was promoted by Eddie Charlton who won the 16-man event at Melbourne. Six of the competitors were Australian.

Year	Winner	Runner-up	Score
1976	Eddie Charlton	Ray Reardon	31-24

Highest break
104 Paddy Morgan

Coral UK Championship

Now the Tennents UK Open, it started as the Super Crystalate UK Professional Championship and was open only to holders of UK passports. First held in 1977 its venue was the Blackpool Tower Circus and new professional Patsy Fagan took the first prize of £2000.

Coral Racing became sponsors in 1978 when the venue was moved to the Guildhall at Preston. One of the most outstanding matches at the new venue was that between Terry Griffiths and Rex Williams in 1978. New professional Griffiths led 8-2 before throwing away his lead to lose 9-8.

The champion a year later was Steve Davis who won his first major title. He has since gone on to become the most successful player of the modern era.

Terry Griffiths beat Alex Higgins in one of the sport's great finals in 1983 when the Welshman won 16-15 after Higgins missed an easy black that would have set up a certain victory for the Ulsterman.

The 1983 final was even more dramatic, and again Higgins was involved. This time he came from 7-0 down to beat Steve Davis 16-15 (the full report of the match can be found on p. 44).

The 1984 championship was accorded ranking status and full results and reports on subsequent finals can be found on p. 69.

Year	Winner	Runner-up	Score
1977	Patsy Fagan	Doug Mountjoy	12-9
1978	Doug Mountjoy	David Taylor	15-9
1979	John Virgo	Terry Griffiths	14-13
1980	Steve Davis	Alex Higgins	16-6
1981	Steve Davis	Terry Griffiths	16-3
1982	Terry Griffiths	Alex Higgins	16-15
1983	Alex Higgins	Steve Davis	16-15

Highest break
139 Graham Miles (1978)
139 Tony Meo (1983)

Dry Blackthorn Cup

Another tournament held just once, it was played at the Wembley Conference Centre, the first snooker tournament at the famous venue. It was promoted by boxing promoter Mike Barrett. Only four players took part and the event was completed in one day.

Year	Winner	Runner-up	Score
1977	Patsy Fagan	Alex Higgins	4-2

Highest break
77 Ray Reardon

Benson and Hedges Irish Masters

Like its English counterpart, the Benson and Hedges Irish Masters is an invitation-only event and is extended to 12 players each year. First

held in 1978, every tournament has been at the Goff's Sales Ring, Kill, Co. Kildare, near Dublin.

It was originally a round-robin style event but changed to its present knockout format in 1981.

Alex Higgins with the new love in his life, Siobhan Kidd, after he became the first Irishman to win the Benson and Hedges Irish Masters, in 1989.

Year	Winner	Runner-up	Score
1978	John Spencer	Doug Mountjoy	5–3
1979	Doug Mountjoy	Ray Reardon	6–5
1980	Terry Griffiths	Doug Mountjoy	9–8
1981	Terry Griffiths	Ray Reardon	9–7
1982	Terry Griffiths	Steve Davis	9–5
1983	Steve Davis	Ray Reardon	9–2
1984	Steve Davis	Terry Griffiths	9–1
1985	Jimmy White	Alex Higgins	9–5
1986	Jimmy White	Willie Thorne	9–5
1987	Steve Davis	Willie Thorne	9–1
1988	Steve Davis	Neal Foulds	9–4
1989	Alex Higgins	Stephen Hendry	9–8

Most wins
4 Steve Davis
3 Terry Griffiths
2 Jimmy White

Most finals
5 Steve Davis
4 Terry Griffiths
3 Doug Mountjoy, Ray Reardon
2 Alex Higgins, Willie Thorne, Jimmy White

Highest break
139 Terry Griffiths (1988)

Champion of Champions

Following his first snooker venture in 1977 with the Dry Blackthorn Cup (see above), boxing promoter Mike Barrett returned to the Wembley Conference Centre with the *Daily Mirror* sponsored Champion of Champions in 1978. Like the Dry Blackthorn, it was a four-man event played over a single day. A crowd of 1800 watched the final.

Not held in 1979 it returned in 1980 and to a new home, the New London Theatre, a former home of the Benson and Hedges Masters. The 10-man event was unsponsored and it did not return in 1981.

Year	Winner	Runner-up	Score
1978	Ray Reardon	Alex Higgins	11–9
1979	Not held		
1980	Doug Mountjoy	John Virgo	10–8

Highest break
128 Steve Davis (1980)

Jimmy White Versus Stephen Hendry: A Truly Great Match

What a shame these two exciting players had to meet each other in the 2nd round of the 1988 world championship. Their clash at The Crucible was a truly memorable one and was a game worthy of the final itself.

Such was the outstanding potting skill of both players that the 25-frame match produced no fewer than 26 breaks in excess of 40; 21 over 50; nine over 70; and three centuries. Perhaps that final statistic is the most surprising of the lot–*only* three centuries.

Such was the interest in the match that the BBC showed the final session live on Saturday morning. In going its full distance the match ate into *Grandstand* by more than half an hour. But even Des Lynam was captivated by the match.

Hendry had a break of 78 in taking the first frame; White levelled it and then went to 3–1. He managed to keep his nose two frames in front at the end of the opening session and led 5–3. That was soon increased to 6–3 upon resumption of the second session but then Hendry turned it on with some outstanding snooker to win six consecutive frames in which he compiled 125 and 101 breaks. White won the last frame of the day to reduce the arrears to 7–9.

Hendry won on the black to take the first frame of the Saturday morning's play. But then it was the Englishman's turn to give one of his finest displays as breaks of 62, 50, 78 and 71 gave him a four-frame streak and put him back in front at 11–10. With four frames remaining, the match was destined to go the full distance, and it did.

'That's another fine mess you've gotten me into,' thinks Jimmy White (right) as he contemplates his next shot.

Right: *At the end of a brilliant match, White scraped home by just one frame.*

Both men were playing snooker to the highest level. The player who got the first opening was guaranteed to make a big break and in frame 22 that honour fell to Hendry who compiled his third century of the match (108). White got in with a 64 break to make it 12–11, but the Scot drew level again with a 48 break and so the match was finely poised at 12–all.

With the tension building up to its peak, White attempted a long red under great pressure. In true White style he sank it and that gave him the opportunity to develop another big break which he did. And his 86 was enough to give him victory and bring an end to yet another dramatic and entertaining match this great tournament seems constantly to produce.

Forward Chemicals Tournament

Another event which lasted just one year. It was sponsored by the Widnes-based chemical company Forward Chemicals and was run along the lines of the Park Drive 2000 with four invited professionals playing each other three times with the top two meeting in the final at Manchester's Royal Exchange Theatre.

Year	Winner	Runner-up	Score
1979	Ray Reardon	John Spencer	9–6

Highest break
122 John Spencer

Holsten Lager Tournament

Yet another event which lasted just one year. But how close it came to immortality in the snooker records.

Played at the Fulcrum Centre, Slough, it was covered by Thames Television. However, the cameras were not rolling for the afternoon session of John Spencer's match against Cliff Thorburn. Had they been they would have witnessed the first televised maximum break. Spencer's 147, the first in tournament play, was never officially ratified because of the 'over generous' pockets.

Year	Winner	Runner-up	Score
1979	John Spencer	Graham Miles	11–7

Highest break
147 John Spencer

John Spencer with the Holsten Lager Trophy, during which he compiled the first competitive 147 break.

● ● ● ● ● ● ● ● ● ● ● ● ● ● ●

JOHN SPENCER

Born: 18 September 1935, Radcliffe, Lancashire

In the early-1970s John Spencer was one of the finest players, and his potting skills were second-to-none.

Although he started playing snooker at the age of 15 it was not until 1963 that he started playing seriously. Three years later he was the English amateur champion and runner-up to Gary Owen in the world amateur championship. Spencer turned professional in 1968 and the following year beat Gary Owen to win the world professional title.

He beat his great rival Ray Reardon to win the first Benson and Hedges Masters in 1975, and in 1977 he won the first Embassy World Professional Championship at The Crucible.

John Spencer and *Pot Black* were synonymous with snooker in the 1970s and Spencer won the event three times.

His last individual success was in the 1980 Wilson's Classic, and in 1981 he was a member of the England team that won the World Cup. Since then he has had problems with his eyesight, but on occasions can still show why he was one of the best players nearly 20 years ago.

● ● ● ● ● ● ● ● ● ● ● ● ● ● ●

The Crucible before the start of play . . . and before the dividing partition comes down between the two tables.

Below The 'Voice of Snooker' Whispering Ted Lowe.

Snooker, Davis-eye-view style.

Below One of the game's great talents, Scotland's Stephen Hendry.

Right Alex Higgins returned to winning ways in 1989 after a few lean years. But despite his spell in the wilderness he remained the game's biggest box office draw.

Above . . . another Fleet Street reporter trying to get an Alex Higgins scoop. But my word, don't they start them young these days!

Above, right The 1985 World Champion, Dennis Taylor. He's not a bad golfer either.

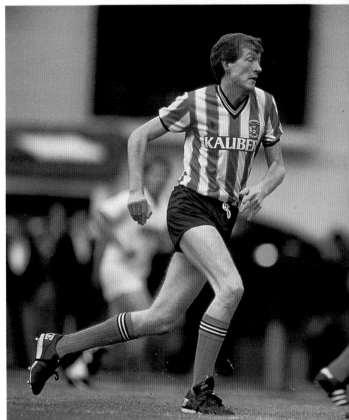

Left Jimmy White: he certainly is one of snooker's 'Masters'.

Right Fortunately Steve Davis doesn't rely on his knees to win him any prizes! He is seen here taking part in a charity football match to raise money for the Hillsborough disaster fund.

Mandy Fisher, the former number one of ladies' snooker. She has had to make way for Allison Fisher (no relative) in recent years.

Bolton's Tony Knowles is one of the game's biggest attractions.

Above Steve James smiling . . .

Left Former world champion John Spencer. This is the 1975 version complete with many extras, like side-burns.

Left, below Joe Johnson not only surprised a lot of people by beating Steve Davis to capture the 1986 world title but a year later he reached the final again.

Below One of the game's senior referees, John Williams.

The two are synonomous: Steve Davis and the Embassy World Championship.

Bombay International

The first professional tournament held in India, it was a six-man round-robin tournament. The £2000 first prize went to the player with the most wins. In 1980 the top two players after the round-robin event contested the final to see who took the increased first prize of £3000.

1979 1st John Spencer 4 wins; 2nd Dennis Taylor 3 wins
1980 John Virgo beat Cliff Thorburn 13–7

Highest break
123 Cliff Thorburn (1980)

Tolly Cobbold Classic

Before they became sponsors of the English professional championship the Suffolk brewers Tolly Cobbold sponsored a popular eight-man tournament played at Ipswich each year from 1979.

The Classic was inaugurated following the success of a four-man event at the Ipswich Corn Exchange in 1978. In its first three years the eight men were divided into two groups with the leaders playing each other in the final. It became a straight knockout event in 1981. The final Classic was held in 1984 when the sponsors widened their horizons.

Year	Winner	Runner-up	Score
1979	Alex Higgins	Ray Reardon	5–4
1980	Alex Higgins	Dennis Taylor	5–4
1981	Graham Miles	Cliff Thorburn	5–1
1982	Steve Davis	Dennis Taylor	8–3
1983	Steve Davis	Terry Griffiths	7–5
1984	Steve Davis	Tony Knowles	8–2

Most wins
3 Steve Davis
2 Alex Higgins

Most finals
3 Steve Davis
2 Alex Higgins, Dennis Taylor

Highest break
119 Terry Griffiths (1980)

Winfield Australian Masters

First held in 1979 as a *Pot Black* style event it was devised especially for television with each match being over a single frame. It was expanded to a multi-frame tournament in 1983 and the following year, for the first time, it moved out of the Channel 10 television studios and was played at the Parramatta Leagues Club in Sydney.

In 1986 it reverted to a short-frame format and after the 1987 event the tournament was discontinued.

Year	Winner	Runner-up	Score*
1979	Ian Anderson	Perrie Mans	*
1980	John Spencer	Dennis Taylor	*
1981	Tony Meo	John Spencer	*
1982	Steve Davis	Eddie Charlton	*
1983	Cliff Thorburn	Bill Werbeniuk	7–3
1984	Tony Knowles	John Virgo	7–3
1985	Tony Meo	John Campbell	7–2
1986	Dennis Taylor	Steve Davis	3–2
1987	Stephen Hendry	Mike Hallett	*

* 1979–82 aggregate score over three frames; 1987 aggregate score over five frames

Most wins
2 Tony Meo

Most finals
2 Steve Davis, Tony Meo, John Spencer, Dennis Taylor

Highest break
134 Tony Meo (1985)

Limosin International

The first major professional event in South Africa for more than ten years, it was played at the Good Hope Centre, Cape Town. Eight players took part and the event was well supported and received television coverage.

Year	Winner	Runner-up	Score
1979	Eddie Charlton	John Spencer	23–19

Highest break
120 Cliff Thorburn
(Silvino Francisco made a 137 during a 'dead frame' after beating Perrie Mans.)

Kronenbrau 1308 Classic

A four-man event held a week after the Limosin International. It was played in Johannesburg and involved Eddie Charlton, Ray Reardon, Perrie Mans and Jimmy van Rensburg.

Year	Winner	Runner-up	Score
1979	Eddie Charlton	Ray Reardon	7–4

Highest break
Not recorded

Fersina Windows World Cup

Inaugurated in 1979 the event has had more sponsors and titles than any other professional event. The full list of sponsors and venues is as follows:

1979	State Express World Cup	Haden Hill LC, Birmingham
1980	State Express World Cup	New London Theatre, London
1981–3	State Express World Team Classic	Hexagon Theatre, Reading
1984	Not held	
1985	Guinness World Cup	Bournemouth International Centre
1986	Car Care Plan World Cup	Bournemouth International Centre
1987	Tuborg World Cup	Bournemouth International Centre
1988–9	Fersina Windows World Cup	Bournemouth International Centre

Six teams competed in the first tournament, promoted by Mike Watterson, at the Haden Hill Leisure Centre, Birmingham. There was no tournament in 1984 because it was moved from an early- to late-season position in the calendar. The 1985 tournament was the first to contain its current quota of eight teams and for the first time the event was held on a knockout basis.

Year	Winner	Runner-up	Score
1979	Wales	England	14–3
1980	Wales	Canada	8–5
1981	England	Wales	4–3
1982	Canada	England	4–2
1983	England	Wales	4–2
1984	Not held		
1985	All-Ireland	England 'A'	9–7
1986	Ireland 'A'	Canada	9–7
1987	Ireland 'A'	Canada	9–2
1988	England	Australia	9–7
1989	England	Rest of the world	9–8

Most wins (Team)
4 England
3 All-Ireland/Ireland 'A'
2 Wales

Most wins (Individual)
4 Steve Davis (1981, 1983, 1988–9)
3 Alex Higgins (1985–7), Eugene Hughes (1985–7), Dennis Taylor (1985–7)
2 Neal Foulds (1988–9), Terry Griffiths (1979–80), Doug Mountjoy (1979–80), Ray Reardon (1979–80), Jimmy White (1988–9)

The successful Irish trio of Eugene Hughes (second from the left) Dennis Taylor (with trophy) and Alex Higgins (looking happy!) being presented with the World Cup trophy which they won three years in succession, 1985–7.

Most finals (Team)
7 England/England 'A'
4 Canada, Wales
3 All-Ireland/Ireland 'A'

Most finals (Individual)
6 Steve Davis (1981–3, 1985, 1988–9)
4 Terry Griffiths (1979–81, 1983), Doug Mountjoy (1979–81, 1983), Ray Reardon (1979–81, 1983), Kirk Stevens (1980, 1982, 1986–7), Cliff Thorburn (1980, 1982, 1986–7), Bill Werbeniuk (1980, 1982, 1986–7)
3 Alex Higgins (1985–7), Eugene Hughes (1985–7), Tony Knowles (1982–3, 1985), Dennis Taylor (1985–7), Jimmy White (1982, 1988–9)
2 Neal Foulds (1988–9), Tony Meo (1983, 1985), John Spencer (1979, 1981)

Highest break
127 Terry Griffiths (1981)

Padmore/Super Crystalate International

The eight-man tournament at the Gala Baths, West Bromwich was contested for just one year. The original sponsors pulled out four days before the start of the tournament and billiard and snooker traders Padmore and ball manufacturers Super Crystalate helped out at the last minute.

Year	Winner	Runner-up	Score
1980	Alex Higgins	Perrie Mans	4–2

Highest break
106 Willie Thorne

Lada Classic

The Lada Classic was first played in 1982 when it replaced the Wilson's Classic. The Lada itself was last played in 1984 and was replaced by the Mercantile Credit Classic.

The first Wilson's Classic was held in January 1980 and the eight-man event was played over two days at Manchester's New Century Hall. The second event was held in December of the same year and Steve Davis won his second major professional event by beating Dennis Taylor at Blighty's, Farnworth, near Bolton.

After Lada took over the sponsorship in 1982 the event was moved to the Oldham Civic Centre, and it was there during his match with John Spencer that Steve Davis recorded the first televised maximum.

The field was enlarged to 16 in 1983 when Warrington's Spectrum Arena became the

Lada's new home. It was the last time the event was contested as a non-ranking tournament.

It became a ranking event in 1984 and all results for that year and all subsequent events as the Mercantile Credit Classic can be found on pages 66–69.

Year	Winner	Runner-up	Score
1980 (Jan)	John Spencer	Alex Higgins	4–3
1980 (Dec)	Steve Davis	Dennis Taylor	4–1
1982	Terry Griffiths	Steve Davis	9–8
1983	Steve Davis	Bill Werbeniuk	9–5

Highest break
147 Steve Davis (1982)

Welsh Professional Championship

Wales was the first of the four home countries to revive its national professional championship on a regular basis. The championship was first

Welshman Terry Griffiths reached his second world final in 1988 but he could not match his first appearance nine years earlier when he lifted the title.

played in the 1920s but it was more than 50 years before Ray Reardon and Doug Mountjoy met, in 1977, for an 'unofficial' Welsh professional title.

The Ebbw Vale Leisure Centre staged the official revived championship in 1980 which was sponsored by cider producers H.P. Bulmer and Co., using their Woodpecker name. The full list of sponsors and venues is as follows:

1980–3	Woodpecker	Ebbw Vale Leisure Centre
1984	Strongbow	Ebbw Vale Leisure Centre
1985	BCE	Abertillery Leisure Centre
1986	Zetters	Abertillery Leisure Centre
1987	Matchroom	Newport Centre
1988–9	Senator	Newport centre

Year	Winner	Runner-up	Score
1980	Doug Mountjoy	Ray Reardon	9–6
1981	Ray Reardon	Cliff Wilson	9–6
1982	Doug Mountjoy	Terry Griffiths	9–8
1983	Ray Reardon	Doug Mountjoy	9–1
1984	Doug Mountjoy	Cliff Wilson	9–3
1985	Terry Griffiths	Doug Mountjoy	9–4
1986	Terry Griffiths	Doug Mountjoy	9–3
1987	Doug Mountjoy	Steve Newbury	9–7
1988	Terry Griffiths	Wayne Jones	9–3
1989	Doug Mountjoy	Terry Griffiths	9–6

Most wins
5 Doug Mountjoy
3 Terry Griffiths
2 Ray Reardon

Highest break
127 Terry Griffiths (1980)

Most finals
8 Doug Mountjoy
5 Terry Griffiths
3 Ray Reardon
2 Cliff Wilson

British Gold Cup

Held once, at the Assembly Rooms, Derby, the tournament belonged to Alex Higgins who compiled breaks of 134 and 135 in his group match against Terry Griffiths and in the final compiled another big break, of 132.

Year	Winner	Runner-up	Score
1980	Alex Higgins	Ray Reardon	5–1

Highest break
135 Alex Higgins

Yamaha International Masters

The Yamaha International Masters started life as the Yamaha Organs Trophy, and replaced the

British Gold Cup. Like its predecessor it was played at the Derby Assembly Rooms.

The original format in 1981 saw 16 players divided into four groups and each match was over only the best-of-three frames. The four group winners then contested a knockout tournament. In 1982 the leading eight players contested two more round-robin groups with the two group winners contesting the final. This same format was adopted in 1983 when the tournament became the Yamaha International Masters. The final tournament in 1984 saw yet another change in format. This time 27 contestants were split into nine groups. The group winners split into three further groups the winners of which contested the three-man round-robin final. All matches were the best-of-three.

The Yamaha was replaced by the Dulux British Open in 1985. For results since then see p. 72.

Year	Winner	Runner-up	Score
1981	Steve Davis	David Taylor	9–6
1982	Steve Davis	Terry Griffiths	9–7
1983	Ray Reardon	Jimmy White	9–6
1984	1st: Steve Davis	2nd: Dave Martin	
	3rd: John Dunning		

Highest break
135 Steve Davis (1982)

English Professional Championship

First held in 1981 it was discontinued until 1985 when it gained sponsorship from the Suffolk brewers Tolly Cobbold and also received a £1000 per entrant contribution towards prize money from the WPBSA. It has been held every year since then and has been noted for producing surprise finalists. Sponsors and venues have been:

1981	John Courage	Haden Hill Leisure Centre, Birmingham
1982–4	Not held	
1985–7	Tolly Cobbold	Corn Exchange, Ipswich
1988	unsponsored	Corn Exchange, Ipswich
1989	unsponsored	Redwood Lodge, Bristol

Year	Winner	Runner-up	Score
1981	Steve Davis	Tony Meo	9–3
1982–4	Not held		
1985	Steve Davis	Tony Knowles	9–2
1986	Tony Meo	Neal Foulds	9–7
1987	Tony Meo	Les Dodd	9–5
1988	Dean Reynolds	Neal Foulds	9–5
1989	Mike Hallett	John Parrott	9–7

Most wins
2 Steve Davis, Tony Meo

MIKE HALLETT

Born: 6 July 1959, Grimsby, Humberside

Mike Hallett has established himself as an outstanding player in the last couple of years as he has climbed the rankings since he first made the top-16 in 1987.

Like John Parrott, Hallett was labelled a 'nearly man'. But in Hallett's case he suffered some big defeats in the finals he managed to reach.

Mike came into the professional ranks in 1979 shortly after captaining England in the Home International championship. However, it took a long time for him to gain the recognition his skill deserved.

He reached the final of the Winfield Masters in 1987 but lost to Stephen Hendry. Towards the end of the year he teamed up with Hendry to win the Fosters World Doubles title. But then followed a sequence of big defeats in finals.

In 1988 Steve Davis beat him 9–0 in the final of the Benson and Hedges Masters. His doubles partner inflicted a 13–2 thrashing on him in the final of the MIM Britannia British Open. And then John Parrott beat him 9–1 in the final of the Pontins Professional Championship.

Hendry beat him 6–1 in the close-season New Zealand Masters, but at the start of the 1988–9 season Mike eventually got his hands on a title when he beat Hendry to win the Fosters Professional Championship and in the second half of the season he beat John Parrott to lift the English professional title.

Grimsby's Mike Hallett has shot up the rankings in recent years and is now well established in the top-16.

Most finals
3   Tony Meo
2   Steve Davis, Neal Foulds

Highest break
139 Tony Knowles (1985)
139 John Virgo (1987)

Langs Scottish Masters

An early-season tournament, the first Masters was held in 1981 at Glasgow's Kelvin Hall and won by 19-year-old Jimmy White, the then youngest winner of a major professional tournament.

The Holiday Inn, Glasgow was the tournament's home in 1982 and the following year it moved to the Skean Dhu Hotel, also in Glasgow. It remained the event's venue (as the renamed Hospitality Inn) until 1987 when the last Masters was played.

Originally a nine-man event, all subsequent Masters were contested by eight men.

In the 1985 tournament Cliff Thorburn compiled breaks of 133 and 142.

Year	Winner	Runner-up	Score
1981	Jimmy White	Cliff Thorburn	9–4
1982	Steve Davis	Alex Higgins	9–4
1983	Steve Davis	Tony Knowles	9–6
1984	Steve Davis	Jimmy White	9–4
1985	Cliff Thorburn	Willie Thorne	9–7
1986	Cliff Thorburn	Alex Higgins	9–8
1987	Joe Johnson	Terry Griffiths	9–7

Most wins
3   Steve Davis
2   Cliff Thorburn

Jimmy White.

Most finals
3 Steve Davis, Cliff Thorburn
2 Alex Higgins, Jimmy White

Highest break
142 Cliff Thorburn (1985)

Jameson International

Played at the Derby Assembly Rooms, the first Jameson International in 1981 was the only one not to receive ranking tournament status. When it was played a second time in 1982 it became the next event after the world championship to be accorded ranking status. It is now known as the Fidelity Unit Trusts International and all results from 1982–8 can be found on p. 57.

Year	Winner	Runner-up	Score
1981	Steve Davis	Dennis Taylor	9–0

Highest break
135 Steve Davis

Northern Ireland Classic

Another 'once-only' tournament. The eight-man invitational Northern Ireland Classic was won by 19-year-old Jimmy White at Belfast's Ulster Hall.

Year	Winner	Runner-up	Score
1981	Jimmy White	Steve Davis	11–9

Highest break
112 Dennis Taylor

Scottish Professional Championship

First held before the last war, like its Irish counterpart, it was held on a challenge basis and dominated by one man, Walter Donaldson. It was discontinued until 1979 when Eddie Sinclair met 'Anglo' Chris Ross in a challenge for the revived title. But in 1981, after six more Scots joined the professional ranks the first knockout-style championship was organized.

There was no tournament in 1984 because the event moved from an early- to late-season fixture. Venues and sponsors have been:

1981	unsponsored	Cumbernauld Theatre, Kildrum
1982	Tartan Bitter/ *Daily Record*	Glen Pavilion, Dunfermline
1983	unsponsored	Glasgow University
1984	Not held	
1985	unsponsored	Marco's Leisure Centre, Edinburgh
1986	Canada Dry	Marco's Leisure Centre, Edinburgh
1987	People's Cars	Steve Davis Club, Glasgow
1988	Swish	Marco's Leisure Centre, Edinburgh
1989	unsponsored	Marco's Leisure Centre, Glasgow

Year	Winner	Runner-up	Score
1981	Ian Black	Matt Gibson	11–7
1982	Eddie Sinclair	Ian Black	11–7
1983	Murdo Macleod	Eddie Sinclair	11–9
1984	Not held		
1985	Murdo Macleod	Eddie Sinclair	11–2
1986	Stephen Hendry	Matt Gibson	10–5
1987	Stephen Hendry	Jim Donnelly	10–7
1988	Stephen Hendry	Murdo Macleod	10–4
1989	John Rea	Murdo Macleod	9–7

Most wins
3 Stephen Hendry
2 Murdo Macleod

Most finals
4 Murdo Macleod
3 Stephen Hendry, Eddie Sinclair
2 Ian Black, Matt Gibson

Highest break
147 John Rea (1989)

Irish Professional Championship

Held for the first time as a challenge competition in 1947, Jackie Rea withstood several challenges over the years until losing to Alex Higgins in 1972. Higgins then successfully defended against Dennis Taylor in 1978 and Patsy Fagan in

1979. Taylor won the title in 1980 and he held off a challenge from Fagan in 1981. However, the event became a knockout tournament in 1982 with seven competitors. There was no championship in 1984. Sponsors and venues of the championship have been:

1982	Smithwicks	Riverside Theatre, Coleraine
1983	Smithwicks	Maysfield Leisure Centre, Belfast
1984	Not held	
1985	Strongbow	Ulster Hall, Belfast
1986	Strongbow	Maysfield Leisure Centre, Belfast
1987	Matchroom	Antrim Forum
1988-9	unsponsored	Antrim Forum

Year	Winner	Runner-up	Score
1982	Dennis Taylor	Alex Higgins	16-13
1983	Alex Higgins	Dennis Taylor	16-11
1984	Not held		
1985	Dennis Taylor	Alex Higgins	10-5
1986	Dennis Taylor	Alex Higgins	10-7
1987	Dennis Taylor	Joe O'Boye	9-2
1988	Jack McLaughlin	Dennis Taylor	9-4
1989	Alex Higgins	Jack McLaughlin	9-7

Most wins
4 Dennis Taylor
2 Alex Higgins

Most finals
6 Dennis Taylor
5 Alex Higgins
2 Jack McLaughlin

Highest break
132 Alex Higgins (1983)

Highland Masters

Played just once, at the Eden Court Theatre, Inverness, it was an eight-man event. Steve Davis and Alex Higgins were both beaten 6-0 in their semi-finals by Ray Reardon and John Spencer, respectively.

Year	Winner	Runner-up	Score
1982	Ray Reardon	John Spencer	11-4

Highest break
119 John Spencer

Foster's World Doubles

Inaugurated in 1982 as the Hofmeister World Doubles it was initially played at the National Recreation Centre, Crystal Palace. But in 1983 it moved to the Derngate Centre, Northampton, which became the event's permanent home until

it was discontinued in 1987. Foster's became the tournament's sponsors in its final year.

It was the first serious attempt to play doubles since just after the war when Joe Davis and Walter Donaldson used to play exhibition matches against Fred Davis and John Pulman.

Players took it in turn to visit the table and the highest break prize consisted of the highest combined break made by the two players in any one match.

Year	Winners	Runners-up	Score
1982	Steve Davis/ Tony Meo	Terry Griffiths/ Doug Mountjoy	13-2
1983	Steve Davis/ Tony Meo	Tony Knowles/ Jimmy White	10-2
1984	Alex Higgins/ Jimmy White	Cliff Thorburn/ Willie Thorne	10-2
1985	Steve Davis/ Tony Meo	Ray Reardon/ Tony Jones	12-5
1986	Steve Davis/ Tony Meo	Mike Hallett/ Stephen Hendry	12-3
1987	Mike Hallett/ Stephen Hendry	Cliff Thorburn/ Dennis Taylor	12-8

Most wins
4 Steve Davis, Tony Meo

Most finals
4 Steve Davis, Tony Meo
2 Mike Hallett, Stephen Hendry, Cliff Thorburn, Jimmy White

Highest break
217 Steve Davis/Tony Meo (1986)

LEP Hong Kong Masters

The first Hong Kong Masters consisted of three of Barry Hearn's players, Steve Davis, Tony Meo and Terry Griffiths, plus Doug Mountjoy and two local players. It was sponsored by cognac distillers Camus between 1983 and 1986. In 1987, under the sponsorship of Riley's, it formed the second leg of the shortlived World Series (see p. 110). The sponsors in 1988 were LEP, who also became the new sponsors of the Matchroom Trophy.

Year	Winner	Runner-up	Score
1983	Doug Mountjoy	Terry Griffiths	4-3
1984	Steve Davis	Doug Mountjoy	4-2
1985	Terry Griffiths	Steve Davis	4-2
1986	Willie Thorne	Dennis Taylor	8-3
1987	Steve Davis	Stephen Hendry	9-3
1988	Jimmy White	Neal Foulds	6-3

Highest break
140 Terry Griffiths (1983)

The World Championship's Humble Beginnings

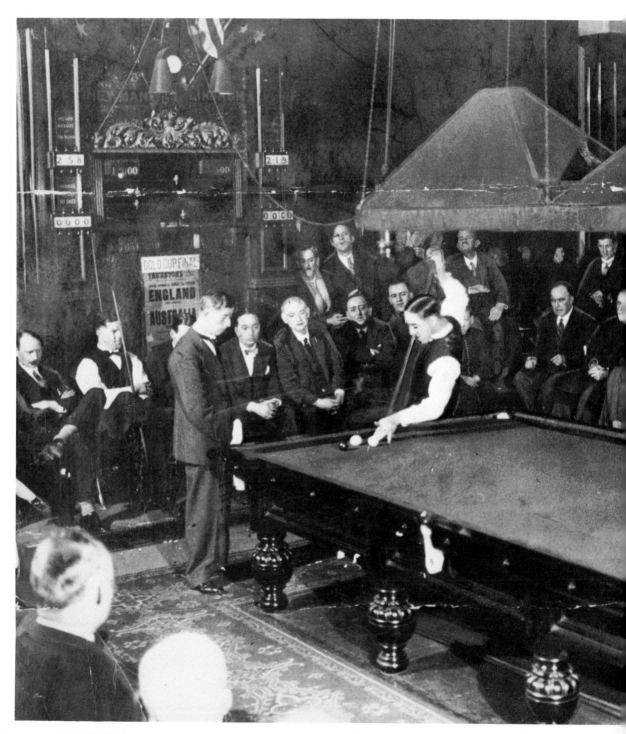

Thurston's Hall, home of the world championship eight times between 1930–40.

Every year more than 130 hopefuls set out on the road that takes the last 32 players to The Crucilbe Theatre every spring, From there, it is a 17-day battle to see who becomes the world professional snooker champion and take with it a cheque for over £100,000. But how different it was in the early days of the championship.

When Joe Davis collected the winner's trophy after beating Tom Dennis at Camkin's Hall, Birmingham, in the inaugural final in 1927, his winner's cheque amounted to £6 10s (£6.50). The trophy, however, is the same. It was acquired in 1927 by the Billiards Association and Control Club for £19 taken from the players' share of the prize money. It remained their property (later as the B & SCC) until it was presented to the WPBSA in 1986.

A far cry from the 130-plus entrants of today, the first championship consisted of ten entrants, and on 26 November 1926 Melbourne Inman and Tom Newman met in the first match at Thurston's Hall, London, the capacity of which was not much over 100. The first final was promoted by George Camkin (whose billiard hall staged the final). He refereed the final as well! Davis won the tournament, and his highest break was a mere 57.

The tournament remained a season-long affair with the final generally played in May. The competition still struggled to gain in popularity and continued to be less popular than its billiards counterpart. The number of competitors gradually dwindled from ten in the first year to a mere two in 1931 when Joe Davis and Tom Dennis did battle at the Lounge Billiard Hall, Nottingham. It was, in fact, the back room of Dennis's public house. Three years

later Davis played Tom Newman in the final and again they were the only two competitors.

The tournament attracted a pre-war record 15 entrants in 1939. In the immediate post-war years it went through a mini-boom, probably because the invincible Joe Davis, the 15-times champion, retired from the championship after winning in 1946. But then a further decline set in and after Horace Lindrum and Clark McConachy contested the two-man championship in 1952 that was the last championship until revived on a challenge basis in 1964.

Since the advent of colour television, and since the event moved to The Crucible Theatre, it has gained in popularity and status and become one of Britain's premier sporting events. It was a different story in the backroom of Tom Dennis's Nottingham pub in 1931.

The game's two biggest attractions, Jimmy White (left) and Alex Higgins . . . taken when they were both a bit younger.

Canadian Professional Championship

A form of professional championship had existed in Canada for many years but it was not until 1983 that it was officially recognized for the first time.

Year	Winner	Runner-up	Score
1983	Kirk Stevens	Frank Jonik	9–8
1984	Cliff Thorburn	Mario Morra	9–2
1985	Cliff Thorburn	Bob Chaperon	6–4
1986	Cliff Thorburn	Jim Wych	6–2
1987	Cliff Thorburn	Jim Bear	8–4
1988	Alain Robidoux	Jim Wych	8–4

Highest break
128 Jim Bear (1983)

ALEX HIGGINS

Born: 18 March 1949, Belfast

A one-time apprentice jockey, Alex Higgins started playing snooker at the age of 11 when one of his haunts was Belfast's Jampot club. He won the Northern Ireland amateur championship in 1968 and in 1971 turned professional.

Higgins had an immediate impact on the professional game and in his first world championship in 1972 beat such notable men as Jackie Rea, John Pulman and Rex Williams before he lined up against John Spencer in the final. The 23-year-old Higgins won and remains the youngest winner of the title.

He emerged as the biggest attraction in snooker in the 1970s but had to wait until 1982 before regaining his world title. In between, however, he won the Benson and Hedges Masters in 1978 and 1981, and the British Gold Cup in 1980.

After winning the Irish professional title and Coral UK Championship in 1983, Higgins did not win another individual title until 1989 when he regained the Irish Championship. He was, however, a member of the three Irish teams that won the world team championship between 1985 and 1987. He had earlier teamed up with Jimmy White to win the 1984 Hofmeister world doubles title.

A troubled life away from the snooker table has seen a decline in his play in recent years but the 1988–9 season saw him reach the final of the Rothmans Grand Prix and become the first Irish winner of the Benson and Hedges Irish Masters.

Costa Del Sol Classic

The first attempt to promote professional snooker on Spain's Costa Del Sol proved a success. The 12-man event was played initially at the Fuengirola and Torremolinos Snooker Centres before moving to the 380-seater Las Palmeras Hotel, Torremolinos for the final. Dennis Taylor won the first prize of £600.

Year	Winner	Runner-up	Score
1984	Dennis Taylor	Mike Hallett	5–2

Highest break
105 Joe Johnson

Foster's Professional Championship

An early season tournament it was first held in 1984 as the Carlsberg Challenge. It became known as the Carling Challenge in 1987 before assuming its present style in 1988. It is a four-man knockout event played in the studios of Radio Telefis Eireann in Dublin.

Year	Winner	Runner-up	Score
1984	Jimmy White	Tony Knowles	9–7
1985	Jimmy White	Alex Higgins	8–3
1986	Dennis Taylor	Jimmy White	8–3
1987	Dennis Taylor	Joe Johnson	8–5
1988	Mike Hallett	Stephen Hendry	8–5

Highest break
140 Dennis Taylor (1987)

Professional Snooker League

A 12-man round-robin tournament played at varying venues around Britain during the 1983–4 season. The cost outweighed the amount of sponsorship and the event was a financial disaster. The eventual winner, John Virgo, received no prize money.

1st	John Virgo	16 pts
2nd	Dennis Taylor	15 pts
3rd	Eddie Charlton	15 pts

Highest break
136 Alex Higgins
136 Bill Werbeniuk

Australian Professional Championship

The Australian championship was revived in 1984 after the WPBSA announced its £1000-a-man sponsorship of all national championships. Like other national events, the Australian championship had previously been held but only on a spasmodic challenge basis with Eddie Charlton dominating the event. The last time he met a challenge was in 1978. Since 1984, however, he has seen his domination of Australian snooker

The chairman of the WPBSA, John Virgo.

● ● ● ● ● ● ● ● ● ● ● ● ● ● ●

JOHN VIRGO

Born: 3 April 1946, Salford, Greater Manchester

As an amateur, John Virgo was groomed in the tough schooling around the Manchester area which bred so many good players in the mid-seventies. Virgo was one of them.

The under-16 and under-19 champion, he teamed up with Paul Medati to win the national pairs title in 1976. The following year Virgo turned professional but had to wait until 1979 for his first major title, the Coral UK Championship at Preston when he beat Terry Griffiths 14–13 in the final.

Although consistently among the top-16, John Virgo has never won another major title, and has not appeared in a ranking final. His last win was in the shortlived Professional Snooker League in 1984 which, sadly for him, did not carry any prize money.

Away from the snooker table John serves as the chairman of the WPBSA, a position he took in 1987 after Rex Williams's retirement.

● ● ● ● ● ● ● ● ● ● ● ● ● ● ●

diminish with the arrival of the likes of John Campbell and Warren King.

Year	Winner	Runner-up	Score
1984	Eddie Charlton	Warren King	10-3
1985	John Campbell	Eddie Charlton	10-7
1986	Warren King	John Campbell	10-3
1987	Warren King	Eddie Charlton	10-7
1988	John Campbell	Robbie Foldvari	9-7

Highest break
130 Warren King (1985)

Labbatt's Canadian Masters

Inaugurated in 1985 as an eight-man event it was held in the CBC Television Studios in Toronto. After two years of BCE sponsorship the event was sponsored by Labbatt in 1987 when it became the third and last leg of the ill-fated World Series (see p. 110). The Masters was sponsored by BCE again in 1988 when it was granted ranking status and became the first ranking event outside Britain. (Details of this latter tournament can be found on p. 78.)

Year	Winner	Runner-up	Score
1985	Dennis Taylor	Steve Davis	9-5
1986	Steve Davis	Willie Thorne	9-3
1987	Dennis Taylor	Jimmy White	9-7

Highest break
143 Steve Davis (1986)

Camus Singapore Masters

One of the stopping-off points on Barry Hearn's tour of the Far East. It was sponsored by cognac distillers Camus.

Year	Winner	Runner-up	Score
1985	Steve Davis	Terry Griffiths	4-2

Highest break
Not recorded

Camus Thailand Masters

Another of the Matchroom team's Far Eastern ventures it was held on two occasions. In the second tournament, local hero James Wattana beat

Dennis Taylor, Steve Davis and Terry Griffiths to take the first prize.

Year	Winner	Runner-up	Score
1985	Dennis Taylor	Terry Griffiths	4-0
1986	James Wattana	Terry Griffiths	2-1

Highest break
141 Steve Davis (1985)

Kit Kat Break for World Champions

This unique eight-man tournament consisted only of former world champions: Fred Davis, Steve Davis, Dennis Taylor, Alex Higgins, John Spencer, Ray Reardon, Terry Griffiths and Cliff Thorburn.

The event was the idea of Roger Lee, a member of the Brothers Lee, the singing/comedy trio who found fame through television's *Generation Game*. The tournament, which carried a £10,000 first prize, was held at the East Midlands Conference Centre, Nottingham.

Year	Winner	Runner-up	Score
1985	Dennis Taylor	Steve Davis	9-5

Highest break
126 Dennis Taylor

BCE Belgian Classic

With snooker rapidly gaining in popularity in Belgium, table manufacturers BCE sponsored the first, and only, Belgian Classic which was an eight-man invitational event.

Year	Winner	Runner-up	Score
1986	Terry Griffiths	Kirk Stevens	9-7

Highest break
121 Terry Griffiths

Brazilian Masters

After an exploratory visit to Brazil in 1985, Barry Hearn returned with Steve Davis and Tony Meo to take part in the inaugural four-man Masters. Played on a 9 ft table with only six reds, the two Englishmen competed in a round-robin tournament against two local players. Steve Davis was undefeated and won the first title. There was also a 'Test Match' which England won 3-2. The following year local player Roberto Carlos beat Steve Davis 18–14 to take the title.

Winners

1986	Steve Davis
1987	Roberto Carlos

Camus Malaysian Masters

Held at Kuala Lumpur, the Malaysian Masters was launched in 1986 following the success of the Matchroom tour of the Far East the previous year.

Year	Winner	Runner-up	Score
1986	Jimmy White	Dennis Taylor	2–1

Highest break
91 Steve Davis

Camus China Masters

In terms of television viewing figures the inaugural Camus China Masters was a huge success with figures in excess of 100 million. It was inaugurated in 1986 after a successful exhibition by Dennis Taylor and Steve Davis in Canton the year before.

Year	Winner	Runner-up	Score
1986	Steve Davis	Terry Griffiths	3–0

Highest break
Not recorded

LEP Matchroom Trophy

The in-house tournament for the members of Barry Hearn's Matchroom team, it was inaugurated in 1986 and played at the Cliffs Pavilion, Southend. It acquired an outside sponsor, LEP, for the first time in 1988 when the first prize was £50,000.

Year	Winner	Runner-up	Score
1986	Willie Thorne	Steve Davis	10–9
1987	Dennis Taylor	Willie Thorne	10–3
1988	Steve Davis	Dennis Taylor	10–7

Highest break
141 Dennis Taylor (1987)

Matchroom League

A ten-man round-robin tournament played between January and May. Matches are played at different venues around Britain and on the Continent at such places as Reykjavic in Iceland and Turku in Finland. All matches are over eight frames, thus making a draw a possibility. Three points are awarded for a win and one for a draw.

Inaugurated in 1987 it was sponsored by Rothmans in its first two years but was without an outside sponsor in 1989. The seven Matchroom players and Cliff Thorburn (not a Matchroom player at the time) made up the original eight-man complement. It was increased to ten in 1988 when the eight Matchroom players were joined by Stephen Hendry and Joe Johnson. In 1989 Dennis Taylor and Joe Johnson were 'relegated' after finishing 9th and 10th in 1988. Their places were taken by Alex Higgins and John Parrott. Higgins and Terry Griffiths both lost their League places at the end of the 1989 League and Jimmy White held on to his place only after beating Steve Davis in the final match of the League. It was Davis's only defeat in nine matches.

1987	1st	Steve Davis	13 pts
	2nd	Neal Foulds	12 pts
	3rd	Jimmy White	11 pts
1988	1st	Steve Davis	21 pts
	2nd	Stephen Hendry	18 pts
	3rd	Willie Thorne	15 pts
1989	1st	Steve Davis	24 pts
	2nd	John Parrott	19 pts
	3rd	Stephen Hendry	19 pts

Highest break
147 Tony Meo (1988)
147 Cliff Thorburn (1989)

British Caledonian Tokyo Masters

Held for the first time in 1987 it was one of the three legs of the World Series (see p. 110) actually completed. Part of Dennis Taylor's prize as winner was a samurai warrior's helmet!

Year	Winner	Runner-up	Score
1987	Dennis Taylor	Terry Griffiths	6–3

Highest break
118 Terry Griffiths

'Mine's better than theirs,' says Willie Thorne at the presentation of the prize vases after the Kent Cup tournament in China.

World Series

This proposed eight-leg worldwide series of events was launched in 1987 but after three legs the series discontinued. The three legs that were completed were the Tokyo Masters, Hong Kong Masters and Canadian Masters. (For details of the results of those tournaments see the appropriate individual entries.)

The leading positions at the time of the abandonment of the series were:

1. Dennis Taylor   22 pts
2. Steve Davis   13 pts
3. Jimmy White   12 pts

Highest break
127 Dennis Taylor (Canadian Masters)

Kent Cup

China's first major event, it was first held in 1987 when Barry Hearn took members of his team to play in the televised event at the Peking Sports Stadium. The eight British players who made the trip in 1988 were all members of Howard Kruger's Framework team.

Year	Winner	Runner-up	Score
1987	Willie Thorne	Jimmy White	5–2
1988	John Parrott	Martin Clark	5–1

Highest break
134 Steve Davis (1987)

Fiat Snooker/Pool Triathlon

A snooker and pool challenge match between American pool champion Steve Mizerak and Steve Davis in 1987, and Mizerak and Jimmy White in 1988. Played over three legs consisting of straight pool, snooker and nine-ball pool, Mizerak has won both titles. It was held at the Palace Hotel, St Moritz in 1987, and at the Deauville Casino the following year.

Year	Winner	Runner-up	Score
1987	Steve Mizerak	Steve Davis	2–1
1988	Steve Mizerak	Jimmy White	6–4

New Zealand Lion Brown Masters

The most prestigious professional event ever held in New Zealand the televised competition was played at the Parliament's Legislative Council Chambers in Wellington. Total prize money amounted to £40,000.

Year	Winner	Runner-up	Score
1988	Stephen Hendry	Mike Hallett	6–1

Highest break
113 Joe Johnson

Steve Davis holds aloft the inaugural Everest World Match-Play trophy. With it went snooker's first £100,000 winner's cheque.

Below: Steve Davis (wearing cap) and Steve Mizerak during their Fiat Snooker/Pool Triathlon at St Moritz in 1987. Rex Williams is on the left. Judging by Mizerak's outfit somebody told him it was a fancy-dress tournament. Mind you, what does Steve look like in that cap?

Everest World Match-Play Championship

This was the third event since 1952 to incorporate 'Match-Play' in its title. This latest venture was open to the top 12 players based on 1987–8 performances. Played at the International Hall, Brentwood, it was the first time that snooker's top prize was in six figures (£100,000).

Year	Winner	Runner-up	Score
1988	Steve Davis	John Parrott	9–5

Highest break
135 John Parrott

Dubai Duty Free Masters

Another Barry Hearn venture. All eight Matchroom players plus eight locals competed in the 16-man tournament at the Al Nasr Stadium. Neal Foulds returned from a lean spell to beat Steve Davis in the final.

Year	Winner	Runner-up	Score
1988	Neal Foulds	Steve Davis	5–4

Highest break
107 Willie Thorne

111

WPBSA Non-Ranking Tournaments

In 1988–9 the WPBSA promoted three non-ranking tournaments open to players who did not make the last 32 of early season ranking tournaments. The first event was at Marco's Leisure Centre, Glasgow, the second at Pontins, Brixham, and the third at the Excelsior Club, Leeds.

Year	Winner	Runner-up	Score
1988 (1)	Gary Wilkinson	Alex Higgins	5–4
1988 (2)	Paddy Browne	Peter Francisco	5–1
1988 (3)	David Taylor	Steve Meakin	9–1

Highest break
128 Alex Higgins (2)

Norwich Union Grand Prix

Norwich Union returned to snooker sponsorship after an absence of 14 years. The Grand Prix, open to the eight Matchroom members, involved them, four at a time, playing a series of knockout tournaments across Europe in Belgium, France, Spain and Italy. The four winners then played in the final which was held at the Beach House Playa Hotel in Monte Carlo. Steve Davis had one of the best wins of his career in coming back from 1–4 to beat Jimmy White 5–4 in the final.

Year	Winner	Runner-up	Score
1988	Steve Davis	Jimmy White	5–4

Highest break
136 Steve Davis

Continental Airlines London Masters

Played throughout the 1988–9 season at London's Café Royal. Each evening offered dinner-suited guests the benefits of top-class cuisine followed by top-class snooker. Eight invited players took part in a knockout tournament.

Year	Winner	Runner-up	Score
1989	Stephen Hendry	John Parrott	4–2

Highest break
89 Stephen Hendry

CHAPTER FIVE

The Great Rivalries

Snooker is no different to any other sport in arousing interest through its personal rivalries. Steve Davies versus Alex Higgins clashes were a major feature of the early 1980s, so were the Steve Davis–Terry Griffiths matches. Today it is Davis versus the young pretender, Stephen Hendry. But days gone by also had their rivalries, none greater than the clashes between Ray Reardon and John Spencer. This chapter looks at some of the great snooker rivalries over the past 20 years. The players concerned have obviously met each other in matches other than those listed. For example, Steve Davis and Stephen Hendry have twice met in a series of exhibition challenge matches. These are not included, nor are competitive meetings in matches of less than eight frames. (* Indicates a ranking tournament.)

Ray Reardon versus John Spencer

When Ray Reardon and John Spencer were drawn together in the pre-televised stage of the 1988 Fidelity International it was a nostalgic reunion for two men who played an important role in snooker's revival in the late-sixties/early-seventies. Spencer won that particular battle to keep his nose in front in their personal battles. Surprisingly, despite dominating snooker for so long in the 1970s, they never met in the world championship final although they met in the semi-final stage three times.

1970	World Championship (semi-final)	Reardon won 37–33
1971	World Championship (semi-final)	Spencer won 34–15
1973	World Championship (semi-final)	Reardon won 23–22
1975	Norwich Union Open (final)	Spencer won 10–9
1975	Benson and Hedges Masters (final)	Spencer won 9–8
1975	World Championship (quarter-final)	Reardon won 19–17
1977	*Embassy World Championship (quarter-final)	Spencer won 13–6
1979	Forward Chemicals Tournament (final)	Reardon won 9–6
1981	Benson and Hedges Masters (quarter-final)	Spencer won 5–1
1981	*Embassy World Championship (2nd round)	Reardon won 13–11
1982	Highland Masters (final)	Reardon won 11–4
1983	Lada Classic (1st round)	Spencer won 5–3
1988	*Fidelity Unit Trusts International (3rd round)	Spencer won 5–4

The Reardon–Spencer rivalry is one of the oldest in the modern game.

113

Dennis Taylor versus Cliff Thorburn

Taylor and Thorburn are good friends, and are both members of the Barry Hearn Matchroom team. Their rivalry goes back to 1973 when they played each other in the world championship. For both of them it was their debut match in the

championship. As far as all the rivalries in this chapter go, these two are the most evenly matched; Taylor has a slight advantage with nine wins to Thorburn's eight.

1973	World Championship (1st round)	Thorburn won 9–8
1977	*Embassy World Championship (semi-final)	Thorburn won 18–16
1979	Bombay International (round-robin)	Taylor won 6–5
1980	Bombay International (semi-final)	Thorburn won 6–4
1982	*Jameson International (2nd round)	Taylor won 5–2
1983	*Jameson International (2nd round)	Thorburn won 5–3
1984	Benson and Hedges Irish Masters (quarter-final)	Taylor won 5–2
1984	*Rothmans Grand Prix (final)	Taylor won 10–2
1985	Benson and Hedges Masters (1st round)	Thorburn won 5–3
1985	*Embassy World Championship (quarter-final)	Taylor won 13–5
1985	*Goya Matchroom Trophy (semi-final)	Thorburn won 9–5
1987	Benson and Hedges Masters (semi-final)	Taylor won 6–5
1987	Matchroom League	Taylor won 5–3
1987	Benson and Hedges Irish Masters (quarter-final)	Taylor won 5–1
1987	Lang Scottish Masters (1st round)	Thorburn won 5–2
1987	Labbatts Canadian Masters (semi-final)	Taylor won 8–5
1988	Matchroom League	Thorburn won 6–2

Steve Davis versus Alex Higgins

The rivalry between Steve Davis and Alex Higgins is well publicized, so is the fact that it is a long time since Higgins last beat Davis in a major tournament. It was Higgins who was on the receiving end in the 1980 Coral UK Cham-

pionship when Davis won his first major title. But Alex gained revenge in the same championship three years later when he won 16–15 after trailing 7–0, in one of snooker's finest-ever finals.

1980	*Embassy World Championship (quarter-final)	Higgins won 13–9
1980	Coral UK Championship (final)	Davis won 16–6
1981	*Embassy World Championship (2nd round)	Davis won 13–8
1981	Jameson International (semi-final)	Davis won 9–8
1981	Northern Ireland Classic (1st round)	Davis won 5–2
1982	Benson and Hedges Irish Masters (semi-final)	Davis won 6–2
1982	Langs Scottish Masters (final)	Davis won 9–4
1983	*Embassy World Championship (semi-final)	Davis won 16–5
1983	Langs Scottish Masters (semi-final)	Davis won 6–2
1983	Coral UK Championship (final)	Higgins won 16–15
1984	Benson and Hedges Irish Masters (semi-final)	Davis won 6–4
1984	Langs Scottish Masters (semi-final)	Davis won 6–4
1984	*Jameson International (quarter-final)	Davis won 5–1
1984	*Coral UK Open (final)	Davis won 16–8
1985	*Mercantile Credit Classic (2nd round)	Davis won 5–2
1985	Benson and Hedges Masters (1st round)	Higgins won 5–4
1985	Benson and Hedges Irish Masters (semi-final)	Higgins won 6–2
1985	*Rothmans Grand Prix (5th round)	Davis won 5–0
1985	Kit Kat Break for Champions (semi-final)	Davis won 6–1

1986	*Dulux British Open (semi-final)	Davis	won	9–3
1986	BCE Canadian Masters (semi-final)	Davis	won	8–2
1986	*Tennents UK Open (semi-final)	Davis	won	9–3
1987	*Tennents UK Open (5th round)	Davis	won	9–2
1988	*Mercantile Credit Classic (5th round)	Davis	won	5–0
1988	Benson and Hedges Irish Masters (semi-final)	Davis	won	6–2
1988	*Rothmans Grand Prix (final)	Davis	won	10–6
1989	*Anglian British Open (4th round)	Davis	won	5–0
1989	Matchroom League	Davis	won	5–3

Steve Davis versus Terry Griffiths

Steve Davis and Terry Griffiths have been teammates and rivals for a long time. In the early 1980s they seemed to meet in most tournaments, and at that time there was nothing like the Davis monopoly of their matches as there is today.

Their meeting in the 1988 Embassy World Championship final revived memories of those confrontations at the beginning of the decade. But consistent with recent results, Davis was the winner again.

1980	*Embassy World Championship (2nd round)	Davis	won	13–10
1980	Coral UK Championship (semi-final)	Davis	won	9–0
1981	*Embassy World Championship (quarter-final)	Davis	won	13–9
1981	Northern Ireland Classic (semi-final)	Davis	won	9–6
1981	*Coral UK Championship (final)	Davis	won	16–3
1982	Lada Classic (final)	Griffiths	won	9–8
1982	Benson and Hedges Masters (final)	Davis	won	9–5
1982	Yamaha International Masters (final)	Davis	won	9–7
1982	Benson and Hedges Irish Masters (final)	Griffiths	won	9–5
1982	Coral UK Championship (quarter-final)	Griffiths	won	9–6
1983	Tolly Cobbold Classic (final)	Davis	won	7–5
1983	Benson and Hedges Irish Masters (semi-final)	Davis	won	6–2
1984	*Lada Classic (quarter-final)	Davis	won	5–4
1984	Benson and Hedges Irish Masters (final)	Davis	won	9–1
1984	*Embassy World Championship (quarter-final)	Davis	won	13–10
1985	*Embassy World Championship (quarter-final)	Davis	won	13–6
1985	BCE Canadian Masters (1st round)	Davis	won	5–4
1986	BCE Belgian Classic (1st round)	Griffiths	won	5–2
1986	Matchroom Trophy (semi-final)	Davis	won	6–2
1986	*Rothmans Grand Prix (5th round)	Davis	won	5–2
1987	Matchroom League		drew	4–4
1987	Benson and Hedges Irish Masters (semi-final)	Davis	won	6–2
1987	*Embassy World Championship (quarter-final)	Davis	won	13–5
1988	Matchroom League		drew	4–4
1988	Benson and Hedges Masters (quarter-final)	Davis	won	5–0
1988	*Embassy World Championship (final)	Davis	won	18–11
1988	*Rothmans Grand Prix (semi-final)	Davis	won	5–3
1988	*BCE Canadian Masters (quarter-final)	Davis	won	5–3
1989	Matchroom League	Davis	won	7–1

Steve Davis.

Steve Davis versus Jimmy White

Although Steve Davis has had the better of their meetings, Jimmy White is one player who goes into a match with Davis on near-level terms. When White first beat Davis in the 1981 Langs Scottish Masters he was only 19 and the youngest winner of a senior professional tournament. Since then the two men have been engaged in some memorable matches and none was finer than the 1984 Embassy World Championship, and 1987 Mercantile and Tennents UK finals, all of which were won by Davis. But Steve will perhaps savour his 5–4 win over Jimmy in the 1988 Norwich Union Grand Prix final at Monte Carlo as one of his best over Jimmy when he came back from the brink of defeat at 1–4 to clinch victory.

1981	*Embassy World Championship (1st round)	Davis won 10–8
1981	Langs Scottish Masters (semi-final)	White won 6–5
1981	Northern Ireland Classic (final)	White won 11–9
1981	Coral UK Championship (semi-final)	Davis won 9–0
1983	Coral UK Championship (semi-final)	Davis won 9–4
1984	*Embassy World Championship (final)	Davis won 18–16
1984	Langs Scottish Masters (final)	Davis won 9–4
1984	*Coral UK Open (quarter-final)	Davis won 9–4
1985	*Goya Matchroom Trophy (quarter-final)	White won 5–3
1985	*Coral UK Open (semi-final)	Davis won 9–5
1986	*Mercantile Credit Classic (quarter-final)	White won 5–2
1986	Benson and Hedges Masters (semi-final)	White won 6–3
1986	*Embassy World Championship (quarter-final)	Davis won 13–5
1986	BCE Canadian Masters (1st round)	Davis won 5–2
1987	*Mercantile Credit Classic (final)	Davis won 13–12
1987	Matchroom League	White won 5–3
1987	*Embassy World Championship (semi-final)	Davis won 16–11
1987	*Tennents UK Open (final)	Davis won 16–14
1988	Matchroom League	Davis won 8–0
1988	Matchroom Championship (semi-final)	Davis won 6–4
1988	*Fidelity Unit Trusts International (final)	Davis won 12–6
1988	*BCE Canadian Masters (final)	White won 9–4
1988	Everest World Match-Play (semi-final)	Davis won 9–5
1988	Norwich Union Grand Prix (final)	Davis won 5–4
1989	Matchroom League	White won 6–2

Terry Griffiths versus Cliff Thorburn

For a match full of true grit and determination then a meeting between Terry Griffiths and Cliff Thorburn will delight the purists. They have engaged in some long and tough matches over the years but, surprisingly, Griffiths has not beaten Thorburn in a major tournament since the 1982 Lada. It was during their match in the 2nd round of the 1983 Embassy that Cliff compiled the first 147 maximum break in the world championship. The match went on until 3.51 a.m., the latest finish of a world championship match.

1979	Canadian National Exhibition Open (final)	Thorburn won 17–16
1980	Champion of Champions (round-robin)	Griffiths won 8–1
1980	Benson and Hedges Masters (quarter-final)	Griffiths won 5–3
1981	Benson and Hedges Irish Masters (semi-final)	Griffiths won 6–5
1982	Lada Classic (1st round)	Griffiths won 5–1
1983	Benson and Hedges Masters (quarter-final)	Thorburn won 5–3
1983	*Embassy World Championship (2nd round)	Thorburn won 13–12
1983	Langs Scottish Masters (1st round)	Thorburn won 5–1
1984	*Jameson International (semi-final)	Thorburn won 9–8
1985	*Mecantile Credit Classic (quarter-final)	Thorburn won 5–4
1985	*Rothmans Grand Prix (quarter-final)	Thorburn won 5–1
1986	Benson and Hedges Masters (quarter-final)	Thorburn won 5–2
1986	*BCE International (5th round)	Thorburn won 5–4
1987	Matchroom League	Griffiths won 6–2
1988	Matchroom League	drew 4–4
1989	Matchroom League	Griffiths won 5–3

Alex Higgins versus Jimmy White

The Whirlwind and the Hurricane – what a lethal combination. When these two play, don't blink you might miss something. Higgins and White are two of the biggest attractions in snooker because their outward and often brash approach to the game is exciting to watch. Sadly, the two men have not been drawn together as often as the public would have liked. But when they have, they have produced some exhilarating snooker. Their first meeting was perhaps the best match between the two when Higgins won the Embassy World Championship semi-final 16–15 after coming back from 13–15 to reach the final. After building a 3–0 lead in the series, Higgins hasn't beaten White since the 1983 Langs Scottish Masters.

Alex Higgins.

1982	*Embassy World Championship (semi-final)	Higgins won 16–15
1983	Benson and Hedges Irish Masters (quarter-final)	Higgins won 5–2
1983	Langs Scottish Masters (1st round)	Higgins won 5–3
1985	Benson and Hedges Irish Masters (final)	White won 9–5
1985	Carlsberg Challenge (final)	White won 8–3
1985	Langs Scottish Masters (1st round)	White won 5–0
1985	*Coral UK Open (5th round)	White won 9–6
1986	Carlsberg Challenge (1st round)	White won 5–1
1987	Langs Scottish Masters (1st round)	White won 5–3
1989	Matchroom League	White won 5–3

Steve Davis versus Stephen Hendry

Many men have posed a threat to Steve Davis in recent years, but most have failed to dislodge him as champion. However, Stephen Hendry has proved to be the exception and has started getting the measure of Davis. After soundly beating Davis in the semi-final of the 1988 Tennents, Hendry followed up with another semi-final win in the Benson and Hedges Masters at Wembley, and again in the Benson and Hedges Irish Masters a couple of months later. But Davis reasserted his superiority with an emphatic 16–9 win in the 1989 world championship semi-final at The Crucible.

1987	*Mercantile Credit Classic (semi-final)	Davis won 9–3
1987	Hong Kong Masters (final)	Davis won 9–3
1987	*Rothmans Grand Prix (5th round)	Hendry won 5–2
1988	Matchroom League	drew 4–4
1988	*Mercantile Credit Classic (quarter-final)	Davis won 5–3
1988	*BCE Canadian Masters (semi-final)	Davis won 9–5
1988	*Tennents UK Championship (semi-final)	Hendry won 9–3
1989	Benson and Hedges Masters (semi-final)	Hendry won 6–3
1989	Benson and Hedges Irish Masters (semi-final)	Hendry won 6–4
1989	Matchroom League	Davis won 5–3
1989	*Embassy World Championship (semi-final)	Davis won 16–9

The World Professional Billiards and Snooker Association

The boardroom at the WPBSA's Bristol headquarters.

The World Professional Billiards and Snooker Association is the governing body of all professional players of both billiards and snooker.

It was formed out of the old Professional Billiard Players Association which was formed on 26 July 1946 with Joe Davis as its first chairman. The Association fell into disuse as the professional game declined in the 1950s and 1960s and it was not until April 1968 that it was formally revived.

Following a meeting at the Berners Hotel, London, the old Association was restructured and renamed as the World Professional Billiards and Snooker Association (WPBSA). Mike Green was appointed the Association's first secretary and membership consisted of just eight professionals. Today there are in excess of 140 members. Turnover in the Association's first season was approximately £20; in 1970-1 it was still only a meagre £24 17s 11d. Today it is more than £5 million.

The WPBSA was formed for the purpose of organizing all professional events and to act as the disciplinary body of the professional game. Today it has its own promotions company, WPBSA Promotions Ltd, which was formed

as a wholly-owned subsidiary in 1983.

Of the 140-plus members, only 128 are classed as tournament-playing members. The rest are classed as non-tournament members and are eligible only to compete in the Embassy World Championship. They can, however, take the place of tournament players in other WPBSA events if any of the 128 tournament players withdraw or are not eligible.

At one time, membership to the WPBSA was by application when playing and disciplinary records of the individual were prime considerations before acceptance, or rejection. Today, a series of pro-ticket events gives the leading non-professional players the opportunity to gain professional status and thus become eligible to take part in the ranking events.

Mike Green retired as the Association's secretary in 1984 and was replaced by Martyn Blake. At the same time the Association's offices moved from Birmingham to Bristol. Rex Williams was chairman of the Association for 13 years until resigning in 1987 when he was replaced by fellow professional John Virgo.

John Virgo (centre), the WPBSA chairman with fellow committee members Ian Doyle (Stephen Hendry's manager, left) and Ray Reardon, during a press conference.

CHAPTER SIX

World Rankings

A ranking system was first introduced by the WPBSA in 1976. Its purpose was to seed players in the world championships, although the previous year's winner and runner-up were automatically seeded 1 and 2.

To arrive at the first ranking table a player's performances since the 1974 world championship were calculated. This means, effectively, the first ranking event was the 1974 world championship, even if the players were not aware of it at the time.

The first ranking system gave five points to the world champion, four to the runner-up, three to each losing semi-finalist and so on, down to one point for players who lost in the last 16. This system remained unaltered until 1982 when two more tournaments, the Jameson International

and Professional Players' Tournament, were designated ranking events. At the end of the 1982–3 season the rankings were calculated on the previous three years' world championship performances (as before) plus performances from the two new events. The points for the 1983 world championship, however, carried double points. As the two new events stood the test of time their past three years' results were incorporated into the ranking points.

The number of ranking tournaments was increased to six in the 1984–5 season and at the end of that season the points system was

When the ranking system was first introduced in 1976 Welshman Ray Reardon was number one.

restructured into its present format which is as follows:

Losers in round 1	no. of frames won
Losers in round 2	1 'A' point
Losers in round 3	1 merit point
Losers in round 4 (last 32)	1 ranking point
Losers in round 5 (last 16)	2 ranking points
Losers in quarter-final	3 ranking points
Losers in semi-final	4 ranking points
Beaten finalist	5 ranking points
Winner	6 ranking points

However, the points allocation is different for the world championship, and is as follows:

Losers in pre-preliminary rounds	no. of frames won
Losers in round 1	1 'A' point
Losers in round 2	1 merit point
Losers in round 3	2 merit points
Losers in round 4 (last 32)	1 ranking point or 2 merit points*
Losers in round 5 (last 16)	2 ranking points
Losers in quarter-final	4 ranking points
Losers in semi-final	6 ranking points
Beaten finalist	8 ranking points
Winner	10 ranking points

* Players who had to qualify for this stage will receive the ranking point if eliminated. But players exempt to this stage receive two merit points if beaten.

To allow new professionals more chance of making an impact on the ranking list, the previous two years only of all ranking tournaments are now included (as opposed to three) and at the end of each season a new ranking list is devised. The order of preference when drawing up the list takes the following into account:

1 Ranking points
2 Merit points
3 'A' points
4 Frames won

If players are level on ranking points then it shall be decided by the player with the most merit points in the last season. If still level then it shall be by the one with the most 'A' points in the latest campaign, and down to the one with most frames won. If still level, then performances from the last world championship are taken into account. And if still level, the ranking tournament immediately before that, and so on.

The number of qualifying tournaments was increased to eight in 1988-9 with the addition of the first two overseas ranking tournaments, the BCE Canadian Masters and ICI European Open. The number will be increased again in 1989-90 with the addition of further overseas tournaments, to the ever-increasing fixture list, in Hong Kong, Thailand, and Dubai.

The ranking list is drawn up immediately after each world championship and remains in force throughout the following season. Players ranked 1-32 are exempt until the last qualifying round of each ranking tournament (world championship excepted), players ranked 33-64 are exempt until the previous round, while players ranked 65-128 come into a tournament at the first preliminary round. In the world championship, players ranked 1-16 are exempt until The Crucible stage of the tournament.

Technically, the ranking list alters as the season progresses. Provisional lists are drawn up after each tournament during the season. This is done because all points obtained two seasons earlier will be wiped out during the current season and new points are constantly added, although the new table does not come into force until after the world championship.

In all ranking tournaments the defending champion is seeded number one and the remainder of the players are seeded according to their ranking position.

The following is a list of the all-important top 16 in the rankings year-by-year since their introduction in 1976, with previous ranking in brackets from 1977 and number of points:

1976				1977				1978			
1	Ray Reardon (Wal)	15		1	(1)	Ray Reardon (Wal)	12		1	(1)	Ray Reardon (Wal)	12
2	Alex Higgins (Ire)	9		2	(8)	John Spencer (Eng)	9		2	(10)	Perrie Mans (SAf)	8
3	Eddie Charlton (Aus)	8		3	(3)	Eddie Charlton (Aus)	9		3	(3)	Eddie Charlton (Aus)	8
4	Fred Davis (Eng)	6		4	(9)	Dennis Taylor (Ire)	8		4	(2)	John Spencer (Eng)	8
5	Graham Miles (Eng)	6		5	(2)	Alex Higgins (Ire)	8		5	(6)	Cliff Thorburn (Can)	7
6	Rex Williams (Eng)	6		6	(13)	Cliff Thorburn (Can)	7		6	(9)	Fred Davis (Eng)	6
7	Perrie Mans (SAf)	5		7	(15)	John Pulman (Eng)	5		7	(5)	Alex Higgins (Ire)	6
8	John Spencer (Eng)	5		8	(5)	Graham Miles (Eng)	4		8	(4)	Dennis Taylor (Ire)	6
9	Dennis Taylor (Ire)	5		9	(4)	Fred Davis (Eng)	4		9	(8)	Graham Miles (Eng)	5
10	Gary Owen (Eng)	4		10	(7)	Perrie Mans (SAf)	4		10	(7)	John Pulman (Eng)	5
11	John Dunning (Eng)	4		11	(6)	Rex Williams (Eng)	4		11	(19)	Patsy Fagan (RoI)	3
12	Jim Meadowcroft (Eng)	3		12	(16)	David Taylor (Eng)	3		12	(17)	Bill Werbeniuk (Can)	3
13	Cliff Thorburn (Can)	3		13	(10)	Gary Owen (Eng)	3		13	(12)	David Taylor (Eng)	3
14	Bill Werbeniuk (Can)	3		14	(—)	Doug Mountjoy (Wal)	2		14	(14)	Doug Mountjoy (Wal)	3
15	John Pulman (Eng)	3		15	(12)	Jim Meadowcroft (Eng)	2		15	(20)	Willie Thorne (Eng)	2
16	David Taylor (Eng)	2		16	(11)	John Dunning (Eng)	2		16	(15)	Jim Meadowcroft (Eng)	2
(Number of qualifying events: 1)				(Number of qualifying events: 1)				(Number of qualifying events: 1)			

World Rankings

It's all go being the world's number one player.

1982			
1	(4)	Ray Reardon (Wal)	9
2	(11)	Alex Higgins (Ire)	8*
3	(1)	Cliff Thorburn (Can)	8
4	(2)	Steve Davis (Eng)	7
5	(8)	Eddie Charlton (Aus)	6
6	(10)	Kirk Stevens (Can)	6
7	(6)	Doug Mountjoy (Wal)	6
8	(7)	David Taylor (Eng)	5
9	(9)	Bill Werbeniuk (Can)	4
10	(21)	Jimmy White (Eng)	3
11	(15)	Perrie Mans (SAf)	3
12	(14)	John Spencer (Eng)	3
13	(5)	Dennis Taylor (Ire)	3
14	(3)	Terry Griffiths (Wal)	3
15	(20)	Tony Knowles (Eng)	2
16	(22)	Willie Thorne (Eng)	2

(Number of qualifying events: 1)

* Minus 2 points deducted 1980–1 season

1983			
1	(4)	Steve Davis (Eng)	17
2	(1)	Ray Reardon (Wal)	15
3	(3)	Cliff Thorburn (Can)	13
4	(15)	Tony Knowles (Eng)	13
5	(2)	Alex Higgins (Ire)	11*
6	(5)	Eddie Charlton (Aus)	11
7	(6)	Kirk Stevens (Can)	10
8	(9)	Bill Werbeniuk (Can)	10
9	(14)	Terry Griffiths (Wal)	8
10	(8)	David Taylor (Eng)	8
11	(10)	Jimmy White (Eng)	8
12	(7)	Doug Mountjoy (Wal)	7
13	(13)	Dennis Taylor (Ire)	7
14	(19)	John Virgo (Eng)	7
15	(24)	Tony Meo (Eng)	6
16	(12)	John Spencer (Eng)	6

(Number of qualifying events: 3)

* Minus 2 points deducted 1980–1 season

1984			
1	(1)	Steve Davis (Eng)	32
2	(4)	Tony Knowles (Eng)	21
3	(3)	Cliff Thorburn (Can)	20
4	(7)	Kirk Stevens (Can)	19
5	(2)	Ray Reardon (Wal)	18
6	(6)	Eddie Charlton (Aus)	18
7	(11)	Jimmy White (Eng)	17
8	(9)	Terry Griffiths (Wal)	16
9	(5)	Alex Higgins (Ire)	13
10	(15)	Tony Meo (Eng)	12
11	(13)	Dennis Taylor (Ire)	12
12	(18)	Willie Thorne (Eng)	11
13	(16)	John Spencer (Eng)	10
14	(8)	Bill Werbeniuk (Can)	10
15	(12)	Doug Mountjoy (Wal)	9
16	(10)	David Taylor (Eng)	8

(Number of qualifying events: 4)

Tony Knowles, who came so close to toppling Steve Davis from the no. 1 position in the mid-eighties.

World Rankings

1985			
1	(1)	Steve Davis (Eng)	59
2	(3)	Cliff Thorburn (Can)	36
3	(2)	Tony Knowles (Eng)	34
4	(11)	Dennis Taylor (Ire)	32
5	(4)	Kirk Stevens (Can)	29
6	(5)	Ray Reardon (Wal)	25
7	(7)	Jimmy White (Eng)	23
8	(8)	Terry Griffiths (Wal)	23
9	(9)	Alex Higgins (Ire)	20
10	(10)	Tony Meo (Eng)	19
11	(12)	Willie Thorne (Eng)	19
12	(6)	Eddie Charlton (Aus)	19
13	(17)	Silvino Francisco (SAf)	15
14	(16)	David Taylor (Eng)	13
15	(15)	Doug Mountjoy (Wal)	13
16	(19)	Joe Johnson (Eng)	11

(Number of qualifying events: 6)

1986			
1	(1)	Steve Davis (Eng)	59
2	(2)	Cliff Thorburn (Can)	41
3	(4)	Dennis Taylor (Ire)	35
4	(3)	Tony Knowles (Eng)	32
5	(7)	Jimmy White (Eng)	30
6	(9)	Alex Higgins (Ire)	27
7	(11)	Willie Thorne (Eng)	26
8	(16)	Joe Johnson (Eng)	25
9	(5)	Kirk Stevens (Can)	24
10	(8)	Terry Griffiths (Wal)	22
11	(10)	Tony Meo (Eng)	17
12	(13)	Silvino Francisco (SAf)	17
13	(23)	Neal Foulds (Eng)	15
14	(15)	Doug Mountjoy (Wal)	14
15	(6)	Ray Reardon (Wal)	13
16	(27)	Rex Williams (Eng)	12

(Number of qualifying events: 6)

1987			
1	(1)	Steve Davis (Eng)	61
2	(5)	Jimmy White (Eng)	46
3	(13)	Neal Foulds (Eng)	38
4	(2)	Cliff Thorburn (Can)	38
5	(8)	Joe Johnson (Eng)	33
6	(10)	Terry Griffiths (Wal)	30
7	(4)	Tony Knowles (Eng)	29
8	(3)	Dennis Taylor (Ire)	25
9	(6)	Alex Higgins (Ire)	25
10	(12)	Silvino Francisco (SAf)	22
11	(7)	Willie Thorne (Eng)	22
12	(16)	Rex Williams (Eng)	20
13	(17)	John Parrott (Eng)	18
14	(14)	Doug Mountjoy (Wal)	17
15	(29)	Dean Reynolds (Eng)	16
16	(27)	Mike Hallett (Eng)	16

(Number of qualifying events: 6)

Joe Johnson and Steve Davis shake hands before the start of the 1987 world championship. Davis 'owed Johnson one' for his defeat a year earlier and he got his revenge with an 18–14 win.

1988

1	(1)	Steve Davis (Eng)	59
2	(2)	Jimmy White (Eng)	44
3	(3)	Neal Foulds (Eng)	34
4	(23)	Stephen Hendry (Sco)	33
5	(6)	Terry Griffiths (Wal)	33
6	(4)	Cliff Thorburn (Can)	33*
7	(13)	John Parrott (Eng)	30
8	(7)	Tony Knowles (Eng)	28
9	(16)	Mike Hallett (Eng)	24
10	(8)	Dennis Taylor (Ire)	23
11	(5)	Joe Johnson (Eng)	23
12	(10)	Silvino Francisco (SAf)	22
13	(11)	Willie Thorne (Eng)	19
14	(18)	Peter Francisco (SAf)	18
15	(19)	John Virgo (Eng)	17
16	(17)	Cliff Wilson (Wal)	16

(Number of qualifying events: 6)

* 2 points deducted

1989

1	(1)	Steve Davis (Eng)	64
2	(7)	John Parrott (Eng)	48
3	(4)	Stephen Hendry (Sco)	46
4	(2)	Jimmy White (Eng)	43
5	(5)	Terry Griffiths (Wal)	39
6	(9)	Mike Hallett (Eng)	33
7	(6)	Cliff Thorburn (Can)	33*
8	(10)	Dennis Taylor (Ire)	29
9	(13)	Willie Thorne (Eng)	28
10	(24)	Doug Mountjoy (Wal)	25
11	(11)	Joe Johnson (Eng)	24
12	(8)	Tony Knowles (Eng)	24
13	(15)	John Virgo (Eng)	22
14	(31)	Tony Meo (Eng)	20
15	(22)	Dean Reynolds (Eng)	19
16	(32)	Steve James (Eng)	17

(Number of qualifying events: 8)

* Minus 2 points deducted 1987–8 season

After a couple of 'oh-so-near' years, it eventually came good for Liverpool's John Parrott in 1988–9.

Rankings Miscellany

Most seasons in top-16

(Maximum: 14)
14 Dennis Taylor, Cliff Thorburn
12 Alex Higgins, Doug Mountjoy
11 Terry Griffiths, Ray Reardon
10 Eddie Charlton, Steve Davis, David Taylor
9   John Spencer

New top-16 players

Since the first ranking list in 1976 the following players have subsequently earned a place in, or returned to the top-16:

1977 Doug Mountjoy
1978 Bill Werbeniuk*, Patsy Fagan, Willie Thorne
1979 Terry Griffiths, John Virgo
1980 Kirk Stevens, Steve Davis
1981 None
1982 Jimmy White, Tony Knowles, Willie Thorne*
1983 Tony Meo, John Virgo*
1984 Willie Thorne*
1985 Silvino Francisco, Joe Johnson
1986 Rex Williams*, Neal Foulds
1987 John Parrott, Dean Reynolds, Mike Hallett
1988 Stephen Hendry, Peter Francisco, Cliff Wilson, John Virgo*
1989 Doug Mountjoy*, Tony Meo*, Dean Reynolds*, Steve James

* Indicates a player returned to the top-16.

For ungentlemanly conduct at the Herringthorpe Leisure Centre on 24 February 1981 Alex Higgins had two points deducted from him. Had

he not had those points deducted, which were carried forward (because the ranking system at that time took into account performances in the three previous seasons), Higgins would have topped the rankings in 1982. As it is, he has never been number one.

When Stephen Hendry first came into the top-16 in 1988 he entered at No. 4, the highest position by a top-16 debutant. Terry Griffiths (8th in 1979) is the only other player to come into the top-16 in the first eight.

Rankings (Top-16 Summary)

	76	77	78	79	80	81	82	83	84	85	86	87	88	89
Ray Reardon	1	1	1	1	1	4	1	2	5	6	15	–	–	–
Alex Higgins	2	5	7	11	4	11	2	5	9	9	6	9	–	–
Eddie Charlton	3	3	3	3	3	8	5	6	6	12	–	–	–	–
Fred Davis	4	9	6	6	8	12	–	–	–	–	–	–	–	–
Graham Miles	5	8	9	9	16	16	–	–	–	–	–	–	–	–
Rex Williams	6	11	–	–	–	–	–	–	–	–	16	12	–	–
Perrie Mans	7	10	2	7	7	15	11	–	–	–	–	–	–	–
John Spencer	8	2	4	4	15	14	12	16	13	–	–	–	–	–
Dennis Taylor	9	4	8	2	6	5	13	13	11	4	3	8	10	8
Gary Owen	10	13	–	–	–	–	–	–	–	–	–	–	–	–
John Dunning	11	16	–	–	–	–	–	–	–	–	–	–	–	–
Jim Meadowcroft	12	15	16	–	–	–	–	–	–	–	–	–	–	–
Cliff Thorburn	13	6	5	5	2	1	3	3	3	2	2	4	6	7
Bill Werbeniuk	14	–	12	12	10	9	9	8	14	–	–	–	–	–
John Pulman	15	7	10	14	–	–	–	–	–	–	–	–	–	–
David Taylor	16	12	13	15	9	7	8	10	16	14	–	–	–	–
Doug Mountjoy	–	14	14	13	14	6	7	12	15	15	14	14	–	10
Patsy Fagan	–	–	11	16	–	–	–	–	–	–	–	–	–	–
Willie Thorne	–	–	15	–	–	–	16	–	12	11	7	11	13	9
Terry Griffiths	–	–	–	8	5	3	14	9	8	8	10	6	5	5
John Virgo	–	–	–	10	12	13	–	14	–	–	–	–	15	13
Kirk Stevens	–	–	–	–	11	10	6	7	4	5	9	–	–	–
Steve Davis	–	–	–	–	13	2	4	1	1	1	1	1	1	1
Jimmy White	–	–	–	–	–	–	10	11	7	7	5	2	2	4
Tony Knowles	–	–	–	–	–	–	15	4	2	3	4	7	8	12
Tony Meo	–	–	–	–	–	–	–	15	10	10	11	–	–	14
Silvino Francisco	–	–	–	–	–	–	–	–	–	13	12	10	12	–
Joe Johnson	–	–	–	–	–	–	–	–	–	16	8	5	11	11
Neal Foulds	–	–	–	–	–	–	–	–	–	–	13	3	3	–
John Parrott	–	–	–	–	–	–	–	–	–	–	–	13	7	2
Dean Reynolds	–	–	–	–	–	–	–	–	–	–	–	15	–	15
Mike Hallett	–	–	–	–	–	–	–	–	–	–	–	16	9	6
Stephen Hendry	–	–	–	–	–	–	–	–	–	–	–	–	4	3
Peter Francisco	–	–	–	–	–	–	–	–	–	–	–	–	14	–
Cliff Wilson	–	–	–	–	–	–	–	–	–	–	–	–	16	–
Steve James	–	–	–	–	–	–	–	–	–	–	–	–	–	16

Welshman Wayne Jones was the surprise finalist in the 1989 Mercantile Credit Classic and performances like that will surely make him a top-16 player in the near future.

CHAPTER SEVEN

The Non-professional Game

As from 1 July 1973 all snooker players who were not professionals ceased to be called amateurs. That move followed a resolution passed by the then world governing body of the amateur game, the Billiards and Snooker Control Council (B & SCC), the previous November. It ruled that players who were not professionals should be called non-professionals, although major events such as the English championship and the world championship are still affectionately called the 'English Amateur' and 'World Amateur' championships.

In the years before the arrival of Joe Davis in the 1920s, the amateur game was considerably stronger than the professional game, but it still had to take second place to the more popular billiards. The English Amateur Snooker Championship dates to 1916 and makes it the oldest established snooker tournament in the world.

In the late-fifties and early-sixties, when the professional game went through a slump, the amateur game continued to thrive and the English Amateur continued to remain a prestigious event.

There is no restriction on the amount of prize money a non-professional can win. Pro-am events are very popular and are often won by the non-professional players who receive a start from their professional opponents.

Prior to 1986 a non-professional player had to apply to the WPBSA for acceptance as a professional. But since then a series of pro-ticket events has been introduced. This is a series of tournaments which can lead to any non-professional gaining membership to the WPBSA.

The B & SCC was for a long time regarded as the world governing body of both the professional and amateur game. It has long since lost its control of the professional game, and in recent years it has lost its title as world governing body of the non-professional game. That title now belongs to the International Billiards and Snooker Federation (IBSF).

The B & SCC was formed following a meeting on 31 January 1885 when professional billiards players and traders decided to form an association, which they called the Billiards Association. One of their prime functions was to formulate the rules of billiards. The rules of snooker were formulated in 1900. The Billiards Control Club was founded in 1908 and its task was to organize championship events. The Control Club and Association merged in 1919 to form the Billiards Association and Control Club. In 1971 the name was changed to its present style, thus incorporating the word 'snooker' in its title for the first time.

The IBSF was formed in 1971. It was originally called the World Billiards and Snooker Council but changed to its present name in 1973. It was formed by members who were not happy that the B & SCC should be responsible for the game at both English and international level, and their prime function was to take over the running of

Stan Brooke, chairman of the Billiards and Snooker Control Council (B&SCC) which is based in Leeds.

the world amateur championships of both billiards and snooker. The world amateur snooker championships had been in existence since 1963.

Since its formation the IBSF has gradually had a bigger say in the running of the sport at international level and in 1984 became the world governing body. The B & SCC is responsible only for the game in England. However, the IBSF has agreed that it will make no changes to the rules of snooker without consultation with the B & SCC which remains the rule maker of the game at both non-professional and professional level.

In 1988 the IBSF deleted the word 'amateur' from its constitution and formed its own promotions company, World Snooker Promotions Ltd with the aim of promoting more events worldwide. It will also encourage entries from WPBSA members as well as non-professionals; a move that is the first step towards making snooker 'open'. From 1989 the world amateur championship will be called the IBSF World Championship.

World Amateur Championship

Inaugurated in 1963, 37 years after its billiards counterpart, the World Amateur Championships are now held every year. They were originally held three years apart and then biennially until becoming an annual event in 1985. The championships are staged in a different country each year as predecided by the IBSF, which organizes the championships.

Each member nation of the IBSF, and there are currently 35, is entitled to send two players to the championship, which does not offer any prize money. The players are split into eight groups and they play each other once within each group. The top two in each group then take part in a knockout competition.

In the first two championships there were only single groups and the player at the head of the table at the end of the round-robin series was declared champion. In 1968 there were two groups and two from each contested two semi-finals and a final. In 1970, however, the two group winners only met in the final. Between 1974 and 1986 the knockout stage of the competition started at the quarter-finals but since 1987 there has been a pre-quarter-final knockout stage involving 16 players.

1963 Calcutta, India

1 Gary Owen (Eng)
2 Frank Harris (Aus)
3 Mohammed Lafir (Cey)
4 Tony Monteiro (Ind)
5 Wilson Jones (Ind)

Highest break
71 Gary Owen

1966 Karachi, Pakistan

1 Gary Owen (Eng)
2 John Spencer (Eng)
3 Bill Barrie (Aus)
4 Mohammed Lafir (Cey)
5 Bert Demarco (Sco)
6 Hamid Karim (Pak)

Highest break
118 Gary Owen

1968 Sydney, Australia

Semi-finals Max Williams (Aus) beat Jimmy van Rensburg (SAf) 8–7; David Taylor (Eng) beat Paddy Morgan (RoI) 8–3

Final David Taylor beat Max Williams 8–7

Highest break
96 David Taylor

1970 Edinburgh, Scotland

Final Jonathan Barron (Eng) beat Sid Hood (Eng) 11–7

Highest break
65 Jack Rogers (RoI)

1972 Cardiff, Wales

Semi-finals Ray Edmonds (Eng) beat Jonathan Barron (Eng) 8–6; Mannie Francisco (SAf) beat Arvind Savur (Ind) 8–7

Final Ray Edmonds beat Mannie Francisco 11–10

Highest break
101 Ray Edmonds

1974 Dublin, Ireland

Quarter-finals Ray Edmonds (Eng) beat Lou Condo (Aus) 4–3; Pascal Burke (RoI) beat Mohammed Lafir (Sri) 4–3; Eddie Sinclair (Sco) beat Winston Hill (NZ) 4–2; Geoff Thomas (Wal) beat Alwyn Lloyd (Wal) 4–2

Semi-finals Ray Edmonds beat Eddie Sinclair 8–4; Geoff Thomas beat Pascal Burke 8–2

Final Ray Edmonds beat Geoff Thomas 11–9

Highest break
104 Alwyn Lloyd

1976 Johannesburg, South Africa

Elimination match Terry Griffiths (Wal) beat Roy Andrewartha (Eng) 4–0

Quarter-finals Paul Mifsud (Mal) beat Ray Edmonds (Eng) 5–1; Silvino Francisco (SAf) beat Mannie Francisco (SAf)

5–1; Jimmy van Rensburg (SAf) beat Terry Griffiths 5–3; Doug Mountjoy (Wal) beat Ron Atkins (Aus) 5–1

Semi-finals Doug Mountjoy beat Silvino Francisco 8–2; Paul Mifsud beat Jimmy van Rensburg 8–4

Final Doug Mountjoy beat Paul Mifsud 11–1

Highest break
107   Doug Mountjoy

1978 Rabat, Malta
Elimination match Joe Grech (Mal) beat Dale Kwok (NZ) 4–0

Quarter-finals Kevin Burles (Aus) beat Bob Paquette (Can) 5–4; Kirk Stevens (Can) beat Paul Mifsud (Mal) 5–0; Joe Johnson (Eng) beat Alwyn Lloyd (Wal) 5–0; Cliff Wilson (Wal) beat Joe Grech 5–4

Semi-finals Cliff Wilson beat Kirk Stevens 8–2; Joe Johnson beat Kevin Burles 8–4

Final Cliff Wilson beat Joe Johnson 11–5

Highest break
101   Joe Johnson

1980 Launceston, Australia
Quarter-finals Jimmy White (Eng) beat Steve Newbury (Wal) 5–4; Paul Mifsud (Mal) beat John Campbell (Aus) 5–3; Ron Atkins (Aus) beat James Giannaros (Aus) 5–3; Arvind Savur (Ind) beat Alwyn Lloyd (Wal) 5–3

Semi-finals Jimmy White beat Paul Mifsud 8–6; Ron Atkins beat Arvind Savur 8–6

Final Jimmy White beat Ron Atkins 11–2

Highest break
128   Eugene Hughes (RoI)

1982 Calgary, Canada
Quarter-finals Terry Parsons (Wal) beat Malcolm Bradley (Eng) 5–0; Wayne Jones (Wal) beat Tony Kearney (RoI) 5–1; Joe Grech (Mal) beat Paddy Browne (RoI) 5–3; Jim Bear (Can) beat Paul Mifsud (Mal) 5–2

Semi-finals Terry Parsons beat Wayne Jones 8–5; Jim Bear beat Joe Grech 8–7

Final Terry Parsons beat Jim Bear 11–8

Highest break
103   Terry Parsons

1984 Dublin, Ireland
Quarter-finals O. B. (Omprakash) Agrawal (Ind) beat Dilwyn John (Wal) 5–4; Jon Wright (Eng) beat Alf Micallef (Mal) 5–1; Chris Archer (Eng) beat Tony Drago (Mal) 5–4; Terry Parsons (Wal) beat Glen Wilkinson (Aus) 5–2

One of the many top class players to come out of India, Omprakash 'OB' Agrawal, the 1984 world amateur snooker champion.

Semi-finals O. B. (Omprakash) Agrawal beat Jon Wright 8–5; Terry Parsons beat Chris Archer 8–3

Final O. B. (Omprakash) Agrawal beat Terry Parsons 11–7

Highest break
132   Tony Drago

1985 Blackpool, England
Quarter-finals Paul Mifsud (Mal) beat Terry Whitthread (Eng) 5–2; Joe Grech (Mal) beat Geet Sethi (Ind) 5–2; Robert Marshall (Eng) beat Jim McNellan (Sco) 5–1; Dilwyn John (Wal) beat Mark Bennett (Wal) 5–2

Semi-finals Paul Mifsud beat Joe Grech 8–4; Dilwyn John beat Robert Marshall 8–4

Final Paul Mifsud beat Dilwyn John 11–6

Highest break
115   Terry Whitthread

1986 Invercargill, New Zealand
Quarter-finals Paul Mifsud (Mal) beat Sanjay Sawant (Ind) 5–2; Geoff Grennan (Eng) beat John Griffiths (Wal) 5–2; Kerry Jones (Wal) beat Brady Gollan (Can) 5–1; Gay Burns (RoI) beat Michael Colquitt (IoM) 5–0

Semi-finals Paul Mifsud beat Gay Burns 8–5; Kerry Jones beat Geoff Grennan 8–7

Final Paul Mifsud beat Kerry Jones 11–9

Highest break
118   Geoff Miller (Aus)

1987 Bangalore, India
Pre-quarter finals Darren Morgan (Wal) beat Bjorn L'Orange (Nor) 5–0; James Wattana (Tha) beat Mario Lanoye (Bel) 5–3; Alain Robidoux (Can) beat Michael Henson (FRG) 5–1; Jim Allan (Sco) beat Peter Hawkes (Aus) 5–3; Paul Mifsud (Mal) beat Joseph Swail (Ire) 5–3; Geet Sethi (Ind) beat Jeffrey White (Can) 5–2; Joe Grech (Mal) beat Seamus McClarey (Ire) 5–0; Udon Kaimuk (Tha) beat James Long (RoI) 5–3

Quarter-finals Darren Morgan beat James Wattana 5–3; Alain Robidoux beat Jim Allan 5–4; Geet Sethi beat Paul Mifsud 5–4; Joe Grech beat Udon Kaimuk 5–4

Semi-finals Darren Morgan beat Alain Robidoux 8–5; Joe Grech beat Geet Sethi 8–3

Final Darren Morgan beat Joe Grech 11–4

Highest break
129   Alain Robidoux
129   James Wattana

1988 Sydney, Australia
Pre-quarter finals Ron Jones (Wal) beat Bjorn L'Orange (Nor) 5–0; Drew Henry (Sco) beat Paul Mifsud (Mal) 5–3; Brady Gollan (Can) beat Paul Doran (Ire) 5–0; Jim Allan (Sco) beat Nopadol Nopachorn (Tha) 5–2; James Wattana (Tha) beat Michael Colquitt (IoM) 5–0; Jason Peplow (Mal) beat Lim

Koon Guam (Sin) 5–0; Paul Dawkins (Wal) beat John Buckley (Rol) 5–1; Barry Pinches (Eng) beat Steve Ventham (Eng) 5–0

Quarter-finals James Wattana beat Ron Jones 5–0; Barry Pinches beat Brady Gollan 5–0; Jason Peplow beat Paul Dawkins 5–4; Drew Henry beat Jim Allan 5–1

Semi-finals James Wattana beat Jason Peplow 8–2; Barry Pinches beat Drew Henry 8–5

Final James Wattana beat Barry Pinches 11–8

Highest break
135 Brady Gollan
(Jason Peplow broke the old championship record with a break of 134 the day before Gollan's 135)

Records
Most wins
2 Ray Edmonds, Paul Mifsud, Gary Owen

Most finals
3 Paul Mifsud
2 Ray Edmonds, Gary Owen

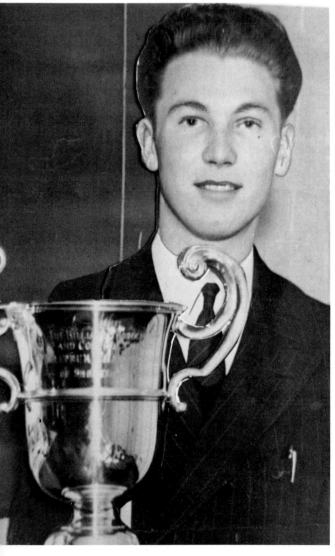

The Non-professional Game in England

English Amateur Championship

The most prestigious of all national championships, many of today's professionals have added their name to the list of illustrious winners.

First held in 1916 as the Amateur Snooker Championship, it became known as the English Amateur Championship in 1921 and is still affectionately known by that name even though the word 'amateur' no longer exists in snooker constitution.

In the early days of the championship, frame scores, rather than number of frame won, counted towards the eventual result. Today, with nearly 1000 hopefuls setting out on the long road to the final each spring, matches are played on a regionalized basis initially before the northern

● ● ● ● ● ● ● ● ● ● ● ● ● ● ●

JOHN PULMAN

Born: 12 December 1923, Teignmouth, Devon

As an unknown in 1946, John Pulman became the then youngest winner of the English amateur championship. He turned professional later that same year and soon established himself as capable of living with the 'big boys' of the day such as Joe and Fred Davis and Walter Donaldson.

He won the prestigious *News of the World* title in 1954 and 1957, and was twice runner-up in the Professional World Match-Play championship before eventually lifting the crown in 1957.

When the world championship was revived on a challenge basis in 1964 Pulman and Fred Davis met for the title; Pulman won 19–16. He successfully fended off subsequent challenges from Rex Williams (twice), Fred Davis (twice), Jimmy van Rensburg and Eddie Charlton.

Since the championship reverted to a knockout event Pulman has only once reached the final, in 1970, when he lost to Ray Reardon.

An expert coach, Pulman's experience is now used behind the microphone where he is a summarizer for ITV.

● ● ● ● ● ● ● ● ● ● ● ● ● ● ●

A very young looking John Pulman, aged 22. Seen here after winning the 1946 English Amateur title.

and southern champions eventually meet for the title at a varying venue each year.

The first trade sponsors of the championship, which is organized by the B & SCC, were table manufacturers BCE in 1983. The championship was sponsored by the WPBSA in 1985 and since 1986 BCE have again been the sponsors.

The Amateur Snooker Championship
Winners:

1916	Charles N. Jacques
1917	Charles N. Jacques
1918	'T. N. Palmer' (pseudonym)
1919	S. H. Fry
1920	A. R. Wisdom

English Amateur Championship
Finals:

1921	M. J. Vaughan	384–378	Sidney Fry
1922	Jack McGlynn	423–301	C. Cox, Jnr
1923	Walter Coupe	432–337	E. Forshall
1924	Walter Coupe	413–333	H. G. Olden
1925	Jack McGlynn	392–308	W. L. Crompton
1926	W. Nash	383–356	'F. T. Leaphard' (pseudonym used by Fred Morley)
1927	Ollie Jackson	4–2	A. W. Casey
1928	Pat Matthews	5–4	Frank Whittall
1929	Laurie Steeples	5–4	Frank Whittall
1930	Laurie Steeples	5–1	Frank Whittall
1931	Pat Matthews	5–4	Harry Kingsley
1932	W. E. Bach	5–3	Ollie Jackson
1933	E. Bedford	5–1	Albert Kershaw
1934	Charles Beavis	5–2	Pat Matthews
1935	Charles Beavis	5–3	Duggie Hindmarch
1936	Pat Matthews	5–3	Charles Beavis
1937	Kingsley Kennerley	6–3	W. H. Dennis
1938	Pat Matthews	6–1	Kingsley Kennerley
1939	Percy Bendon	6–4	Kingsley Kennerley
1940	Kingsley Kennerley	8–7	Albert Brown
1941–5	Not held		
1946	John Pulman	5–3	Albert Brown
1947	Chizzy Morris	5–1	Charley Kent
1948	Sidney Battye	6–4	Tommy Postlethwaite
1949	Tommy Gordon	6–4	Sydney Kilbank
1950	Alf Nolan	6–5	Gary Owen
1951	Rex Williams	6–1	Percy Bendon
1952	Charles Downey	6–1	Jack Allen
1953	Tommy Gordon	6–5	George Humphries
1954	Geoff Thompson	11–9	Cliff Wilson
1955	Maurice Parkin	11–7	Alf Nolan
1956	Tommy Gordon	11–9	Ray Reardon
1957	Ron Gross	11–6	Stan Haslam
1958	Marcus Owen	11–8	Jack Fitzmaurice
1959	Marcus Owen	11–5	Alan Barnett
1960	Ron Gross	11–4	John Price
1961	Alan Barnett	11–9	Ray Edmonds
1962	Ron Gross	11–9	Jonathan Barron
1963	Gary Owen	11–3	Ron Gross
1964	Ray Reardon	11–8	John Spencer
1965	Pat Houlihan	11–3	John Spencer
1966	John Spencer	11–5	Marcus Owen
1967	Marcus Owen	11–4	Sid Hood
1968	David Taylor	11–6	Chris Ross
1969	Ray Edmonds	11–9	Jonathan Barron
1970	Jonathan Barron	11–10	Sid Hood
1971	Jonathan Barron	11–9	Doug French
1972	Jonathan Barron	11–9	Ray Edmonds
1973	Marcus Owen	11–6	Ray Edmonds
1974	Ray Edmonds	11–7	Patsy Fagan
1975	Sid Hood	11–6	Willie Thorne
1976	Chris Ross	11–7	Roy Andrewartha
1977	Terry Griffiths	13–3	Sid Hood
1978	Terry Griffiths	13–6	Joe Johnson
1979	Jimmy White	13–10	Dave Martin
1980	Joe O'Boye	13–9	Dave Martin
1981	Vic Harris	13–9	George Wood
1982	Dave Chalmers	13–9	Malcolm Bradley
1983	Tony Jones	13–9	John Parrott
1984	Steve Longworth	13–8	Wayne Jones
1985	Terry Whitthread	13–4	Jim McNellan
1986	Anthony Harris	13–9	Geoff Grennan
1987	Mark Rowing	13–11	Sean Lanigan
1988	Barry Pinches	13–6	Craig Edwards
1989	Nigel Bond	13–11	Barry Pinches

Most wins
4 Pat Matthews, Marcus Owen
3 Jonathan Barron, Tommy Gordon, Ron Gross
2 Charles Beavis, Walter Coupe, Ray Edmonds, Terry Griffiths, Charles N. Jacques, Kingsley Kennerley, Jack McGlynn, Laurie Steeples

Most finals
5 Jonathan Barron, Ray Edmonds, Pat Matthews, Marcus Owen
4 Ron Gross, Sid Hood, Kingsley Kennerley
3 Charles Beavis, Tommy Gordon, John Spencer, Frank Whittall
2 Alan Barnett, Percy Bendon, Albert Brown, Walter Coupe, Terry Griffiths, Ollie Jackson, Charles N. Jacques, Jack McGlynn, Dave Martin, Alf Nolan, Gary Owen, Ray Reardon, Chris Ross, Laurie Steeples

Highest break
142 Jim Allan (1989)

British Isles Junior Championships

This championship was a stepping-stone for many of today's top professionals, and the winning of the under-16 or under-19 title is a major British honour.

An under-16 billiards championship has existed since 1922 when the first winner was Walter Donaldson. A boys snooker championship was inaugurated, thanks to enthusiasts from Scunthorpe, in 1944. The Humberside town staged the tournament until 1949 when it moved to a permanent home at Burroughes and Watts in London. However, there were two championships that year; one at Scunthorpe and one in London. That same year saw the introduction of the under-19 championship, also at Burroughes and Watts.

When Burroughes Hall closed in 1966 the

The Junior Championships have provided a springboard for many of to-day's top pros. These youngsters all competed in the championships in the 1950s. From left to right: Mark Wildman, Maurice Chapman, Rex Williams, Clive Everton (wearing glasses), Eddie Sinclair and Dennis Breese.

championships lapsed but were revived thanks largely to the efforts of Clive Everton in 1968. Since 1975 the championships have been organized by the B & SCC, and since 1988 have been sponsored by Dudley Snooker.

	Under-16	Under-19
1944	Gary Owen	—
1945	Ron Baker	—
1946	D. Thomas	—
1947	Maurice Knapp	—
1948	Rex Williams	—
1949	(S) Rex Williams	
	(L) D. Lewis	Aubrey Kemp
1950	Marcus Owen	Jack Carney
1951	Marcus Owen	Rex Williams
1952	Mark Wildman	Cliff Wilson
1953	J. Board	Cliff Wilson
1954	David Bond	Mark Wildman
1955	Peter Shelley	W. McGivern
1956	Anthony Hart	Eddie Sinclair
1957	Peter Shelley	Harry Burns
1958	David Bend	Wally West
1959	James Doyle	David Root
1960	Norwood Cripps	David Bend
1961	Not held	Ian Rees
1962	John Virgo	Tony Matthews
1963	John Hollis	Tony Matthews
1964	David Clinton	Joe Fisher
1965	John Maugham	John Virgo
1966	John Terry	John Hollis
1967	Not held	
1968	Edward Stone	John Maugham
1969	Phillip Hughes	John Terry
1970	Willie Thorne	John Terry
1971	John Mills	Joe Johnson
1972	John Mills	Tony Knowles
1973	Peter Bardsley	Willie Thorne
1974	Stephen Holroyd	Tony Knowles
1975	Mike Hallett	Eugene Hughes
1976	Wayne Jones	Ian Williamson
1977	Jimmy White	Ian Williamson
1978	Danny Adds	Tony Meo
1979	Tony Pyle	Joe O'Boye
1980	Terry Whitthread	Tommy Murphy
1981	Chris Hampson	Dean Reynolds
1982	Steve Ventham	Neal Foulds
1983	Stephen Hendry	Mark Thompson
1984	Brian Morgan	Martin Clark
1985	Barry Bunn	Wayne Rendle
1986	Dave Grimwood	Barry Pinches
1987	Jamie Woodman	Mark Johnston-Allen
1988	Dave Grimwood	Joe Swail
1989	Ronnie O'Sullivan	Paul McPhillips

(S) Played at Scunthorpe
(L) Played at London

Most wins (under-16)
2 Dave Grimwood, John Mills, Marcus Owen, Peter Shelley, Rex Williams

Most finals (under-16)
2   David Bond (1954, 1956), Dave Bonney (1976–7), Dave Grimwood (1986, 1988), John Hollis (1963–4), John Mills (1971–2), Marcus Owen (1950–1), John Parrott (1979–80), Peter Shelley (1955, 1957), Willie Thorne (1969–70), Steve Ventham (1981–2), Rex Williams (1948–9)

Most wins (under-19)
2   Tony Knowles, Tony Matthews, John Terry, Ian Williamson, Cliff Wilson

Most finals (under-19)
3   David Bend (1958–60), Ian Williamson (1976–8), Cliff Wilson (1951–3)
2   John Hollis (1965–6), Tony Knowles (1972, 1974), Tony Matthews (1962–3), Tommy Murphy (1980–1), Marcus Owen (1952–3), Ian Rees (1960–1), Brian Rowswell (1983–4), John Terry (1969–70), Mark Wildman (1954–5)

Winners of both titles
David Bend, John Hollis, John Maugham, John Terry, Willie Thorne, John Virgo, Mark Wildman, Rex Williams

Home International Championship

Following the success of an international between England and Wales at Port Talbot in 1969, a three-nation Home International Championship was launched in the 1970–1 season when those two countries were joined by a team from the Republic of Ireland. Scotland joined the championship the following season and the Isle of Man joined in 1978, the same year that Pontins agreed to stage the championship. The event ceased to be a season-long affair and was played during the Pontins Autumn Festival of Snooker at their Prestatyn Camp.

The number of competing nations was increased to its current complement of six in 1979 when Northern Ireland became the last addition.

A Junior Home International Championship was launched in 1985, and the following year the main event moved from Prestatyn to Pontins' Heysham camp. Since 1988 the championship has been sponsored by Matchroom and played at the Lido Hotel, Douglas, Isle of Man.

The junior event is sponsored by the *Daily Mirror* and has its home at Pontins' Hemsby camp in Norfolk.

Both championships are open to non-professional players only who are selected to represent their country.

Senior Championship

Year	Winner	Runner-up
1970–1	England	Wales
1971–2	England	Wales
1972–3	England	Wales
1973–4	England	Wales
1974–5	Wales	England
1975–6	Wales	England

Senior Championship

Year	Winner	Runner-up
1976–7	England	Wales
1977–8	Wales	England
1978	England	Wales
1979	England	Wales
1980	Wales	England
1981	Wales	England
1982	Wales	England
1983	Wales	England
1984	Wales	England
1985	Wales	England
1986	England	Wales
1987	England	Northern Ireland
1988	England	Northern Ireland

Highest break
141   Martin Clark (Eng), 1986

Junior Championship

Year	Winner	Runner-up
1985	England	Scotland
1986	Wales	Northern Ireland
1987	Wales	England
1988	Republic of Ireland	Wales

Highest break
120   Ken Doherty (RoI), 1988

Inter-Counties championship

Organized by the B & SCC, the Inter-Counties Snooker Championship was launched in 1973–4. A billiards championship was introduced the following year. Counties affiliated to the B & SCC only are allowed to enter a four-man team. An Inter-Counties Under-23 tournament was added in 1979–80. It later became for under-21s and in 1986–7 it became an under-19s competition.

Some of today's top professionals have appeared in winning teams: John Virgo (1976), Ray Edmonds (1977), Tony Meo and Steve Davis (1978), Jimmy White (1979), Neal Foulds and Dave Gilbert (1982), Steve Duggan (1983), Barry West (1983, 1984), Jon Wright (1986).

Senior finals

1974	Glamorgan	5–1	Lincolnshire
1975	Greater London	9–7	Cornwall
1976	Lancashire 'A'	9–5	Greater London 'A'
1977	Lincolnshire	9–3	Cornwall
1978	London	9–2	Yorkshire
1979	London	9–3	Durham
1980	Hampshire	5–2	Merseyside
1981	Durham	5–0	Wessex
1982	London	5–1	Staffordshire
1983	Yorkshire	5–3	Essex
1984	Yorkshire	5–4	Devon
1985	Devon	5–0	Lincolnshire
1986	London	5–2	Staffs and West Midlands
1987	Kent	5–3	Yorkshire
1988	Essex	5–4	Lancashire
1989	Merseyside	5–1	Surrey

Most wins (team)
5 London/Greater London
2 Yorkshire

Most wins (individual)
3 Roger Brown (London) 1978–9, 1982
2 Tony Emmott (Yorkshire) 1983–4, Geoff Foulds (London) 1975, 1978, Peter Oakley (Yorkshire) 1983–4, Barry West (Yorkshire) 1983–4

Most finals (team)
6 London/Greater London
4 Yorkshire
3 Lincolnshire
2 Cornwall, Devon, Durham, Essex, Lancashire, Staffordshire (including one as Staffs and W. Midlands)

Most finals (individuals)
3 Roger Brown (London) 1978–9, 1982, Geoff Foulds (London) 1975–6, 1978, Peter Oakley (Yorkshire) 1978, 1983–4

Under-19 finals
1980	Essex	5–4	Gloucestershire
1981	Cornwall	5–3	Yorkshire
1982	Surrey	5–4	Essex
1983	Staffordshire	5–3	Devon
1984	London	5–1	Derbyshire
1985	East Sussex	5–2	North East
1986	Staffs and West Midlands	5–3	East Sussex
1987	Staffs and West Midlands	5–3	Devon
1988	Yorkshire	5–1	Avon
1989	Yorkshire	5–2	Devon

UK Pairs Championship
Held since 1975 it has survived in recent years despite not currently attracting a sponsor. Over the years, however, such people as Coral, Guinness and San Miguel have lent their name to the competition which is under the auspices of the B & SCC.

Finals
1975	Mario Berni/ John Selby	3–1	Frank McCourt/ George Wood
1976	Paul Medati/ John Virgo	3–2	Dennis Hughes/ Billy Kelly
1977	Roger Bales/ Clive Everton	3–0	Dickie Laws/ John Pike
1978	Dave Martin/ Don Reed	3–1	Dickie Laws/ John Pike
1979	Steve Newbury/ Cliff Wilson	3–2	Jack Fitzmaurice/ Maurice Suckling
1980	Harry Burns/ Doug French	3–1	Tony Green/ Dave Grimmer
1981	Roger Coles/ Bill Oliver	3–0	Harry Burns/ Doug French
1982	John Griffiths/ Zenon Lembicz	3–2	Roger Coles/ Bill Oliver
1983	Gary Keeble/ Martin Smith	3–2	David Hoggarth/ Gary Thomas
1984	Paul Fryatt/ Tony Putnam	3–2	Eddie Hobson/ Alan Trigg
1985	Tony Emmott/ Martin Unsworth	3–0	Rob Brown/ Peter Redmond

1986	Paul Fryatt/ Tony Putnam	3–1	Ken Owers/ Steve Meakin
1987	Stan Brooke/ Paul Cavney	3–2	Geoff Laney/ Graham Lee
1988	Dave Harold/ Barry Pinches	3–1	David Rippon/ Neil Mosley
1989	Jason Weston/ Matthew Paffett	3–1	Paul Cavney/ Michael Stocks

British Isles Under-21 Championship
Held just once, in 1986, it was a B & SCC organized event and the final was played during the Hastings Snooker Festival.

Final
1986	Jeff Cundy	5–3	Vince McCluskey

BCE Grand Masters
An over-50s event organized by the B & SCC, the first competition was held in 1987. It is a popular annual event.

Finals
1987	Malcolm Cowley	5–3	Charlie Gay
1988	John Griffin	4–3	Maurice Chapman
1989	John Halcrow	4–2	Peter Marshall

UK Amateur Championship
Held just once, more than 1500 entrants took part in the competition sponsored by Rothmans who put up £18,000 worth of prize money. The final was held at Breaks, Solihull.

Final
1987	Stefan Mazrocis	5–2	Paul Cavney

The Non-professional Game Worldwide
ISBF World Junior Championship
Inaugurated at Hastings 1987 it is the world championship for under-21-year-olds. The 1988 championship was held in Thailand.

Finals
1987	Jonathan Birch (Eng)	4–1	Stefan Mazrocis (Eng)
1988	Brian Morgan (Eng)	6–1	Jason Peplow (Mal)
1989	Ken Doherty (RoI)	11–5	Jason Ferguson (Eng)

Highest break
147 Gary Hill (Eng), 1989

Malta's Paul Mifsud has been one of the top amateurs for more than 20 years. He has won over 20 national titles at billiards and snooker and has been a dual world champion at both games. He turned professional in 1983 but reverted back to amateur status a year later.

European Amateur Championship

First held at Schveningen, Holland, in 1988 it is a world championship style event with the 26 entrants split into four qualifying groups. Held every two years the 1990 championship will be in Belgium.

Final
1988 Stefan Mazrocis (Eng) 11–7 Paul Mifsud (Mal)

Highest break
109 Jonathan Birch (Eng), 1988

Asian Championship

With Asia being one of the great growth areas of snooker, the Asian Championship has become one of the most prestigious non-professional events outside Great Britain. The championship was first held in 1984 and the organization is similar to the world championship, with the competitors divided into groups for a round-robin tournament prior to engaging in a knock-out. The venues have been: 1984 Bangkok; 1985 Singapore, 1986 Colombo, Sri Lanka; 1987 Kuala Lumpur; 1988 Colombo, Sri Lanka

Finals
1984	Sakchai Sim-gnarm (Tha)	nk	O. B. Agrawal (Ind)
1985	Gary Kwok (HK)	8–5	Sakchai Sim-gnarm (Tha)
1986	James Wattana (Tha)	nk	Gary Kwok (HK)

1987 Udon Kaimuk (Tha)	8–6	James Wattana (Tha)
1988 James Wattana (Tha)	8–7	Kenny Kwok (HK)

Highest break
112 Udon Kaimu, 1987

National Championships

More than 25 countries worldwide hold annual national championships. Some, like those of Bangladesh, Belgium, Brunei, Holland, Iceland, Sweden and West Germany have all been launched in recent years. But these countries are already making great strides forward. The English amateur championship is the oldest snooker competition in the world, and that is followed by the Northern Ireland, Republic of Ireland, Wales, South African and Indian national championships which were all launched before the last war.

Country	Year inaugurated	Most titles
All-Ireland	1935	4 Seamus Fenning (RoI) 1935–6, 1939, 1954
		4 J. Stevenson (Ire) 1951–3, 1955
Australia	1953	8 Max Williams 1961, 1966–8, 1970–3
Bangladesh	1985	2 Reshdul Ameen 1985, 1988
Belgium	1984	4 Mario Lanoye 1984–5, 1987–8
Brunei	1988	1 Eddy Lim 1988
Canada	1979	3 Alain Robidoux 1983, 1985, 1987
Egypt	1979	5 Amro Abdul Aziz 1979–82, 1987
Germany, West	1987	2 Michael Henson 1987–8
Holland	1987	2 Rene Dijkstra 1987–8
Hong Kong	1981	6 Kenny Kwok 1981–2, 1984–5, 1987–8
Iceland	1982	3 Kjartank Fridthjofsson 1982–3, 1985
Ireland, Northern	1927	6 J. McNally 1931, 1938–9, 1941, 1945–6
Ireland, Republic of	1927	5 Seamus Fenning 1933, 1935, 1949, 1954–5
India	1939	8 Mohammad Lafir (Sri) 1956–7, 1959, 1961, 1963, 1974–5, 1977
Isle of Man	1980	4 Peter Reynolds 1980–2, 1987
		4 Mike Colquitt 1984–6, 1988
Kenya	1984	not known
Malaysia	1986	1 Peter Chin 1986
		1 Mohammed Loon Hong 1987
		1 Benjamin Choo 1988
Malta	1947	15 Paul Mifsud 1967–71, 1974–6, 1978–9, 1982–3, 1985–6, 1988
Mauritius	1983	2 Christian d'Avoine 1986–7
New Zealand	1945	7 L. Stout 1948–50, 1952–3, 1955–6

Scotland	1946	7 Eddie Sinclair 1960, 1963, 1967–8, 1973, 1975–6
Singapore	1979	5 Lau Weng Yew 1979, 1982–4, 1988
South Africa	1937	11 Jimmy van Rensburg 1953–5, 1957, 1961–3, 1967, 1970, 1972–3
Sri Lanka	1948	18 Mohammad Lafir 1948, 1950, 1952–62, 1964–6, 1969, 1973
Sweden	1984	2 Michael Hallgren 1984–5
		2 Bjorn Bjorkman 1986–7
Thailand	1982	4 Vichien Saengthong 1982–5
Wales	1930	8 Tom Jones 1930–6, 1947
Zimbabwe	1967	6 R. D. Sheridan 1968–71, 1978–9

Sri Lanka's Mohammad Lafir has won a total of 26 national snooker titles; 18 Sri Lankan and 8 Indian. His 18 Sri Lankan titles is a record for any one country.

Professional Ticket Series

Prior to 1986, membership to the WPBSA was by application and, based on various factors, including playing record, the board of the governing body accepted or rejected applications each year. However, since the 1986–7 season, membership has been via a series of pro-ticket tournaments.

The first were held in 1985 and points were awarded for performances over two events. The top eight in the 'league' automatically became members of the WPBSA for the 1986–7 season.

Since then, the system has constantly changed to keep in line with the WPBSA's policy of restricting the number of tournament professionals to 128. Since 1986 the leading players from the pro-ticket series have engaged in a single man-for-man play-off against the lower ranked professionals to see who gains, or retains, full professional status.

The system in operation in the 1988–9 season was as follows. The leading 26 players from the three qualifying pro-ticket tournaments held during 1988 played a knockout tournament in March/April 1989. They played down to the last eight and were then joined by the reigning world amateur champion (James Wattana) and reigning English amateur champion (Barry Pinches). Those ten then engaged in a head-to-head confrontation against the professionals ranked between 119–128 on the up-to-date ranking list. The winners either took up, or retained, full professional status. This is how the pro-ticket series have affected WPBSA membership since their introduction:

Welshman Cliff Wilson is one of the game's great characters and entertainers. He was world amateur champion in 1978.

1985

Venue	Winner		Runner-up
Pontins, Prestatyn	Davie Roe	5–4	Jon Wright
Butlins, Pwllheli	Jon Wright	5–1	David Roe

Top eight finishers after two qualifying events: 1 Jon Wright, 2 David Roe, 3 Ken Owers, 4 Terry Whitthread, 5 Paul Gibson, 6 Steve James, 7 Mark Bennett, 8 Brian Rowswell

The above, together with Nigel Gilbert, took up professional status in 1986–7. Gilbert finished 9th but was allowed in because Whitthread had already been accepted as a professional before the pro-ticket series.

1985–6

Venue	Winner		Runner-up
Pontins, Prestatyn	Anthony Harris	5–1	Tony Putnam
Butlins, Barry Island	Terry Parsons	5–2	Robert Marshall
Butlins, Barry Island	Martin Clark	5–2	Paul Cavney
Pontins, Brean Sands	Gary Wilkinson	5–1	Jim Chambers

Top eight finishers after four qualifying events: 1 Gary Wilkinson, 2 Martin Clark, 3 Anthony Harris, 4 Jim Chambers, 5 Derek Heaton, 6 Jason Smith, 7 Robert Marshall, 8 Eric Lawler

Steve Meakin became eligible for the play-offs because Harris doubly qualified as the English amateur champion. Six play-offs were necessary to bring the WPBSA full membership to 128 but, of the lower ranked professionals, only Maurice Parkin elected to play, the others declined and lost full membership. Parkin lost 10–1 to Meakin and so all nine non-professionals took up professional status in 1987–8.

1986–7

Venue	Winner		Runner-up
Pontins, Prestatyn	Tony Wilson	5–4	Craig Edwards
Warners, Isle of Wight	Nick Terry	5–3	Darren Morgan
Pontins, Brean Sands	Steve Ventham	5–4	Steve Campbell
Pontins, Prestatyn	Nick Terry	5–4	Mark Johnston-Allen

Top eight finishers after four qualifying events: 1 Darren Morgan, 2 Mark Johnston-Allen, 3 Nick Terry, 4 Mick Price, 5 Craig Edwards, 6 Steve Campbell, 7 Tony Wilson, 8 Ian Graham

English amateur champion Mark Rowing also automatically qualified for the play-offs. Darren Morgan doubly qualified as world amateur champion, which allowed Darren Clarke (9th in the table) to take part. Morgan, Rowing and Mark Johnston-Allen all gained professional status without having to engage in a play-off. The other results were as follows:

Nick Terry	10–5	Maurice Parkin*
Mick Price	10–4	David Greaves*
Craig Edwards	10–9	Derek Heaton*
Steve Campbell	10–1	Paul Thornley*
Tony Wilson	10–8	Derek Mienie*
Ian Graham	10–1	Clive Everton*
Robert Marshall*	10–5	Darren Clarke

* Existing professional

1987–8

Venue	Winner		Runner-up
Warners, Isle of Wight	Steve Murphy	5–3	James Wattana
Pontins, Brean Sands	James Wattana	5–1	Duncan Campbell
Pontins, Prestatyn	Jason Ferguson	5–2	Jonathan Birch

The top 26 in the final table after the three qualifying events then played off. However, because Barry Pinches (English amateur champion) and James Wattana (world amateur champion) were exempt, the players who occupied 27th and 28th places joined the knockout competition. The top 26 played down to eight survivors and they, together with Pinches and Wattana, played the ten lowest-ranked professionals. This is how those head-to-head matches went:

Ian Brumby	9–3	Billy Kelly*
Steve Murphy	9–4	Derek Mienie*
Nigel Bond	9–0	Ian Black*
Brian Morgan	9–0	Pascal Burke*
Nick Dyson	9–2	Dave Chalmers*
Brady Gollan	9–2	Patsy Fagan*
Andrew Cairns	9–4	Ian Anderson*

* Existing professional

James Wattana, Barry Pinches and Duncan Campbell all gained professional status because their opponents did not appear for the challenge match.

CHAPTER EIGHT

Women's Snooker

Women's snooker has undergone several changes in recent years, but the biggest significant change came about in 1986 when the game went 'open' thus dropping all distinctions between amateur and professional players.

Current women's star Allison Fisher is talked about as possibly being the first female to enter the male domain of the WPBSA. And through the pro-ticket tournaments she has every chance of fulfilling that ambition. In the pre-war days, however, women played an integral part in the world of professional snooker and Joyce Gardner was as big an attraction as many of her male counterparts of the era. Along with Joe Davis, she did a lot to popularize the sport, and during the war years she helped to raise much needed money for the war effort. Another outstanding female player of the day was Ruth Harrison, and after the war Thelma Carpenter was the star attraction of women's snooker.

The Women's Billiards Association was formed in 1931 when a meeting was held at the Women's Automobile and Sports Association club, Buckingham Palace Road, London, on 20 May. The first British women's billiards championship was organized that year and in 1933 the snooker championship was launched.

The first professional championships were organized in 1934 and Ruth Harrison dominated the snooker event up to the outbreak of the war. However, like the male game, women's professional snooker also went into decline in the 1950s. The professional championship ceased in 1950 but the amateur championship remained

Two present-day stars of the ladies' game, Allison Fisher (left) and Stacey Hillyard.

The star of the ladies' game, Allison Fisher.

ALLISON FISHER

Born: 24 February 1968, Peacehaven, Sussex

If a female player is going to make the break into the male dominated world of professional snooker then Allison Fisher is the most likely candidate. She has proved that she can compete with her male counterparts in the non-professional game, and thanks to the pro-ticket series she has the opportunity to progress into the professional ranks.

She has been playing snooker since the age of seven and in 1985, at the age of 17, she captured the women's world title. She retained the title a year later but defeat by Stacey Hillyard in the 1987 championship was her first defeat by another woman for nearly three years. However, she compensated by winning the UK women's title by beating Mandy Fisher.

She won both titles, the most prestigious in the women's game, in 1988 and in the world championship final she beat the defending champion Ann-Marie Farren 6–1 as she continued to prove that she is one of the most outstanding players women's snooker has ever known.

• • • • • • • • • • • • •

and a new star of ladies snooker emerged in the form of Maureen Barrett (later Maureen Baynton). She eventually turned professional in 1968; the first new professional since the war.

As the late 1970s approached, women's snooker was virtually dormant until Wally West came along to help. A former amateur player, he was installed as chairman of the Women's Billiards and Snooker Association, and set about the task of putting women's snooker back on the map.

Embassy had sponsored a world open to coincide with the men's world championship in 1976, and in 1980 West played his part in organizing the second world open at Hayling Island, this time under the sponsorship of Guinness.

Canada and Australia are two strongholds of women's snooker, apart from Great Britain, and it was the Australian girl Lesley McIlrath, who won the 1980 World Open. A new association, the World Ladies Billiards and Snooker Association, was formed in July 1981, and since then a variety of tournaments have been held; some successful, some not so successful.

Barry Hearn became involved in the women's game in 1983 when he promoted the British Rail Inter-City Mixed Doubles challenge match between Tony Meo and Julie Islip and Steve Davis and Mandy Fisher. It received ITV coverage and was shown on FA Cup Final day. Meo and Islip won.

The £60,000 National Express Grand Prix was launched in 1984. The idea was a good one as the leading female players travelled around Britain playing a series of knockout competitions. Sadly though, the British public were obviously not ready for women's snooker and gave the series the 'thumbs down'. Needless to say it did not return in 1985.

In 1984 the governing body laid down clear guidelines as to what constituted a professional player, and, like the WPBSA, monitored admission into the professional ranks. The formation of LSI (Ladies Snooker International), a promotions company, took many of the leading professionals under its wing and suddenly the women's game was in a state of confusion again. However, the making of the women's game 'open' as from 1 January 1986 has helped stabilize the game. Since then the standard of ladies' snooker has risen, and Allison Fisher has emerged as the most outstanding female player and has a realistic chance of becoming the first lady member of the WPBSA.

Tuborg UK Women's Championship

The first women's tournament after the game went open in 1986. It replaced the national amateur championship.

1986 Allison Fisher   4–2 Stacey Hillyard
1987 Allison Fisher   4–1 Mandy Fisher
1988 Allison Fisher   5–2 Stacey Hillyard

Highest break
85 Allison Fisher (1988)

Women's World Championship

Inaugurated in 1984 as the World Amateur Championship, the word 'Amateur' was dropped in 1986.

1984 Stacey Hillyard (Eng)   4–1 Natalie Stelmach (Can)
1985 Allison Fisher (Eng)   5–1 Stacey Hillyard (Eng)

1986 Allison Fisher (Eng)   5–0 Sue LeMaich (Can)
1987 Ann-Marie Farren (Eng) 5–1 Stacey Hillyard (Eng)
1988 Allison Fisher (Eng)   6–1 Ann-Marie Farren (Eng)

Highest break
84 Allison Fisher (1986)

World Open

First held in 1976 when it was staged alongside the men's world championship at Middlesbrough. It was not held again until 1980 and was discontinued in 1983.

1976 Vera Selby (Eng)   4–0 Muriel Hazeldine
1980 Lesley McIlrath (Aus) 4–2 Agnes Davies (Wal)
1981 Vera Selby (Eng)   3–0 Mandy Fisher (Eng)
1982 Not held
1983 Sue Foster (Eng)   8–5 Maureen Baynton (Eng)

Steve Davis isn't the only person to win loads of trophies, as 1987 women's world champion Ann-Marie Farren shows.

Barry Hearn's Successful Team

With somebody like Barry Hearn at the helm of any business it is guaranteed success. Thankfully, Barry Hearn decided to contribute a large part of his talents to the world of snooker and that has only been good for the game, even though he has been in conflict with the governing body at various times over the years.

Dagenham-born Hearn is a chartered accountant and his first interest in snooker came when a company he worked for acquired the Lucania Snooker Halls. Based at the Romford Lucania, Hearn used to offer financial help to promising young amateurs and in his earlier days used to help such men as Vic and Bob Harris, Danny Adds, and Geoff Foulds (father of Neal). But Hearn's world changed completely one day in March 1976 when his attention was drawn to a youngster who used to play in the Romford Lucania. That youngster was Steve Davis.

The relationship that developed between Hearn and Davis became one of the best in sport. And today their respect for each other has not altered.

Davis is the best player in the world and Hearn foresaw his protégé as a potential world champion. As soon as that day arrived the brilliant business brain of Barry Hearn helped turn Steve Davis into a sporting millionaire as his champion became a very marketable commodity.

Hearn expanded his playing team with the addition of Tony Meo in 1981, and in May 1982, shortly after he sold 16 of the 17 Lucania Halls (he retained the Romford Centre) and formed the new Matchroom organization, he recruited Terry Griffiths as the third member of the team. Matchroom took its name from the plush matchroom facilities at Hearn's Romford base.

Dennis Taylor became the fourth member of the squad shortly after winning the 1985 world championship, and the following year Willie Thorne and Neal Foulds became Matchroom men. The team by now was the strongest in snooker, but two more great players, Jimmy White and Cliff Thorburn, have since been added to make it unquestionably the strongest team in snooker.

But the strength and success of the team extends beyond the eight men who constantly capture the limelight. There is the backroom team at Matchroom's Romford headquarters who are responsible for a wide range of duties ranging from making players' arrangements to attend matches and exhibitions to being polite to the countless telephone calls from people wishing to meet Steve Davis, or Jimmy White, or other members of the team. Like his players, Barry Hearn has also picked the best backroom men and women.

Hearn has diversified his interests into boxing in the past couple of years and has turned the bottom half of the Matchroom snooker hall into a modern gymnasium. He came into snooker knowing he would do the sport good and he has done that. Now it is boxing's turn to feel the full force of the successful Barry Hearn organization.

Matchroom *boss Barry Hearn.*

Right, above: *The team in Dubai.*

Right: *Steve Davis, Barry Hearn, the world championship trophy and some of the* Matchroom *back-room team celebrate yet another triumph for 'The Nugget'.*

National Amateur Championship

Inaugurated in 1933, it was discontinued in 1986 and replaced by the Tuborg UK Women's Championship.

1933	Margaret Quinn
1934	Ella Morris
1935	Molly Hill
1936	Vera Seals
1937	Mrs. E. Morland-Smith
1938	Ella Morris
1939	Agnes Morris
1940–6	Not held
1947	Mabel Knight
1948	Joan Adcock
1949	Rosemary Davies
1950	Pat Holden
1951–2	Rosemary Davies
1953	Rita Holmes
1954–6	Maureen Barrett
1957–9	Rita Holmes
1960	Muriel Hazeldine
1961–2	Maureen Barrett
1963	Rita Holmes
1964	Maureen Baynton (née Barrett)
1965	Mrs S. Jeffries
1966	Maureen Baynton
1967	Helen Futo
1968	Maureen Baynton
1969	Rae Craven
1970–1	Muriel Hazeldine
1972–5	Vera Selby
1976–7	Ann Johnson
1978	Agnes Davies (née Morris)
1979	Vera Selby
1980	Sue Foster
1981	Not held
1982–3	Sue Foster
1984	Not held
1985	Allison Fisher

Most wins

8	Maureen Baynton (née Barrett)
5	Vera Selby
	Rita Holmes
3	Rosemary Davies
	Sue Foster
	Muriel Hazeldine

National Professional Championship

Inaugurated in 1934 it was discontinued after the 1950 championship.

1934–40	Ruth Harrison
1941–7	Not held
1948	Ruth Harrison
1949	Agnes Morris
1950	Thelma Carpenter

Most wins

8	Ruth Harrison

Women's Break Records

The **first century by a woman in tournament play** was by Stacey Hillyard in the Premier Division of the Walter C. Clark League in Bournemouth on 15 January 1985. Playing Bill Scorer she compiled a break of 114 in 15 minutes. It shattered the old women's record of 71 set by Mandy Fisher in 1974. Furthermore, 15-year-old Stacey's break was the first century in the Walter C. Clark League.

The **first half-century by a woman in tournament play** was by Canada's Natalie Stelmach who compiled a 56 in the 1981 Canadian championship. Stelmach is also believed to be the first women to make a century under practice conditions.

The **first century by a woman in an all-women's tournament** was by Allison Fisher who compiled a 103 in the B & SCC Tournament at Loughborough in 1987.

Ann-Marie Farren, winner of the women's world championship in 1987 when she beat Stacey Hillyard 5–1 in the final.

CHAPTER NINE

Miscellaneous Records

Attendances

The game's biggest attendances have all been set at Wembley during the Benson and Hedges Masters. The following are the highest recorded:

2876 Alex Higgins v. Bill Werbeniuk (1st round 1983)
2693 Ray Reardon v. Cliff Thorburn (final 1983)
2690 Steve Davis v. Doug Mountjoy (quarter-final 1983)
2686 Steve Davis v. Doug Mountjoy (quarter-final 1982)
2593 Alex Higgins v. Tony Knowles (1st round 1988)
2580 Alex Higgins v. Doug Mountjoy (1st round 1984)
2569 Doug Mountjoy v. Cliff Thorburn (final 1985)
2567 Terry Griffiths v. Alex Higgins (semi-final 1982)
2566 Steve Davis v. Alex Higgins (1st round 1985)
2563 Steve Davis v. Terry Griffiths (final 1982)
2563 Cliff Thorburn v. Jimmy White (semi-final 1985)
2562 Eddie Charlton v. Alex Higgins (quarter-final 1982)
2556 Doug Mountjoy v. Ray Reardon (semi-final 1983)
2544 Steve Davis v. Tony Meo (1st round 1984)
2543 Terry Griffiths v. Ray Reardon (quarter-final 1982)
2533 Terry Griffiths v. Jimmy White (final 1984)
2523 Cliff Thorburn v. Jimmy White (final 1987)

The **first 2000 crowd to watch a snooker match in Britain** was at Belle Vue, Manchester during the 1972 Park Drive tournament to watch Alex Higgins and John Spencer.

The **lowest known paying attendance for a professional tournament** is one, for the Jim Meadowcroft versus Bernard Bennett 1st round match in the 1982 Professional Players' Tournament at Birmingham.

Awards

The sport's top awards are the WPBSA annual awards. Inaugurated in 1983 by the Association of Snooker Writers, they came under the auspices of the professional governing body in 1985. In 1988 ten awards were made. The winners of all awards have been:

Player of the Year
1983 Steve Davis
1984 Steve Davis
1985 Dennis Taylor
1986 Steve Davis/Joe Johnson (shared title)
1987 Steve Davis
1988 Steve Davis

Left: Snooker's elder statesman, the likeable Fred Davis.

Personality of the Year
1983 Bill Werbeniuk
1984 Dennis Taylor
1985 Dennis Taylor
1986 Joe Johnson
1987 Joe Johnson
1988 Terry Griffiths

Services to Snooker Award
1983 Mike Watterson
1984 Clive Everton
1985 Del Simmons
1986 Rex Williams
1987 Barry Hearn
1988 Howard Kruger

Special Award
1984 Mike Green
1987 Jackie Rea
1988 Fred Davis
(Award not made in 1983, 1985–6)

Young Player of the Year
1985 John Parrott
1986 Stephen Hendry
1987 Stephen Hendry
1988 Stephen Hendry

Overseas Player of the Year
1987 Dene O'Kane (NZ)
1988 Tony Drago (Mal)

Frame of the Year
1987 Jimmy White
1988 Jimmy White/Stephen Hendry (shared)

Most Memorable Performance of the Year
1987 Joe Johnson (for reaching his second successive world championship final)
1988 Steve James (for his run in the world championship)

Highest Televised Break of the Year
1987 Jimmy White (144, Tennents UK Championship)
1988 Steve Davis (140, Fidelity Unit Trusts International) and Steve James (140, Embassy World Professional Championship)

Billiards Player of the Year
1987 Norman Dagley
1988 Norman Dagley

Breaks

The **earliest recorded century break** was in 1915 when William Murray, manager of the Collingwood Billiard Hall, Newcastle upon Tyne, made a break of 103.

The **first televised century** was made by current professional Mark Wildman in 1960 when he was an amateur. The event, organized by the BA & CC was a North versus London pairs match. The first match in the four-week series was played on 7 November 1960. Wildman compiled a break of 108 when playing with partner George Gibson against Geoff Lockwod and Stan Haslam.

The **first official total clearance** was by Sidney Smith in compiling a break of 133 in the 1936-7 *Daily Mail* Gold Cup. (Murt O'Donoghue had a 134 clearance in 1929 but the break was never ratified.)

The **first player to make 1000 century breaks in public** was Horace Lindrum who reached that milestone in March 1970.

The **first officially recognized century break by an amateur** was by Kingsley Kennerley in 1939.

Progressive official break record
89	Tom Newman	(1919)
96	Joe Davis	(1925)
100	Joe Davis	(1928)
105	Joe Davis	(1930)
109	Joe Davis	(1933)
114	Joe Davis	(1933)

Del Simmons (right) of the WPBSA won the Services to Snooker Award at the WPBSA's annual awards ceremony in 1985. Alex Higgins is still looking for his first award . . .

114	Horace Lindrum	(1936)
131	Horace Lindrum	(1936)*
133	Sidney Smith	(1936)*
135	Joe Davis	(1937)
137	Joe Davis	(1938)
138	Joe Davis	(1938)
140	Joe Davis	(1947)
141	Joe Davis	(1949)
144	George Chenier	(1950)
146	Joe Davis	(1950)
146	Joe Davis	(1954)
147	Joe Davis	(1955)

* Compiled on the same day

Since then, nine other men have compiled official maximums. Details can be found in the feature 'The Maximum Men' which can be found on p. 52.

The **highest official break by an amateur** is 147 by Geet Sethi in the Indian Championship on 21 February 1988.

There have been three instances of **16-red clearances**. Alex Higgins was the first to perform the feat in an exhibition against Willie Thorne at the Leicester YMCA in 1976. Cliff Thorburn did so in

● ● ● ● ● ● ● ● ● ● ● ● ● ● ● ●

WILLIE THORNE

Born: 4 March 1954, Leicester

Willie Thorne.

As a junior, Willie Thorne had one of the best records amongst all current professionals. He was the under-16 billiards and snooker champion in 1970, the under-19 billiards champion in the three years between 1971 and 1973, and under-19 snooker champion in 1973. With that pedigree behind him he turned professional in 1974 but had to wait ten years for the success he had enjoyed in his younger days.

The proprietor of the popular Willie Thorne Snooker Centre in Leicester, his only successes as a professional had been in winning the Pontins Open in 1980 and the Pontins Professional title in 1984. That latter title was the start of a run that took Willie to his first ranking title when he beat Cliff Thorburn 13-8 to win the 1985 Mercantile Credit Classic.

Thorne has since reached two other ranking finals, the Coral UK Open and Dulux British Open, both in 1985-6, and on both occasions he lost to Steve Davis.

Now a member of the Matchroom team, Willie was the first winner of the Matchroom trophy in 1986. He is the champion at maximums and has made over 100 in practice and exhibition conditions. He has compiled one in tournament play, against Tommy Murphy in the 1987 Tennents UK Championship.

● ● ● ● ● ● ● ● ● ● ● ● ● ● ● ●

practice against Geoff Foulds in 1983, and on 27 April 1988 at the Woodland Snooker Centre, Doncaster, while practising against England amateur champion Mark Rowing, Steve Duggan had a 16-red clearance in compiling a break of 148. He was the only one of the three men to compile a break in excess of 147.

The youngest person to compile a maximum break was Gary Hill of Wolverhampton who was 20 yr 249 day when he compiled a 147 in the World Junior Championship at Reykjavik, Iceland on 5 June 1989.

The first player **to compile a century break in three consecutive frames in tournament play** was Steve Davis in the final of the 1988 Fidelity Unit Trusts International at Stoke-on-Trent. Remarkably, Doug Mountjoy emulated the feat less than ten weeks later in the final of the Tennents UK Championship against Stephen Hendry.

Mike Watterson, the man who took the world championship to The Crucible, once compiled **three maximum breaks in 24 hours**. After com-

piling no fewer than 19 15-red/15-black clearances during his long career, Watterson had never gone on to compile a maximum. But at 2.30 p.m. on Saturday 21 January 1984 at Newbould, Chesterfield, he compiled his first ever 147 against local amateur David Poxon. The following day at 1.15 p.m. he compiled his second maximum, and two frames later, at 1.40 he made it a remarkable hat-trick.

In an exhibition match at the Kempsey-Crescent Head Country Club, New South Wales on 5 July 1967 Eddie Charlton played two frames against local players. In the first he broke, potted a red and **made a break of 135**. In the second frame he broke again and **made a 137 clearance**. In both frames neither opponent went to the table. **Charlton scored 272 without reply**.

Fines

The record fines imposed by the WPBSA on its members have been:

£12,000 on Alex Higgins for head-butting a WPBSA official in 1986. He also received a five-tournament ban.

£12,000 on Steve Davis for refusing to give press conferences during the 1988 Rothmans Grand Prix.

£10,000 on Cliff Thorburn for failing a drugs test in 1988. He also received a two-tournament ban.

£8000 on Dennis Taylor for refusing to give press conferences during the 1988 Rothmans Grand Prix.

Longest frames/matches

The world championship final is currently played over the best-of-35 frames. In the four finals immediately after the war it was over the best-of-145 frames!

The original 'grinder', Australia's Eddie Charlton. Playing with Bill Werbeniuk in the 1985 Hofmeister World Doubles the first frame of their match against Les Dodd and Jim Bear took 76 minutes to complete!

The **longest frame in a senior tournament** was in the 1985 Hofmeister World Doubles match between Bill Werbeniuk and Eddie Charlton and Les Dodd and Jim Bear. The first frame of their 3rd round match took 76 minutes to complete.

The 14th frame of the Australian Professional Championship final in 1988 between John Campbell and Robbie Foldvari took 71 minutes. It is the **longest frame in a major individual match**.

The **longest frame in the Embassy World Championship** took 69 minutes to complete. It was in the 18th frame of the 2nd round match between Cliff Thorburn and Doug Mountjoy in 1980. It took 21 minutes to sink the brown!

The **latest finish** of a major match was in the 1983 world championship 2nd round match between Cliff Thorburn and Terry Griffiths. It finished at 3.51 a.m. The final session lasted 6 hr 25 min, **the longest single session** in the world championship.

Miscellaneous

The **first woman to referee a championship match in Britain** was Rae Craven of Putney who officiated at the English Amateur Championship match between W. G. Smith and G. F. Hodges on 24 February 1963.

Money winners

Steve Davis in 1988–9 was the first player **to win more than £500,000** in a single season.

Snooker's **first £100,000 1st prize** was won by Steve Davis when he beat John Parrott in the final to win the inaugural Everest World Match-Play title in 1988. When he won the 1986 UK Open, Steve Davis became the **first player to win over £1 million in a career.**

Oldest

The **oldest person to reach a major final** is John Dunning. He was 56 yr 11 mth when he reached the final of the Yamaha International Masters in 1984. (See also world championship and ranking tournaments for other oldest players.)

My word, what a collection . . . from left to right: Ray Reardon (just!), Alex Higgins, John Pulman, Cliff Thorburn and Bill Werbeniuk. The picture was taken in 1975.

Quickest frames/matches

The **quickest frame in a ranking tournament** was completed in just three minutes. It was the fifth frame of the 3rd round match in the 1988 Fidelity Unit Trusts International at Trentham Gardens, Stoke-on-Trent, between Tony Drago and Danny Fowler on 31 August 1988. Drago won the frame 62–0 and the match 5–3.

Danny Fowler was also on the receiving end when Jimmy White beat him 5–0 in the Rothmans Grand Prix on 12 October 1988. The match was completed in 53 minutes to make it the **quickest ever match in a ranking tournament**.

Youngest

Jimmy White is **the youngest winner of the world amateur title**. He was 18 yr 191 days when he won the title at Launceston, Australia, in 1980.

The **youngest winner of the world professional title** is Alex Higgins who was 22 yr 345 days when he won in 1972.

The **youngest winner of a national professional title** is Stephen Hendry who was just 17 yr 2 mth when he won the Scottish title for the first time in 1986. (See also world championship and ranking tournaments for other youngest players records.)

Stephen Hendry, the youngest winner of a senior professional title, the Scottish Professional Championship in 1986. He is seen here with a look-alike orange after he had his new 'spiky' haircut. Naturally his fellow pros nicknamed him Spike.

Index